T3-BPD-583

PRINTERS' ADVERTISING THAT WORKS

"GLASS, CHINA, & REPUTATION, ARE EASILY CRACKED, & NEVER WELL MENDED."
BENJAMIN FRANKLIN
JUNE 1974
SUNDAY
24 MONDAY
TUESDAY
WEDNESDAY
THURSDAY
FRIDAY
SATURDAY
KEEP
IDGE
LIN
JOHN H. HARLAND
from

PRINTERS' ADVERTISING THAT WORKS

William T. Clawson
President,
Clawson Ideas, Inc.

North American Publishing Company • Philadelphia

Dedicated to Richard B. Tullis

Inquiries should be addressed to North American Publishing Company, 401 North Broad Street, Philadelphia, Pennsylvania 19108.

Library of Congress Catalog Number: 75-24819
ISBN: 0-912920-43-2
Order Number: 120

Printed in the United States of America

"He who whispers down a well
About the things he has to sell,
Will not make the shining dollars
Like he who climbs a tree and hollers."

Table of Contents

Acknowledgements

Thanks to the many printers who so kindly sent samples of their work and answered many questions when they were asked.

Then, acknowledgement is made to the following persons who helped locate material and offered helpful suggestions:

Jane S. Birch, Sales Consultant
Prentice-Hall, Inc.

Irvin J. Borowsky, President
North American Publishing Company

James F. Burns, Jr., Editor
Printing Impressions

Robert J. Buzogany, Public Relations Department
The Procter & Gamble Company

Mary Claffey, Secretary
North American Publishing Company

Kenneth J. Costa, Director, Member Service
Radio Advertising Bureau, Inc.

John Jay Daly, Vice President
Direct Mail Marketing Association

E. W. Evans, Vice President
Miller Printing Machinery Company

Joanne Galvin, Analyst
Commercial Credit Corporation

Arthur Gratz, President
Herbick & Held

Norman F. Guess, Vice President
The Dartnell Corporation

Joseph H. Hennage, President
Hennage Creative Printers

E. R. Howard, Manager
Printing Industries of Northern California

Mildred Howie, Publicist
Public Relations

Bertram Korn, Jr.
Printing Impressions

Burt M. Langhenry
Director of Public Relations

Mary McIntyre Secretary
Miller Printing Machinery Company

Dotty Newhouse, Asst. Director of Public Relations
Specialty Advertising Association International

Joseph Palastak, Executive Director
Transit Advertising Association

Alan S. Perry, Vice President/Director of Marketing
Institute of Outdoor Advertising

Arlyn Powell
Houghton Mifflin Company

Nancy R. Rice, Administrative Assistant, Public Relations
Printing Industries of America, Inc.

Ruth Scherm, Public Relations
General Foods Corporation

Gar K. Ingraham, National Retail Sales Promotion
and Advertising Manager
Sears, Roebuck and Co.

I. Gregg Van Wert, Director of Communications
National Association of Printers and Lithographers

Lillian M. Vidakovich, Secretary
Harris-Intertype Corporation

Introduction

In 1949 there was the first meeting of record of the Self-Advertising Awards Committee. It is known that Jim Bracket, then president of PIA, and Art Wetzel, chairman of the board, were participants and originators of this meeting. In the spring of 1952, Printing Industries of America sent out a questionnaire to determine what the members would like to discuss at their Annual Convention. One of the items was printers' and lithographers' self-advertising. Mr. Dick Tullis, then president of Miller Printing Machinery Company, approached PIA's Board of Directors with a unique plan for a PIA Printers' Self-Advertising Program which consisted of offering prizes of up to $1,000 and replicas of Benjamin Franklin statues. The first contest was in 1953.

This program was developed through the efforts of Dick Tullis and Bill Clawson, who was Miller's advertising manager, and they were the moving forces behind getting the PIA Self-Advertising Awards Program off. Bill, who is a very talented guy, developed, with the approval of Dick Tullis, the procedures and the rules for the contest, the selection of judges and actually handled the program for the first couple of years. He made many visits to local PIA associations showing the contest winners.

In 1958 the contest stopped and there was no awards program for 1959.

Over the years, some printers, including myself, have been convinced that advertising could help them increase their businesses. But even today, among all those who depend on advertising as a source of business, printers, as well as advertising agencies, fail to use their own medicine.

I accepted the chairmanship of the committee in 1960 for a revitalization of the Self-Advertising Awards Program and, with the help of a lot of dedicated industry members, this program has grown each year for the last fifteen years.

There are still thousands of printers who do not use advertising. When business becomes weak they wonder why on one knows they are in business. They wonder why their salesmen can't make effective cold calls. This is one reason why this book has been written—to convince the printers who do not advertise that advertising will help them to increase or keep their businesses.

You will see by studying the table of contents that the first five chapters are general subjects to help answer questions about creating printers' advertising. The last chapter is the longest, and contains many successful case histories which should provide the impetus for every printing and publishing firm in America to get a successful advertising program for their firm. This book should be must *reading for every sales and advertising manager in the industry.*

I congratulate you, Irvin J. Borowsky, for publishing this much needed book for the industry.

Joseph H. Hennage
Chairman, PIA Awards Programs

Preface

There are thousands of printers who do very little advertising. They have all the tools at their fingertips. Their apathy to advertising is unbelievable to this writer, as well as to so many others who know from its use that advertising pays. When business becomes weak these printers wonder why no one knows they are in business. They wonder why their salesmen can't make effective cold calls. They wonder why a few telephone calls or a postal card mailing doesn't bring customers to their doors.

So, we believe this is an excellent time to publish this book. From leading indicators of business, we glean that we are coming out of a recession, a depression, an unfavorable business condition or whatever you wish to call it. Business has been weak, and thousands of printers, especially the small ones, have felt the crunch.

Now is the time for printers who haven't advertised to start. Never again let a business slow-down find your company wondering why no one knows it exists. Advertising alone won't keep you out of trouble but it will surely help. The many side effects of advertising are unbelievable and unknown to those who don't advertise.

This book was written for everyone in the printing or graphic arts industry. It was written for those who contemplate going into the printing industry. It was written for anyone who doesn't believe in advertising.

To narrow that down a bit—it was also written for decision makers in the printing industry who have made or can make the big decision to advertise. We definitely are trying to convince the owner or manager that good advertising will work for printers. We firmly believe that printing volume and quality can be expanded through advertising.

So few people in our printing plants know or understand advertising or really appreciate its value, although they work with it every day. So, this book was written for some printers' salesmen, for the production people, for the delivery man, for the printing student, for the secretaries, for everyone in printing.

This was written for the small or medium-sized printer who wants to grow or who wants to stay in business when business gets rough.

For the printers who are advertising, this book should help them find some new ideas, thought provokers and new ammunition to improve their programs now in existence. Many of the ideas and examples in the last chapter can be adapted for large or small organizations.

We hope that in the first chapter the reader will find enough reasons to want to advertise that he will keep reading. We have listed in this chapter 17 points to help anyone understand why advertising should be used by a printer. The person who already uses advertising may also find some ideas or copy slants for future campaigns.

The second chapter, "How To Get Started," is just that. To the neophyte or student we hope it will be helpful. To those who have already started to advertise, we suggest that you do not skip this chapter. There is an illustration of how a not too fictitious company established its goal that could be helpful to any company.

A listing of advertising media can be found in Chapter Three. It should be reviewed by everyone interested in advertising. Of necessity, we have made most of the descriptions short. Printers doing specialized work should check this chapter carefully.

Direct mail advertising seems to be the most logical advertising medium for printers, so we have taken an entire chapter (Four) to discuss this method. You will find 26 ways that direct mail advertising can be used by printers. There is also a list of 14 suggestions that may help you to create a new or different piece of direct mail advertising. We hope this chapter will assist in getting ideas or creativity started.

Today, Chapter Five is of extreme importance. With postage rates sky rocketing, it is very important that everyone pays attention to his mailing lists. "How To Build A Mailing List" will help you if you are just starting or if you have a list and decide that you better start all over again. Mailing lists are important and don't let anyone tell you otherwise.

Chapter Six, entitled "Printers' Advertising," is where the real meat is. We suggest that you read every subject or category until you at least get the gist of the advertising piece described. If the idea can't be adapted for your plant or operation then go on to the next.We realize that many of these ideas can't be copied word for word but we sincerely believe that almost every one of them can be adapted for most printers. We reviewed in some detail the advertising pieces that we have seen and know to have been successful. We can say that this advertising has been tested. It is printers' advertising that works.

You will see by studying the index that the six chapters are general subjects to help answer questions about creating printers' advertising. We have tried to make the index useful by cross references to many types of printers' advertising. We hope our language or descriptions are the same as yours so that you will find the index of value in discovering various forms, ideas or reasons why we sincerely believe advertising will work for printers.

Good reading!

—William T. Clawson

CHAPTER 1
WHY ADVERTISE?

Advertising exists to serve salesmen. Salesmen are still the key links between sellers and buyers.

To those who have used advertising, or to those in the advertising profession, "Why advertise?" seems like a rhetorical question. However, there are many printers who really ask the question and want an answer.

One printer we know says he has a nice home, a car in running condition, a wife and children who are dressed well, they haven't wanted for food, so he doesn't want any more business than he has. Another printer says he gets enough business right through the front door and he doesn't have to advertise. Another man is sure that advertising costs too much. Like all unfamiliar tasks, there are many reasons, excuses or alibis for failure or neglect.

If you are doing a poor job of printing because of old equipment, or if your organization is making errors of performance, or if employees can't follow instructions, then don't advertise. Advertising will never help those situations. However, if you are proud of your profession, if you are doing a good job, if you are glad that you are a printer, then tell the world or, at least, your community.

We have always been on the outside, but close by and looking in. We think printing is a great profession. Perhaps the grass just looks greener on the other side of the fence. But we don't believe that is so in this case. We know the men and women who are in the business and they are a great group with real character. There are very few phonies.

We believe every printer should open this book about once a week and read the following words that were written by Donald Behrens, away back in 1963, for Bermingham & Prosser Company's publication, *Friendly Adventurer.* This would surely remind any printer that he is in a meaningful profession and he should be glad.

"I've been in groups where men have been talking about their work. There have been doctors and lawyers and businessmen of all types. But, as for me, I'm glad that I'm a printer.

"These men boast of their accomplishments . . . of their challenges overcome . . . of their long hours and hard work . . . of their battles won over obstacles, competition, disease and the minds of men. But, as for me, I'm glad that I'm a printer.

"For, where would the doctor be if he didn't have the accumulated printed knowledge that has come down through the years because of printers like me? What would the lawyer do without the record of his law? The minister without his Bible? The businessman without his catalogs and price lists and training materials?

"These men make their contributions . . . receive their due rewards . . . find justified satisfaction in their jobs. But, as for me, I'm glad that I'm a printer.

"My work makes people happy. It stimulates their minds. It challenges their ambitions. It feeds their souls. It makes them sing. It contributes to their well-being from the cradle to the grave.

"My work makes people sad. And yet, along with this sadness it brings the comfort of the poets, philosophers and great thinkers to lift men out of their sadness and help them find new inspiration and desire in moments of dejection.

"My work is a challenge. Because people in America refuse to stand still. They demand the impossible. They have new ideas that they want presented in new and different ways. They demand new perfection in printed messages. They experiment with new papers, products, and methods of communication that challenge the ingenuity of the most creative individual. They expect miracles of delivery.

"Above all, my work is satisfying. It gives me a sense of accomplishment. I know that in my work I am helping people in their lives and their work. My satisfaction comes from the sparkling eyes of the young girl announcing her approaching wedding. It comes from the grateful smile of the young businessman who has finally found a way to let the world know about his 'amazing new ideas.'

"My work is painting ideas in the minds of men. My brush is the printing press. And I'm glad that I'm a printer."

Let us first define advertising so we know what we are writing about. The Random House *Dictionary of the English Language* defines the word advertise as follows: "1. to describe or present (a product, organization, idea, etc.) in some medium of communication in order to induce the public to buy, support or approve of it. 2. to call public attention to." The second definition is excellent as far as we are concerned. Some advertising doesn't and never was intended to "induce the public to buy." Only direct response or mail order advertising is conceived and written to induce the public to buy and some printers, especially trade shops as we know them, use that type of advertising. However, the majority of printers should use advertising to call public attention to their companies and what they can produce. The salesmen should do the selling.

The phrase "to call public attention to," as far as this book is concerned, will include promotion and publicity, which is all part of printers' advertising. We realize that many professional advertising people, especially those working in some advertising agencies, want to separate sales promotion, public relations and publicity from advertising. However, for our purpose, since so many printers are in the category of small businessmen, we are going to try to encompass all phases of calling the public's attention to printers.

A printer should advertise if, for no other reason, than to provide his market with information about the types of printing he can produce, the characteristics of that printing, the services he can perform, the costs and where the printing or services can be purchased.

Visualize a world without any forms of advertising. How would you know what things were available? Think of the number of salesmen needed and the time necessary to get around to tell everyone about the things that could be purchased. How would you know where to buy a car with a particular feature that you wanted? The cost of hunting for goods would be enormous and the results disappointing.

In order to be more specific we will continue with reasons, in our estimation, why printers should advertise. We know that advertising direction depends on the company's product and goals. Therefore, these reasons will not be in order of their value to any particular company. We hope the printer who doesn't advertise will find at least four or five good reasons why he should, for there is no doubt in our minds that printers can expand their markets or just their local business by advertising.

1. Advertise to create a favorable atmosphere in which a sale can be made. In other words, prepare the ground for a salesman to call. If you have ever made a cold call on a prospect where none of your company's advertising preceded you, we are sure you appreciate the famous McGraw-Hill advertisement. The illustration was a severe photograph of a businessman sitting in a swivel chair and staring straight at you. The copy read:

"I don't know who you are.
"I don't know your company.
"I don't know your company's products.
"I don't know what your company stands for.
"I don't know your company's customers.
"I don't know your company's record.
"I don't know your company's reputation.
"Now, what is it you wanted to sell me?"

Advertising can answer these questions in a prospect's mind before the salesman calls on him. Advertising will save a salesman's time. If the prospect knows the answers to these questions, the salesman can start in by asking for an order. He doesn't have to use his valuable time to describe his company and its products.

If the advertising preceding the salesman has been novel, provocative or entertaining, as well as informative, it creates a talking point or a starting point for the call. The salesman doesn't have to talk about the weather or the poor showing of the local baseball team.

2. Advertise to get a response indicating interest so the response can be followed up by a telephone call or a visit by a salesman. This response puts the prospect into position for personal selling. The response is mostly received through a business reply card on or inserted in the advertisement.

This is one job that advertising can do very well. It can act as a bird dog. It can find those old customers or new prospects who are interested in a particular type of your printing or service.

3. Advertise to announce a new product, a new technique, a new address or telephone number, a new employee, a new anything.

This is the only fast, efficient way that we know of to make an announcement. If you move, who will know it except the movers and the mailman? You are almost forced to advertise if you want to stay in business.

New equipment, new processes, new employees are, for many, a welcome excuse to advertise or to get publicity. Every time you can favorably get your company name or an executive's name before the public, you have gained a point for the company. Of course, there could be some bad news that you do not want to be connected with. We hope all of our readers will avoid that as they would a plague.

4. Advertise to make a point. Every printer we have ever met knows that his shop, his plant, his organization can do a better job than the printer down the street. If you can prove your point, tell your customers and prospects about it. If your photocomposition looks better than hot composition, demonstrate it in an advertising piece and make your point.

If your costs are lower and you pass on the savings to your customers, tell them about it. You may be able to print better halftones than your competitor's. You may have a bindery or some machinery that excels in some particular phase of printing. Tell the buyers of printing about it through advertising. Your salesmen are no doubt the best, but they may forget some points that you want to get across. So, put those sales points in an advertising piece that will help to back up what the salesman has said in person.

5. Advertise to make good mental impressions. Be it a customer or prospect, stimulate their thinking about your printing and your company. Salesmen can do this job but it takes so long for them to get around. Also, each salesman has a different personality and his personality may not be the same as the company's. The mental impression or image your public has about your company is of most importance to your business. There can be as many images as there are individuals who have contact with your public. However, if you establish an image through your advertising and stay with it, you will make the mental impression you want regardless of each company individual because it is printed in black and white. Your company name is signed to it. There is no supposition. A good company image favorably affects many phases of your business. It is like money in the bank. It is what the intangible thing called "good will" is all about. It can be acquired through good advertising.

6. Advertise to make friends. Everyone likes to do business with a friend. The importance of good human relations is nothing new in business or advertising. You may wonder how you can reflect friendliness in advertising. You have to work at it. You can't do it with one or two pieces. It is the warmth of the copy. The attitude of the entire advertising piece. The subtle things you say to make people feel comfortable when they read your advertising. Cold, sophisticated copy with severe, formal illustrations will not do the job. It is an intangible something as simple as a smile or a concerned voice that makes the difference. It is a reflection from the top management down through the organization. If you have it, it will come through in your advertising efforts. There will always be a market for genuine friendliness. "Kindness in words creates confidence." (Lao-Tse)

7. Advertise to involve prospects and customers. Anytime you can get people to participate or become associated in your business you have developed a potential customer. A research project determining what type of printing or bindery equipment a customer or prospect could use can be good advertising if it isn't too involved and complicated. A check-off sheet of what type of printing they buy is another form of advertising. Anything that will give you information to help you better service a prospect is valuable.

Contests of almost any nature can involve prospects. Raffles can get people interested. They can provide leads to salesmen or, at least, something to get a conversation started. A guessing game to see if prospects can estimate the number of impressions your plant will sell in a year, or the cost of a new piece of equipment completely installed in your plant, will get prospects involved and give you an opportunity to develop them as customers.

8. Advertise to keep in contact with customers. Customers are difficult to obtain and often are neglected in order to get new customers. We have known companies who remove good customers' names from their advertising mailing lists because they thought they didn't need to be sold anymore. Another excuse is, "they might think we don't know they are customers if they receive our advertising." If you are afraid of that, send them a note, tell them personally that you want them to see your advertising, that you want to keep them sold.

If salesmen are busy they may neglect your customers. An advertising piece will keep contact. Customers like to be assured that they are dealing with enterprising organizations that are climbing up the ladder of success. Good advertising connotes good business acumen. It puts you in a class with the large successful corporations.

9. Advertise to influence selected groups to action. If you have or if you want to develop a market for a particular form of printing, advertising can be of great assistance. Mailing lists can be obtained or trade magazines used that are directed to doctors, churches, banks, attorneys, jewelers, druggists, nurserymen, you name it. You can at least find a mailing list if you can't find a trade magazine. Some printers believe this is the day of specialization. The quickest way for people to discover your specialty is through advertising.

10. Advertise to help morale and pride of craftsmanship in your employees. We would never direct a piece of advertising to a prospect or customer without also sending it to our employees' homes and posting it on bulletin boards. Employees should know what you are saying about their work. If you are praising their work in your advertising let them know about it. They will try harder. It gives them an incentive that money can't buy.

If you want to keep a clean, neat shop, have an open house for the employees' families as well as your customers. Walk customers through the plant. Introduce them to your employees and, if you can tie in the introduction with a customer's job, be sure to do it. If you have never tried it you will be surprised what it will do for morale.

Pride in the company by the employees is a special dividend you receive from advertising.

11. Advertise to seek and obtain employees. Most business men do not think of a classified ad as an advertisement for the company. Most classified ads aren't. We are suggesting a change. In the first place, make the ad large enough so no one will have to search for it. Then, with a picture of the plant or with just words, describe the place. Let anyone who sees the ad know what you sell. Tell them how many employees you have. Be friendly, and sell your organization. Then tell them what the job is. Make it a selling piece so that even those who don't want to be printers will want, some time, to do business with you.

12. Advertise to keep even with or ahead of your competitors. Some will frown on that suggestion but in some markets that is exactly what you have to do. If your competitor is conducting a strong advertising campaign, you have to either advertise or put on a larger number of salesmen than your competitor if you want to keep even or surge ahead. There are a number of cities in the United States where there are two or three top-flight printing plants in the one city. It becomes a never ending task to keep sales at a profitable volume. The only economical way that they have found to keep business coming in is through a continuing advertising campaign with new ideas, new angles, new gimmicks to get attention and make their points.

13. Advertise to show proof of the quality of your printing. One of the most successful forms of printers' advertising is a sample of a regular job right off the press.

Printing buyers know you will take extra care and patience on your own advertising pieces. They really want to see what your plant is producing every day. They can also see for whom you are working, and if you have customers with excellent reputations, then so much the better. When you use a customer's piece to show the quality of your work you are also complimenting the customer. If you think enough of the customer's layout, design, copy to show it proudly to your prospects, then it must be a good job and he is pleased and satisfied that you think so.

14. Advertise to let everyone know the many types of printing you can produce and the many services you can offer. Unless you are in a very specialized field of printing, now and then you should let everyone in your market know that you exist. Everyone, some time, needs printing. We are not suggesting that you advertise to everyone consistently, because the cost is prohibitive. But at least twice a year there should be an overall effort.

Buying decisions are rarely made by one man, although one man may place the order. Therefore, you want others around the buyer to know of your talents. Advertising to others assists the actual buyer of the printing. It helps to prove to the others that he is purchasing from a wide awake, quality-conscious printer. If something should go wrong with the job, the buyer wants to be able to spread his hands upward and say, "Everybody knows they are the best in the business, even if they did print that gray halftone."

The weekly or monthly advertising can be directed to the regular buyers of printing. Be sure that somehow, and frequently, you tell them about the many types of printing you can produce. If you have a bindery, be sure they know that you can punch holes, collate, fold and do many jobs that perhaps their secretaries are doing. If you have some letterpress equipment, be sure they know that you can emboss and die cut. If you have extra storage space, let them know. You never know what a customer will need and what he can buy from you.

Without advertising, without telling people about your product and its benefits, many potential customers are lost because they remain ignorant of your work.

15. Advertise to educate, to inform your customers and prospects about the character of your printing. Many people do not know why one printing piece looks so attractive and another looks poor. They know there is quality in some pieces that is not in others but they don't know why.

Your advertising can explain broken type, unequal margins, poor register, roller streaks, ghosts, ink coverage, washed out halftones and the many other things that can spoil a printing job. If you have a plant that can eliminate these faults, let people know about it.

16. Advertise to obtain a trial order. The object is to get a potential customer to see how you handle a printing job, to experience your way of doing business. Many buyers of printing are using the same printer because they don't want to bother changing. They aren't getting the best job, he's often late on delivery, but it's easy to give the work to old Joe, who is just around the corner.

The theory of a trial order is the same as that used by manufacturers of consumer products. If the prospect will try the product, it will sell itself and a loyal customer will be made. If you have confidence in your printing and service, advertise to obtain a trial order. It may need a special deal or even a dollars-off coupon, but it is worth it if you can get a new customer.

17. Advertise to establish a brand preference. This is our last point and, perhaps, one that seems "far out" to most printers. It is something that we have wondered about for some time. Why hasn't some company in the printing industry tried to establish, through advertising, a name for itself? In almost every area there is one printer who consistently does top quality work and, of course, charges for it. You can look at the job, no matter what the subject is, and say that there is no doubt it came from Jim Jones' plant. The plant just doesn't turn out sloppy work of any kind.

Most of us will purchase a Westinghouse or General Electric item over one marked Burns Special. Some of us buy, or would like to buy, Cadillac cars. Our wives buy Pillsbury or Gold Medal flour rather than Veverkas flour. Why not establish a brand of printing that is known for its beauty, its quality? A by-line would be shown on every piece. The preference could be built in a community and extended to a state or nation as the company progressed. We don't think that is impossible.

There are, no doubt, many other reasons for advertising, but these 17 points will help anyone to understand the potential value of advertising to printers.

In case you may think these reasons are just one man's biased opinion, we asked three executives of the largest advertisers in the world what their opinion of advertising was, and here are their statements:

Mr. Howard Morgens, Chairman of the Board of Procter & Gamble, the largest advertiser in the world (*Ad Age* reports $275,000,000 a year) says, "We in Procter & Gamble believe that advertising is the most effective and efficient way to sell the consumer. If we should ever find better methods of selling our type of products to the consumer, we'll leave advertising and turn to the other methods. There are certain broad basic reasons for advertising's great effectiveness—reasons which go beyond mere dollars and cents calculations. Advertising can and does create new markets."

C. W. Cook, Chairman of the Board of General Foods Corporation, says, "Advertising plays a vital role in moving goods and services, on one hand, and the people who need and want them, on the other, toward one another." He also said, ". . . critics of advertising don't always understand . . . why, once a product is established, we don't just cut back the advertising and coast. It doesn't work that way. New families . . . new customers . . . are constantly being formed. People move. Incomes rise. Tastes change. Competition will not stand still."

A statement from Sears, Roebuck and Co., the largest user of newspaper advertising in the world: "Sears, naturally, believes in advertising in many forms, because it is the lifeblood of communications to our present and potential customers. As such it has two purposes for us:

1. To do a pre-selling job on merchandise and services, and to sell them on Sears as a place to shop.
2. To attract people to come to our stores, to buy those merchandise items and services they want or need."

Sears, Roebuck and Co., in the last few years, has surely given us one answer to the question, "Why Advertise?" Some of us can remember when, in the forties and early fifties, Sears was considered a catalog house with some big stores scattered around. City folk had a feeling that only farmers and people who lived way back in the hills bought from Sears. At least, we didn't think you could get anything stylish there. The goods were all substantial and wore well, but not what city folk should wear. This picture has all changed and to a great degree because of advertising. Sears ads on floor coverings, clothes, automotive needs and even tools, now appear in the best home furnishing, news and style-conscious magazines. The ads are large and beautiful. Their backgrounds show the finest hotels, fashion salons and country clubs. Everything is in excellent taste. They have sold better quality without saying so in so many words. They have done what we say can be done by any printer. If you are able to produce quality printing you can quickly build an image of a quality house through your advertising.

Advertising volume in 1974 passed the $26 billion mark according to figures compiled for *Advertising Age* magazine by Robert J. Coen, Vice President, McCann-Erickson, New York. Businessmen would not spend that amount of money if they were not convinced that advertising helps produce sales. That is the best answer to the question, "Why Advertise?"

CHAPTER 2
HOW TO GET STARTED

"Advertising doesn't jerk—it pulls.
If it is continuous,
it will exert an irrestible force.
Advertising is no game
for the quitter."

—John Wanamaker

Because advertising is such a controversial, misunderstood thing, the remaining pages in this book could be filled with detailed information about this chapter's subject. In as few pages as possible, we will try to give you the more important procedures for getting started on an advertising program. If we delve into all the complicated historical, motivational, psychological, socioeconomical, geographical and behavioral studies, you will never have time to get started. In fact, you may even be fearful.

Grit Your Teeth

We will assume that your company is small to medium size. We will also assume that it produces a general line of commercial printing and does not specialize. Another important factor will be that it does not have millions of dollars to spend for advertising and promotion. After you get started in advertising, and business increases to huge proportions, then, and only then, will you need to study the many complicated facets of advertising.

You get started in advertising in almost the same manner as you start to swim in a cold body of water. You grit your teeth, hold your breath and jump in. If you don't know anything about advertising, then, as in swimming, you take it in easy steps. First, you must want to swim. That is imperative. You watch and imitate other people. You walk around in the water a little. You hold your nose, close your eyes and try to get your head under the water. You find that it isn't so bad, so you open your eyes under the water. Before you know it, it becomes fun, you dog paddle and you are off. You may not be breaking any speed records but you are doing what some others are doing and making progress. You start advertising just about the same way. But first, you must want to do it.

In discussing and in trying to persuade printers to advertise, we have found that there is hardly anything a printer will not do, in order to avoid the real labor of advertising! That is an exaggeration, but actually, it is not overstated too much. Printers are quite convinced that advertising will help to increase their customers' markets. However, they do not want to try it for their own companies.

As in doing almost anything in this world, you have to want to do something before you can apply yourself and do a skilled job. Advertising is no exception. You have to have good intentions. You have to have a plan. Then you must be interested enough to bring the plan to fruition.

Be Interested

In many companies, top management does not give proper time and thought to the investment it makes in advertising. Advertising is called an expense. If ten thousand dollars are used for advertising and ten thousand dollars are used as a capital investment, on the bottom line of the financial report they are both the same. Both expenditures are investments. One is charged to expense and one is written off by depreciation and expensed in a different manner. It has seemed ridiculous to us that management requires detailed analysis of the expected return on all capital expenditures, but it will turn over large amounts of money to be spent for advertising and never ask for an accounting of results. In many cases, management doesn't have an idea of what the advertising hopes to accomplish, not to mention knowing if anything was accomplished after the money was spent.

Put the Plant in Order

We have often wondered if the real reason that so many printers do not advertise was because they were afraid their regular day in and day out product wasn't good enough. They could get by with some "friendly" customers. To try to sell to large corporations or advertising agencies that had sophisticated buyers, it was another thing. Advertising makes you toe the line quality-wise. We know that there is more than one printing salesman who spends three-fourths of his time selling a customer and picking up the order. In the other fourth of his time he is re-selling the order after it was poorly printed or delivered off schedule.

Actually, a printer should get started on an advertising program by first putting the plant in order. Be sure you have a product that can live up to the usual advertising claims. If you are not producing a good product, all the advertising in the world will not help you. In fact, advertising a poor product or a product that isn't useful will bring out the product's weakness quicker than anything else.

Large manufacturers of consumer goods will test a product in a small market by advertising heavily to see if it can live up to its advertising claims. The advertising will quickly sell the first package or piece to those who are willing to experiment. But will they come back for another package? Is the product good enough to get repeat business? That is what counts and that is why they test the market. Advertising will not help to sell a poor product more than once.

Plan So You Can Measure Results

When you are satisfied that your plant can produce a good product, the next step is to start planning your advertising. We know you have heard that very often. Everything must be planned, planned, planned. It is so necessary when advertising.

The plan should not be only in the head of the company's president. It should not be just in the imagination or in the head of the man who has been assigned the job of taking care of the advertising. The plan should be written down in some detail for everyone to see, understand and refer to from time to time.

A general belief or confidence in the power of good advertising is fine. But you need more than that to have a successful program. Results should be known and measured in order to improve from year to year. A wise printer would not buy a new press without having a fairly good idea of how fast it would run. When it was installed he would keep good records of its production to see if he was getting his money's worth. He should have the same kind of interest in measuring advertising results.

Advertising results are not easy to measure because the effects of advertising may not appear in some cases for years. They are almost impossible to measure unless what you are seeking from advertising has been written and defined. You need objectives. You have read or heard about management-by-objective. This same technique applies to advertising.

Advertising Goals

In writing what you specifically want your advertising to accomplish, you will find many wide differences of opinion within your organization. One executive will want it to build the company name and reputation. The founder will want it to emphasize the length of time the company has been in business. Someone else will want it to sell color work. Another will want it to get rid of that big inventory of 20-pound bond that was bought on speculation for a job that never materialized. Another will want it just to be better than a competitor's advertising. These differences are exactly why the goals should be in writing. Get them resolved before the advertising is planned or prepared. Have everyone agree on one or no more than two goals so that advertising money won't be wasted in trying to go in ten different directions during one campaign.

When you write your goals for advertising they should be specifically for advertising and not marketing. Advertising alone will not increase sales or get the salesmen to open new accounts. These are marketing goals.

If you are conducting a strictly mail-order business, which requires no salesmen, then sales figures can be the measurement of your advertising. In the mail-order business, advertising is the most dominant factor in marketing. The advertising asks for an immediate sale and it is written and produced on an entirely different format from other advertising. Your advertising then is really your catalog or price sheet. Every detail of your product must be clearly described. You leave nothing for a salesman to contribute.

Advertising Means Communication

Advertising is a communication tool. It should be assigned a communication job. It should not be assigned a task that it cannot actually fulfill. For instance, suppose a printer sets a marketing objective to sell more printing. His goal is to get 10% of the printing sales in his community in the next year. Advertising can help in achieving that goal but it can not do the job by itself. Quality printing is important in increasing sales. So are delivery schedules. The number of salesmen hired to do the job will be a factor. Competition must be considered. Price is important. Creativity and all of the things that contribute to a sale can effect the possibility of the printer attaining 10% of the printing sales in his community. So, a marketing goal can not be an advertising goal. Advertising's task is to call public attention to a message (it often is a sales message) that stimulates or leads to action.

The advertising goal for the printer who has a marketing objective to sell more printing in the community could be, "To obtain ten inquiries from 100 known printing prospects in the community."

If, after questioning the company's prospects, it is found that only 5% of the prospects know or have ever heard of the company, a different advertising goal could be established. That goal could be, "To increase by 10% the number of prospects who know the company and its product."

To accomplish the two above advertising goals, a specific communication job is required. It can be done by advertising without depending on other marketing tasks or skills. Either one of the goals can be measured at the end of the year. In the first instance, after the advertising has been started, someone in the organization should keep a record of the business reply cards, letters, phone calls that come in asking for a salesman to call. If a total of ten inquiries come in, the advertising goal has been met.

In the second case, where the goal is to increase by 10% the number of prospects who know the company and its products, another bit of research must be made. When the campaign has been completed, or at the end of a year of advertising, the same questions are asked of the same people who were asked about the company before the advertising was used. You may now find that 20% of the prospects know or have heard of the company. Then there is little doubt that the advertising called public attention to the company. It increased by 15% the number of prospects who knew the company before the use of the advertising campaign. The advertising goal was surpassed by 5%.

Now you also have a rough idea of something else. You know how much the advertising cost to get that result. You know how much time and effort was needed. So, given the same economic climate and the same time frame and a new list of prospects of similar quality, you should get the same results. You could use the same advertising program for this new list of prospects. We would suggest that you increase your budget enough to take care of the usual increase in costs.

If you continue to use the same list of prospects that were used the past year, and if you want a similar result, you will have to increase your budget as well as the creativity of your program. When you work the same list over and over again the resistance to action becomes a little greater. You have to try harder. We have found, however, that inquiries seem to be more productive. The people who want to see your salesmen seem better prepared to buy. They are not just curious.

Measuring Advertising is Difficult

Once more, let us throw in a word of caution. Measuring advertising isn't quite as easy as we have made it sound. We firmly believe that at least you should try to measure results. Our suggestions will give you round, in-the-ball-park figures. This week's advertising or this month's or this year's advertising may not pay off until next year or several years from now. Everyone who receives your advertising may not need printing on the day he sees your advertising. He may not wish to change his present source for printing. There may be five or ten good reasons why he won't act immediately. You must keep informing him, keep asking for action. Even when the prospect does act and you receive an order, keep advertising to him. Advertising assures the customer that he made the right choice, that he had excellent judgment in purchasing printing from your company.

Advertising is not an exact science. So far, no one in advertising has been able to find a formula that will give us a certain result for a certain medium or advertising program. Through testing and measuring we can come up with some facts for one particular company and one particular product. Beware of the man or the agency who will predict the return on a piece of advertising for a particular company unless the advertising has been tested for that company.

There are Many Advertising Goals

There can be many printers' advertising goals other than the two suggested above. What we are trying to emphasize is that in planning you set a goal and that it be an advertising goal that can be measured. None of the following are advertising goals:

To make a profit.
To sell printing.
To sell work for the bindery department.
To earn 5% on our capital investment.
To increase our sales by 12%.
To develop and sell school year books.
To expand use of present facilities.
To capture 8% share of market in two years.

They are either company or marketing objectives.

Advertising's job is to call public attention to your company and your product; to educate prospects so they are aware of your product and understand why it is a good one. These could be advertising goals for a printing company:

Inform 40% of prospects about our new 40" press.
Obtain 30 inquiries from prospects this year.
Increase company identity and favorable attitude among prospects by 10% in the next year.
Raise favorable image of our company from 5% to 10% in next year.
Persuade 20 prospects to visit our plant in six months.

Register cost saving by buying printing from us with 10% of prospects.
Inform 50% of prospects that we have a bindery department.
Get 30% of prospects to recognize that our company produces quality printing.

These are subjects that can be developed by advertising and can be measured. In a number of cases it would be necessary to establish a benchmark before the advertising campaign was used. Then do some opinion research after the campaign has been completed. (See Chapter 6.)

A Fictitious Company and Its Goal

To better illustrate how to determine an advertising goal and to perhaps give you a rough outline of the procedure, we will set up a fictitious city and printing company and work from that. You may find that there isn't too much fiction in this case study. If you recognize any particular company or management group, please accept it as a coincidence.

Our city will be Galvin, Maryland, population 51,000, located in a heavily populated rural district. In other words, there are many small farms around. There's a large city with a population of 69,000 about 35 miles north, and another one with 896,000 people, 50 miles to the south. In and around Galvin, there are 2,451 business establishments. However, there are only 460 business establishments which have a worth of $500,000 or more. There are 14 printers listed in the yellow pages of the telephone book.

Our imaginary printing company will be called Curtis Press, Inc. It is located in a small industrial park on the outskirts of Galvin. The building is modern, brick, one floor, air-conditioned, humidity-controlled, landscaped and makes a nice appearance. There are 16,000 square feet of space.

The equipment consists of three letterpresses, four sheet-fed o?set presses, the two largest presses being 23" x 29" two colors. There's a small typesetting department of two persons and camera, darkroom and platemaking equipment.

The organization consists of a president, two vice presidents, an accountant and estimator, two outside salesmen, two inside salesmen and a production manager. There are a total of 32 employees having service records from two to twenty-two years.

Sales volume has been right around $480,000 for the past two years. They have been getting a fair price for their work. They lose a few jobs to two competitors who need work every now and then. They have been keeping their 15 good customers happy. They print small booklets, short-run publications, catalogs and general commercial printing.

They have room to expand and their financial position is such that they could acquire new equipment if business warranted it. They could operate two shifts if necessary. They are not advertising at the present time. The company depends on the two salesmen to bring in the majority of the work and quite a bit comes in the front door. They have some trouble and must be careful that the credit is good on those jobs that come in unannounced.

The President Makes a Decision

Curt Cart, president of the company, has decided that their sales need a boost. Sales have remained at the same level for over two-and-a-half years. Al Rega, his son-in-law, is the vice president in charge of the marketing end of the business, and he has wanted to try some advertising for some time. The company belongs to the Printing Industries of America organization in the city 50 miles to the south. They have heard at least ten speeches and read many articles on planning. They do plan their capital equipment purchases and try to operate within a budget.

Ted Ways, the vice president in charge of production and the financial end of the business, has been reading quite a bit about marketing and especially advertising. He wants to keep up with Al Rega and not have to accept his word for everything when they prepare budgets. Ted has prepared a list of questions that he has gleaned from many articles and books. The three executives have decided that they will answer these questions and then see where they can go from there. Each one is going to answer the questions on his own and evaluate his answer with a number from 0 to 10. After they have given a few days' thought to these questions they intend to get together, compare answers, discuss and try to arrive at some important conclusions.

An In-House Questionnaire

Here are the questions. For your company or type of business, you may have many more or less.

JUDGE THE QUALITY OF OUR WORK
(0 —Poor; 10—Excellent)

1. Generally speaking, everything that goes out the door, how does it rate? (Do not judge it by our competitors' but by all high quality standards.)
2. How is the creativity that we sometimes provide?
3. How is the art that we provide?
4. How is *our* type composition?
5. How is the cold composition that we buy outside?

HOW DO YOU RATE OUR LETTERPRESS WORK . . .

6. Impression?
7. Color Stability?
8. Halftones?
9. Register?

HOW DO YOU RATE OUR LITHOGRAPHIC PRESS WORK . . .

10. Color Stability?
11. Halftones?
12. Type Reproduction?
13. Register?
14. Hickies, Roller Streaks? (0—Too Many; 10—None)

NOW, PLEASE RATE OUR OTHER WORK.

15. How do you rate our camera work?
16. What about our stripping?
17. How do you rate our plate work?
18. How do you rate our quality control?
19. Do many pieces or sheets of waste get to the customer?
20. Do our cutters deliver absolutely square cuts?
21. How do you rate our folding?
22. How do you rate our collating?
23. How do you rate our stitching?
24. How do you rate our hand work?
25. How do you rate our wrapping?

HOW IS OUR GENERAL HOUSEKEEPING . . .

26. Offices?
27. Plant?
28. Does our delivery truck make a good appearance?

WHAT ABOUT THE MAN WHO MAKES THE DELIVERIES . . .

29. Appearance?
30. Disposition?
31. Hustle?

HOW DO OUR SALESMEN RATE . . .

Joe C.; Henry S.; Bill S.; Dick H.

32. Appearance?
33. Disposition?
34. Graphic arts knowledge?
35. Our plant knowledge?
36. Local industry knowledge?
37. Urgency of an order?
38. Sales ability?
39. Creativity?

HOW ARE OUR BILLING AND COLLECTION PROCEDURES . . .

40. Invoices prepared correctly?
41. Invoices mailed promptly?
42. Overdue accounts handled promptly?
43. Collection of overdue accounts handled firmly but with finesse?
44. After consideration of these questions, do you believe that we can live up to the usual advertising adjectives that will no doubt be used? (Quality House—Real Service—Fine Typography—Good Register—Beautiful Colors—Creativity—Follow Through)

NOW PROCEED WITH THE EVALUATION OF THE IMPORTANCE OF THESE SUBJECTS IN OUR ADVERTISING AND SALES PROMOTION:

(0—No Importance; 10—Top Importance)

COMPANY IMAGE . . .

45. Service?
46. Growth?
47. Progressiveness?
48. Technical know-how?
49. Friendliness?
50. Civic Responsibility?
51. Cooperation? (Suggestions for improvements of customers' printing jobs)
52. Good Character? (Of company and employees)
53. Experience—Age?
54. Add Your Suggestions ______________________

____

____

TO WHOM SHOULD WE AIM OUR ADVERTISING . . .

55. Present Customers?
56. Customers who have left us?
57. The entire community within Galvin?
58. Manufacturing companies in Galvin?
59. Service companies in Galvin?
60. Financial institutions in Galvin?
61. Wholesale outlets in Galvin?
62. Retail outlets in Galvin?
63. Doctors and dentists in Galvin?
64. Attorneys in Galvin?
65. Churches in Galvin?
66. Farms within 25 miles of Galvin?
67. Large corporations in a radius of 50 miles?
68. Large corporations in a radius of 100 miles?
69. Add your Suggestions ______________________

____

____

____

WHAT DO WE WANT OUR ADVERTISING TO DO . . .

70. Completely sell an order?
(Mail order business or printing trade work—we suppy catalog and price list, the customer sends in order. No personal contact except perhaps by phone to clear a production detail.)
71. Inform prospects of our product and services?
72. Inform prospects of some new specialized type of printing?
73. Refute competitive claims?

74. Inform people of the nearness or availability of our plant?
75. Introduce our two outside salesmen and the two inside men?
76. Create what could be called a brand image or, at least, a desire to deal only with us?
77. Build a recognition of our company?
78. Build a reputation for having the most modern type and art department?
79. Demonstrate our creativity?
80. Let prospects know the company we keep?
(Tell them about our customers and show their work)
81. Suggest new uses or novel uses of printing?
82. Get customer to be involved with us?
(Send in a reply card; enter a contest; ask to see the plant; ask to see samples; make inquiries)
83. Aid salesman in seeing prospects?
84. To build confidence and good will?
85. To push our catalog printing?
86. To push our annual report printing?
87. To push our advertising printing?
88. Support our salesmen?
(Back up the statements they make in their sales presentations)
89. Add your suggestions ______________________________

____

Comparing Answers

After answering the 89 questions to the best of their knowledge and beliefs, the three executives met after regular business hours to compare their answers. It was wisely decided by Mr. Carl that they would act as professional businessmen and no one was to spare the horses if they felt strongly about any subject. Proof that each one took that policy at its face value is the time it took to compare each other's opinion and to arrive at one on which they could all agree. The first nine questions took until twelve o'clock the first evening. The next morning they decided that all future meetings would stop at ten o'clock. There were six future meetings! Four of those meetings were devoted to the balance of the first 44 questions. They decided that if they never advertised, the exercise of evaluating their plant was worth the time and effort.

Decisions Made

From the decisions they reached in answering the first 44 questions, they decided to keep only enough hot metal type for some of the imprinting they did as well as for correcting some old type forms that they had. They decided to buy all cold composition in the future. They set up a more formal quality control program. They decided to buy a van-type truck, put the driver in a neat uniform an ask him to cut his hair and keep his face shaved. We understand the young man refused to cut his hair. When he received his bright uniform with flared trousers, the next day he came in with his hair cut. In appreciation, Mr. Carl took him to lunch and told him he was proud to be seen with him. One of the outside salesmen was replaced. Collection procedures on overdue accounts were changed for the better. It was decided to discuss the evaluation procedure with six of the top employees and to answer the same questions within a year. They also decided to go ahead with a modest advertising program.

It was decided that for the first year they would try to develop their company image around progressiveness. They felt that would be the easiest subject for them to sell. They felt that the plant, outside and inside, looked the part. The other subjects were not to be forgotten and they rated them in this order:

1. Progressiveness
2. Technical know-how
3. Employee *esprit de corps* (suggested by Mr. Rega)
4. Growth
5. Service
6. Cooperation
7. Good character
8. Friendliness
9. Civic responsibility
10. Experience—Age

They decided they should advertise, at first, to manufacturing company prospects, present customers and to those who hadn't placed an order within a year. If they could afford it, they wanted to touch the entire community. Their choices were in this order:

1. Manufacturing companies in Galvin.
2. Present customers.
3. Customers who hadn't placed an order within a year.
4. The entire community within Galvin (when they could afford it).
5. Service companies in Galvin.
6. Large corporations in a radius of 50 miles.
7. Wholesale outlets.
8. Retail outlets.
9. Financial institutions.
10. Attorneys.
11. Doctors and dentists.
12. Large corporations in a radius of 100 miles.

They wanted their advertising to build a recognition of their company, its products and its services. Their first ten choices were as follows:

1. Build a recognition of our company.
2. Inform prospects of our product and service.
3. Introduce our two outside salesmen and the two inside men.
4. Get customers involved with us.
5. Support our salesmen.
6. Build confidence and good will.
7. Push our annual report printing.
8. Let prospects know the company we keep.
9. Demonstrate our creativity.

They Start to Write the Goal—But . . .

So, now they had some opinions on which they agreed. The three executives knew about where they wanted to point the company and they were ready to write an adverising goal. Al Rega took on the task. But first, he decided they had to know one thing. He thought he knew the answer, and the salesmen were sure they knew it, but they thought that their opinions might be colored. The question was: How many manufacturing companies in Galvin already thought Curtis Press was a progressive plant with plenty of technical know-how?

So, they decided they would do some research. There are hundreds of research methods. This company was going to do it as quickly and cheaply as possible. Perhaps it isn't the most accurate method but it has been used by a large number of companies including General Motors. Sophisticated researchers probably call it a quick and dirty method. We believe it is good enough. They decided to use a mailed questionnaire with a letter asking for cooperation. They would send it to the same people that they wanted to receive their advertising.

Mailing List

They knew that sooner or later they had to put together a good mailing list or calling list. They had a list that they developed from the telephone book about five years ago. They had added, subtracted and generally defaced it until they didn't have a good list. In fact, they didn't really have a company list of customers. The salesmen knew where their customers were and their addresses. They could get a list from old invoices but nowhere was there an official mailing list or calling list for Curtis Press, Inc.

Companies which sell mailing lists, and there are thousands of them, will not appreciate our describing this next procedure. Research organizations will also complain. In another chapter of this book you will find references and addresses for both types of services. This writing is just one way that a "mythical company" handled the situation.

Al Rega's wife was a worker in a church. He asked her and two other church ladies to compile an up-to-date list of the manufacturing companies in Galvin, as well as a customer list. They were promised five cents a name for the church. On the manufacturing list they wanted companies with a net worth of $250,000 or over. They wanted the names of the president, marketing man, advertising man and buyer of printing. On the customer list they didn't bother with the net worth but they wanted the other information.

The ladies went to a library 50 miles from home and pored through all the manufacturing directories, buyers' guides and city directories that they could find. They wrote their information on 3"x5" cards and some of it was meager. They pored over five years of invoices and sorted and filed them so that a customer's name wouldn't also be on the manufacturers' list. Two of the ladies had unlimited telephones, so if information was missing, and most of it was, they telephoned the company and asked for the information and received it. Al Rega said the conversation at the dinner table every night for over a month was mailing lists. The ladies enjoyed their job and Curtis Press received a beautiful list.

The Research Group

Al Rega then printed some letterheads and envelopes and obtained a mail box at the post office for the Acme Research Group. The Group was the same three ladies. A very short questionnaire was printed asking the following questions:

Have you ever heard of any of the following printing companies?

	Yes	No
Brutout Press, Inc.	☐	☐
Burns Litho Co.	☐	☐
Curtis Press, Inc.	☐	☐
Patterson Printing and Bindery	☐	☐

If there are no check marks in the yes column, please return this sheet in the postage paid envelope enclosed. If you do recognize some of these companies, please proceed.

Is any one of these companies known for its printing techniques and know-how? If so, please place a check mark after the name.

Brutout Press, Inc.	☐	☐
Burns Litho Co.	☐	☐
Curtis Press, Inc.	☐	☐
Patterson Printing and Bindery	☐	☐

Which company or companies are known for progressiveness? Please place a check mark after the name.

Brutout Press, Inc.	☐	☐
Burns Litho Co.	☐	☐
Curtis Press, Inc.	☐	☐
Patterson Printing and Bindery	☐	☐

Thanks for your cooperation. Please return this sheet. Use the postage-paid, addressed envelope enclosed.

The questionnaire was mailed to customers and prospects on the new mailing list with a personalized letter requesting cooperation. A pink questionnaire was sent to customers, a blue one to prospects. There was a 41% return. It was not a fabulous return but it at least gave them a rough idea of what the customers and prospects thought about Curtis Press and three of its best competitors. It was also a benchmark so that another survey could be taken a year or two after the advertising was used and thereby measure the advertising's effectiveness.

The Goal

Now, Al Rega knew what he wanted his advertising to accomplish, so he wrote his goal.

"The Curtis Press market for the next year is 15 present customers, 150 past customers and 980 manufacturing companies in and around Galvin, Md. It is believed that the market is large enough for our marketing goal to be set at a sales volume of $517,500, or a 15% increase over the previous year. Our advertising goal is to increase by 15% the recognition of our company in our selected market. In so doing, we wish to develop a company reputation for progressiveness and technical know-how. We aim to increase these two image characteristics by 10% over our present benchmark survey."

That was it: short, to the point and measurable. Other companies with other management, with more sophisticated study and information, would no doubt have a different goal and, perhaps, set up a different market. This example, at least, will illustrate how an advertising goal can be set.

Planning Again!

After the goal is set, then and only then, can you plan your advertising. We can not emphasize planning too strongly. You will waste your advertising money if you don't plan. If you knock out an advertising piece in December because business is slow, whip one up in March because you discovered that a competitor had advertised, or hustle another advertising piece through in July because someone thought he had a good idea, your advertising cannot be as effective in the long run as it would be if it had been planned, had a theme and was consistent. We used the expressions "knock out," "whip one up," and "hustle" because that is exactly what would happen. You wouldn't have time to put thought and creativity into the program. The pieces would be poor examples of what you are capable of doing.

How Much Should We Spend?

There are two ways to get started with a plan. If you have never advertised, then set a budget and make your plan within the budget. Cost it out as you go. The other method: If you have used a small amount of advertising, then you have an idea of how much advertising it takes to do the job you want. So, you make the plan, then cost it out. If the cost is too high, then you start to eliminate parts of the program with the understanding that you aren't going to do the good job that you wanted to do.

If you are embarking on your first advertising program, how much should you spend to get started? No one really knows how much money should be invested in advertising. Businessmen know that advertising is a cost of doing business. For some it is, perhaps, the single largest expense item (Drugs, cosmetics). The proportion of sales to advertising will also vary within an industry by degree of success. There is one thing that seems certain. In most businesses, products which sell well tend to be advertised more than products which sell poorly.

The Printing Industries of America ratio studies show that the average printing firm spends .35% of its sales volume for advertising. Please remember, these are printers, and printers are notoriously poor users of advertising. One-third of 1% is hardly enough. The same studies show that 8% of the printers who are called profit leaders spend .5%. We wonder what would happen to those profit leaders if they spent 1% or 2% of their sales. Perhaps, then, there would be a PIA category called "capitalists!"

We have had a theory for a long time. We have felt that if a printer would use a heavy advertising program in the first few years of his business life, he would quickly establish himself. We knew it would be difficult. However, we thought it would be worth the effort. In writing this book, we found a man who proved that the theory would work. His name is Robert L. Walker, chairman of the board of Starline Corp., in Albuquerque, N.M. We will let him tell the story:

"As with so many printers, we began operations with a 1250 Multilith and a shingle that proclaimed Starline to be printers. Albuquerque was a sleepy city so far as printers were concerned: The big printers had their traditional customers and the little printers seemed ensnared in working for wages, or less, and complaining of the cut-throat competition. None were advertising to any significant degree.

"Our first full year in business (1958) brought a sales volume of $40,000, with about $3000 spent in direct mail advertising. That $3000 was within a few dollars of all the money we would have made that year (and precisely the amount I had borrowed from my rightfully nervous mother-in-law to initiate, along with a couple of other otherwise gainfully employed relatives, the printing operations.)

"In 1959, we again spent every dime we could find—about $8000, as I recall—on direct mail and our sales volume increased to $80,000. The following year we were able to plunge some $16,000 into advertising, and sales grew to $120,000. In 1961, we spent over $20,000 in direct mail efforts on a sales volume of $180,000."

Since 1961, the advertising budget for Starline has stayed around $20,000, and its business has continued to climb. It went public in 1972. Sales were $886,000. It also moved into a large new plant and installed New Mexico's only four-color press—that's a rags-to-riches story. There's no doubt that it did many things right, but advertising helped to pave the way.

After the first four years of consistent advertising, there was hardly a printing prospect in Albuquerque who hadn't heard of Starline. Leads and inquiries were so numerous that Bob Walker never made a cold call. His days were filled with calling on people who asked him to call. He did the printing at night! He was universally welcomed with friendliness because the people who received his advertising felt they knew him. Mailings were sometimes being made twice a month. He found that printing could be sold on the basis of the results it must produce. Starline had become a local authority on successful direct mail advertising. Clients and prospects regarded the company as more than just printers because of their creative advertising.

Walker says it wasn't particularly pleasant to live those first four or five years eating low on the hog while all that profit was being poured into advertising. However, if given the same existing shoestring capital structure, he is confident he would make the same judgments. Advertising has been and continues to be an absolutely vital selling tool for Starline.

Here are some other remarks of Bob Walker's:

"I am perpetually astonished by the relative non-existence of printers' advertising. The conclusion is inescapable that the printers' best clients, big advertisers invariably, are immeasurably smarter than the printers themselves. Advertising is the only investment of which I am aware that can be totally written off as an expense yet appreciates every time it is used."

We realize that everyone reading this book is not just starting in business. However, in order to make an impression quickly, you should try to use far more than ⅓ of 1% of your sales for advertising.

You will have to make the decision. You know your own situation. Whatever you do, make a decision that you can stay with for the entire year. Don't kill your advertising when business seems to be poor. Grit your teeth and keep it on schedule. Surely you don't stop selling when business is difficult to get. You shouldn't stop advertising.

Who Handles The Advertising?

Your plan should be detailed. Most printers know enough about advertising that they can choose the correct media. There is a chapter that follows on this subject. If the top executive feels that he does not have the time or, perhaps, the knowledge to work out the details of a complete advertising and promotion program, then the best thing to do is to assign a knowledgeable person to do the job. Make it someone's responsibility to plan and handle the work and then let that person do it. And, we should add, fire him if he doesn't do it.

From what we have gleaned, that is the biggest and most forward step in any printer's plan for advertising. The top executive should weigh his responsibilities. No matter how knowledgeable about advertising he is, or thinks he is, if he doesn't have the time to plan it and work the plan, he must give the responsibility to someone else or it won't be accomplished satisfactorily.

Don't let anyone frighten you into thinking that a modest advertising campaign can be handled only by a qualified advertising expert. Any person (Note that we didn't say "any man." Women do outstanding advertising work.) who has been working with printing and is sales-minded can plan and produce good advertising for a printer. Of course, after advertising for a few years and growing to the size of R.R. Donnelley, you will then need someone with a few extra talents to direct your various uses of advertising. But at first, don't let it frighten you. Use good business sense. Use some of your own native creativity and decide to put forth some real effort.

A campaign in some medium other than print will, no doubt, be difficult for the average printer. If the decision has been made to try broadcasting, for instance, then outside assistance will be necessary.

If you are absolutely certain that no one in your organization can handle the advertising, then hire someone from the outside. Hire a one-man agency or a moonlighting agency employee who can afford to give you special attention. Your small account would not be profitable to a large agency, so you would not be satisfied with its work.

Let us repeat. When you give the advertising task to someone, let that person do it. Give him the authority to do the complete job. Since we all read advertising we are all advertising experts. We all know what we like in advertising. Remember, that doesn't make it good advertising. It is what your public likes that counts. You must place great confidence in the person who creates your advertising. If you don't believe he can handle the job, don't give it to him. Be sure he has confidence in himself. If he hasn't had much experience, be sure that he is willing to read or study about advertising. After you have assigned the task to a person, let him do the complete job. Don't criticize small details. Just because your wife doesn't like brown and prefers pink is no reason why an advertising piece printed in brown ink wouldn't be effective.

Many of us like opera and symphony music but that type of music wouldn't exist if it weren't subsidized by huge grants from a few people who enjoy it and in some cases by grants from the government. However, country music, popular music, jazz, the music of Lawrence Welk and Guy Lombardo has flourished for years without any donation. The majority enjoy what some of us call "corn." When you get right down to it, we have seen sophisticated executives enjoying some very corny performances, not only on the stage but in night clubs and yes, in advertising.

Consistent Advertising Pays

When planning your advertising, be sure it is consistent. A folder sent out this month and one some time next year is not consistent and will not keep your name before prospective buyers of printing.

An advertising effort once a month for the average printer is fine, or once every two months if he isn't sure of himself. No one who is interested in increasing his business can afford not to advertise once a month in some medium. People forget quickly. You have to tell them and tell them and then tell them again. Whatever you do in advertising, be consistent, keep hammering away, keep it on schedule. You may not see great results in the first year but keep going. The results will show. We have seen it work.

Getting It Through the Plant

Your plan must have a schedule—a time table. That isn't difficult to put on paper. To make the schedule work is something else. Here's where the person who is directing the advertising must have authority. To some this may be impossible, almost sacrilegious. In order to keep your advertising consistent and on schedule you must put it in the regular production schedule. No other job should have priority over your own advertising. You won't get it out on schedule and you won't get it done if you don't observe that procedure. That is fact, not fiction. It is the greatest handicap your advertising will have.

For the simple reason that they cannot get their own advertising printed in their own plants, a few printers purchase syndicated advertising. This is better than no advertising, but so often it doesn't have the warmth, the personal touch, the local flavor that good advertising needs.

Once this policy of treating your advertising work the same as a good customer's is understood throughout the plant, it becomes easy to live with. But until everyone has tested the order and discovered that top management is in back of the person handling the advertising, it will not by taken seriously.

We caution the advertising man to be sure that his job is a shining example of how everyone in the plant would like to receive a customer's job but rarely does. Instructions should be written and clear. Every i should be dotted and every t crossed. Ink specifications should be given or, at least, an ink swatch provided. Don't ask them to match the Torino cover avocado color or set it in a type "something like" old Pen Print. In other words, give them a layout and the kind of instructions that they can admire and enjoy.

Don't forget that after it is printed it still has to be distributed. It does no good sitting on the shelves. Your plans must also schedule the mailings of plates or negatives to a magazine or whatever media you plan to use.

Summary

To get started in advertising you have to grit your teeth and dive in. You must want to advertise to increase communication with your customers and prospects. You must put the plant in order so you can produce the kind and type of printing that will live up to the usual advertising claims. You must plan your advertising so you can measure the results. You should have an advertising goal. You must assign someone to handle the advertising program and give that person authority. Your advertising should be consistent. In order to get your own advertising through the plant you must put it into your regular production schedule.

CHAPTER 3
ADVERTISING MEDIA

"Advertise, or the chances are
that the sheriff will do it for you!"

—— P. T. Barnum

This chapter will be devoted to advertising media. Almost every medium is after the advertiser's dollar. They all give very convincing arguments and figures. The individual characteristics of each medium must be carefully considered for the job you want to do. Most printers know to whom they want to advertise and where these people are located. Therefore, they do not have to guess or test as much as some other manufacturers or service organizations. We suggest that you consider all the media even if you are very certain you know where you want to advertise. There may be some angle that you have neglected, especially if you are doing specialized printing.

We will try to cover the following general media in this chapter:

Advertising Specialties (Promotion)
Business Publications
Direct Mail
Directories
Farm Publications
Magazines
Newspapers
Outdoor
Packaging
Program, Ticket and Charity Promotion
Promotion
Public Relations
Publicity
Radio
Soundsheets
Television
Theater Screen
Transit
Word of Mouth

Purchase the media that is being read or seen by your prospects. If you do not know what they are you will have to ask. This research will cost more than that done by our mythical company in the last chapter. A mailed, printed form will not do an effective job. Someone will have to go and visit customers and prospects and try to get an honest answer to the question, "What do you read?" In this case, most people will tell you what they think you want to hear or what will make them seem important. Someone must probe and search to get your customers and prospects off guard before you get the answer that is correct for them.

Almost every business man will say he reads *Fortune* magazine and *Wall Street Journal.* Before you believe him, look for used copies around his office. Refer to an article in the last issue of *Fortune* or *Wall Street Journal.* If he doesn't recall it, ask for a copy of the publication so you can show it to him. Perhaps his copy is at home, but keep probing until you are fairly sure he reads whatever he says he reads. It is a difficult task and it will take some skill to get the real facts but it will pay off for your advertising.

Again, as in every phase of advertising, don't let your personal preferences dominate your thinking. If you want to give your message to a youth audience, don't underestimate a flamboyant college newspaper or magazine. You may think it is terrible but your customers might love it.

Measuring Media

Be sure to question the media sales people in detail. You will find the statements and reports very confusing. Ask for facts about the readers or, for broadcasting, the listeners. Question sales representatives until you are sure you have all the facts. Each one will put his best foot forward. It will be up to you to delve into the subject and get the bad news as well as the good. Circulation statements are available from newspapers and magazines. Business papers break down their circulation in many ways. With a computer they can inundate you with figures. Some of the information is useless as far as a printer is concerned, but some of it can be very helpful in determining if the publication is sent to and read by your prospects. These figures are most often audited by one of the four organizations doing this type of work: ABC, Audit Bureau of Circulations; BPA, Business Publications Audit of Circulation, Inc.; CAC, Certified Audit of Circulations, Inc. or VAC, Verified Audit Circulation Corporation.

Sometimes the figures are sworn to by the publisher but not audited. Rarely do you receive figures that haven't been authenticated by some means. If the figures haven't been audited it is likely a local publication that doesn't feel an audit would sell more local advertising, so he foregoes the expense. Be careful of figures that haven't been audited or authenticated in some manner. Some territorial magazines and local shoppers have been known to deliver a lot fewer copies than promised by their salesmen.

You will, no doubt, hear quite a bit about paid circulation and free circulation. The argument has been going on for years. In our experience we have found little difference in the response to advertising and that is what counts. You will have to do some testing to determine that for your own company.

Broadcasting audiences are measured by recognized statistical methods and are based on samples of individuals or households. So few of us have ever been asked if we are or have been listening to a certain program that we are a bit suspicious of broadcasting information. However, it is the only information available so we accept it. The information is audited by two or three groups and each is done with a different technique: Pulse in New York; Arbitron Radio in Beltsville, Md., and Hooper in New York.

Outdoor advertising is also measured. The circulation of an outdoor sign is found by counting the number of people who pass it and have a reasonable chance to see it. They use a figure of one-half the pedestrians and automobiles and a fourth of the passengers using surface transportation. The sales representatives will explain their "impression-opportunities" and how they rely on official federal, state and local traffic counts. The Outdoor Advertising Association of America is the central source of information.

Advertising Specialties

For the printer, advertising specialties can be an effective advertising medium. Specialty advertising employs useful articles such as book matches, combs, memo books, pens and pencils, ash trays, paper weights, calendars, bottle openers, measuring cups, thermometers, paper clips, art calendars and coffee mugs. In fact, almost anything that can be imprinted with the advertiser's name, address and message could be called a specialty advertising item. These pieces are mostly directed to a pre-selected audience and are mailed, or personally given, without cost or obligation as a goodwill or reminder item.

Surveys to determine reactions and the use of advertising specialties are continually being made. You may obtain free copies of the most current surveys from the Specialty Advertising Information Bureau, 740 North Rush Street, Chicago, Illinois 60611.

Specialty advertising is used as reminder advertising or simply to say "Thank you." It works effectively when supplemented by other media.

An item that relates to the printing industry will probably be more effective than one that has no relation. Of course, uniqueness should not be forgotten. No doubt, every printer has distributed rulers at some time or other. But how about something that would give a person an idea of the height of most 6-point, 10-point, 12-point type? Or, a kit to determine paper weight? Hammermill Paper Company's approach includes an imprinted scale for weighing mailing pieces and a slide calculator to determine paper weights per 1000 sheets.

Business Publications

In this section we will be referring to business magazines which are general in nature and business papers which are what we also know as magazines but are specialized business publications. These approximately 2,380 papers or publications are published with many different frequencies. Here is a breakdown:

Monthly	68.6% of total
Bi-monthly	15.4
Bi-weekly	4.8
Quarterly	4.7
Weekly	5.4
Daily	1.1

Their distribution totals 73,182,000 and it is broken down in about the same percentages.

Business magazines are mostly business oriented. Some carry news of general interest but are mostly written for top management people. They carry a large amount of business advertising and the rates are relatively high in comparison to business paper space. Very few printers can afford to advertise in these magazines. A printer should be aiming at the national market before he indulges in this type of advertising.

In the business paper field there are what the advertising people call "horizontal" and "vertical" publications. Horizontal business paper editors try to slant their material to persons with similar duties but in different industries. A magazine written for purchasing agents or maintenance superintendents would be called a horizontal publication. Magazines written for printers or aircraft manufacturers would be called vertical publications. Therefore, if a printer would want to advertise to purchasing agents he should try to find a horizontal business paper sent to purchasing agents. If the printer were interested only in the purchasing agents in his local market, a national publication would give him a large amount of wasted circulation. However, there are a few publications which have regional editions. These magazines permit you to purchase space in an edition that covers only the New England states or the Southern states or wherever you may desire.

In case you hear someone refer to an industrial paper or a professional paper or a trade paper, and he might use the word magazine instead of paper, do not let it confuse you. He is still talking about business papers. Professional papers are edited for professional people who may influence others to buy. Trade papers are mostly for those concerned with retail and wholesale merchandising. Industrial papers which are about half of all the business papers in the United States are written for manufacturing, construction and similar fields.

Farm publications have been separated from this group and are described in another section of this chapter. They have combined consumer-business-editorial matter.

Business papers have smaller circulations than business magazines. Some may only circulate two or three thousand copies. Few have 100,000 circulation. Most are around 50,000 or lower. There are very few manufactured items that are not covered by some type of a business paper.

In making a selection of a business publication you will be exposed to the "paid" and "controlled" circulation argument. The "paid" exponents declare their circulation to be more valuable because no one gets a copy of their publication unless he orders it and pays hard cash for it. The "controlled" circulation magazines argue that they provide more widespread coverage of their specialized field and that reading is not related to payment. Even the U.S. Postal Service has taken a side. "Paid" business papers, as well as newspapers, magazines and some other periodicals, are given the benefit of a special low rate for second class mail. "Controlled" publications must pay relatively higher postal rates.

Whether business publications are paid or controlled, the audit bureaus require that they provide detailed and verified circulation breakdowns for you to study. You will want evidence that qualified recipients receive trade publications regularly. Currently, some 1,475 out of about 2,380 business publications do not have their circulations audited. However, most business paper publishers do submit sworn statements of circulation size.

Advertising space in business publications is customarily quoted by cost per black-and-white page. The rate of the average business paper does not exceed $1,000 per page. Two and four colors are widely available at premiums ranging from 10% to 15% above black-and-white costs per page. Discounts are usually offered, based on continuity and volume.

Printers should examine every medium, including business publications, very carefully before advertising. One main point should be studied—how much waste circulation are you paying for? There may be 3,000 good prospects in a magazine's circulation but in order to reach them, ask yourself if you are paying for 10,000 other persons who do not influence a printing purchase. Study the circulation statements carefully. Discover how many of your prospects receive the magazine you are contemplating. Are they in your market area? Have they subscribed or are they receiving free copies or cut-rate subscriptions, or premiums and special inducements? How many subscriptions are renewed each year? A high renewal percentage is considered evidence of good relationship interest. Are there many copies going out as personal copies or are they just being sent to the company—and the office boy distributes them to whomever he chooses?

Also, get a few copies of the publication and examine its pages. Do you want your advertisement in among those pages? Is the editorial matter interesting or is it filler copy? Is the publication printed in a first class manner? Does it look professional? How much material is written by the paper's own staff? Do they use "bingo cards" (postage-paid, inserted reply cards) for their readers to obtain information from the advertisers? Ask to see some of these cards. Are they coming from curiosity seekers or executives? You will have a difficult time finding out, but ask the question.

Watch for official organs of associations. They may be only promoting the organizations and not be of real interest to the readers. Ask for audited circulation figures or sworn statements of coverage. Study the publication carefully. Note its editorial matter. Check with advertisers who have used the publication—especially printers. Remember, you are not advertising for the good will of a publisher friend. You should want action from your advertising.

Here is a word of caution. Beware of the publication that offers to publish a publicity story for you in return for some paid advertising. Another gimmick is to ask you to pay for the engraving cost to illustrate an article they will write about your company. A legitimate publication that is highly regarded will keep editorial copy and publicity entirely separate from advertising. If you have to pay for a news item, forget it. Either it isn't real news in the first place, or the publication doesn't value its readers or its pages. Never, never accept that type of publicity.

Direct Mail

There's direct mail, direct advertising and mail-order advertising that becomes confusing to some people. Direct mail advertising is sent through the mail, as is mail-order advertising. The principles set down for effective direct mail advertising are often interchangeable with those for mail order. Mail order is used and written to make an immediate sale without benefit of a salesman. Direct mail is used to obtain sales leads, build good will, build acceptance for a product or service and pre-condition prospects in advance of a salesman's call.

Direct advertising is distributed house to house by carriers or handed out by salesmen for the prospect to keep on his desk or in his file for ready reference about your company and its product. It is sometimes called collateral advertising. Every company that advertises uses this form of advertising. It is the booklet, folder or broadside that tells a customer or prospect about your product, how he can use it, your equipment, your employees, your services—in other words, it explains every phase of your business. It is almost a must for any printer. If you don't do any other form of advertising you should have something to leave with the prospect or give to the prospect who comes into your office.

Direct mail communicates directly and personally with individuals. It can be very selective. It is oftentimes referred to as the rifle approach to advertising rather than the shot gun. It is completely flexible, is governed by only a few postal regulations and, of course, good taste and your budget. It is an expensive form of advertising but it can produce great results.

Two out of three users of bulk third-class mail permit holders are small companies doing an annual business of less than $500,000. Ninety percent of bulk permit holders have fewer than 100 employees.

Some media have felt the inroads of direct mail into their profit margins and have launched campaigns against its use. They have coined the phrase "junk mail." As in every other form of advertising, there have been companies who have used direct mail poorly and dishonestly. However, it has been found that everybody enjoys getting mail. It may be very unsophisticated to admit it but surveys have proved that point. Advertising men who have used the medium have nothing but praise for the results they have experienced.

We will not dwell on its many facets here as there is an entire chapter in this book devoted to direct mail. We feel it is the most productive advertising medium for the majority of printers.

Directories

Directory advertising can be beneficial for a printer if its circulation is within the printer's market and it is not necessary to pay for waste circulation. The directory should also be easy to use and be complete so it will be used frequently by buyers. The customer already has the intent to buy when he looks in one of the directories for a printer. He knows what he wants but he does not know where he can get it, or he wishes to investigate several sources. It should be easy to use, be a popular one with a good reputation, and be up to date.

One of the best illustrations of a good directory for a printer is the Yellow Pages of the telephone company directory. They cover a printer's local market. They are well cross-referenced and easy to use. Because, out of habit, most people go to the Yellow Pages for information, they comprise a popular directory. They are kept up to date. It has been said that about 92 million Americans consult the Yellow pages an average of 40 times a year to locate 2,600,000 companies offering products and services in 4,200 classifications. There are 2,094 directories.

There are general industrial directories covering all industries or types of products and services. There are single trade, profession or single industry directories. Then there are directories for products, single or related. Many of the directories follow the same lines as the magazines that publish them.

There are catalog files but very few printers should be in them unless they are selling business forms, books or stationery that can be catalogued.

Large display advertising in directories is questionable because of the cost and the fact that people do not leaf through directories as they do a magazine. A trademark listing or small display ad may give more emphasis to your company, or better describe your product than a one-line listing, but we suggest you question and study the value of large display ads.

Care should be taken in determining circulation of directories. An audited or sworn circulation statement should be requested. Some 'phone solicitations, fake invoices and requests to okay proofs that haven't been ordered are forms of fraud foisted on the unsuspecting. Be sure you are dealing with a reputable company before placing listings or advertising in a directory.

Farm Publications

Farm publications are consumer-business oriented due to the fact that farming has been a family operation. The advertising in these publications is directed to the farm home and the working of the farm. It would be difficult to understand why a printer would advertise in a farm publication unless he were selling egg cartons or some type of farm product packaging that demanded printing.

Farm publications should be evaluated in the same manner as business publications.

Magazines

In advertising circles, magazines are considered to be an excellent medium for consumer products and services. Their circulations run into the millions and their rates are proportionately high. More people than ever are buying and reading these publications. A consumer-type medium is not the place for the average printer's advertising unless the printer has national distribution of a product used by a consumer. Writing paper, greeting cards, art prints and books, no doubt, could be advertised in a national consumer magazine provided the printer was able to make national distribution. The same care in analyzing circulation figures, appearance and editorial policy should be exercised as that suggested for business publications.

One active and recently growing medium that some printers may wish to consider is the city magazine. The number of city or metropolitan magazines being published today is not known. It is estimated that there are over 50. Most are privately owned and are sold because of their readers' "affluence" or "community involvement."

The cost per thousand readers is high because of the small circulation. Caution should be taken in purchasing advertising for the purpose of helping the community. Advertising should be purchased only to keep prospects and customers informed and to excite action. There may be too much waste circulation in the community magazine nearest your plant.

Newspapers

Newspapers are considered the largest medium for advertising, although it seems that we read about newspapers discontinuing publication almost every few months. Although from time to time a newspaper will suspend publication or merge with another, there are new dailies which begin publication. The number of daily newspapers has changed very little since World War II when there were 1,749 dailies published. In fact, the number has increased by only about 25. They get approximately 30% of the advertising dollars spent. Readership is high, especially in well-educated groups. Readership frequency is good because so many Americans have made a habit of reading the newspapers. They set aside special times of the day for their papers. It has been found that even classified ad reading is high. Approximately 85% of the population is reached each week by newspapers.

The printer who wishes to consider newspaper advertising has a number of things to consider. There are dailies with morning, evening, Sunday and zoned editions. Zoned editions are sent to a particular section of the city or county. There are Sunday magazine sections that are very productive and expensive. Then there are weeklies, some published twice a week. There are rural weeklies, suburban, religious, Negro and foreign language weeklies. There are shoppers, which have been cutting into the daily newspapers' advertising revenue. In some areas they have been well managed and very effective. And, of course, the printer must consider circulation. He must decide if he can afford the housewife and student waste circulation in order to get to his prospect who buys printng.

The printer must also think about where he wants his advertising to appear in the paper. The least expensive space is "R.O.P."—run of the paper. That lets the newspaper place the ad wherever it chooses. It may be all by itself right next to editorial matter or it may be squeezed among a large number of ads. It may be on the financial page or on the women's page. The more expensive method is to specify where and when you want your ad and then you pay the price for the extra service.

Another important decision that must be made is the size of the ad and how often it should be run. You must have continuity in your advertising because you need continuity in your sales. Very few printers can have January White Sales or Back-to-School Specials. Their advertising shouldn't be spotty. If ads are going to be placed in a weekly, then every other week is surely the minimum. In a daily newspaper the minimum should be Sunday and at least one other day. Tests will quickly determine how often your ads must appear in order to get results. Every paper, every community will no doubt be different.

The size of the ad must be governed by your budget. A large ad with good artwork and a good message will produce more action than a small one. There are no set rules or formulas to assist you in making this decision. An in-depth study of your budget, and testing of your particular newspaper, is the only way any printer can arrive at an answer for his company's advertising. What will prove right for his operation may not bring results for someone else.

Outdoor Advertising

Outdoor advertising patronized by national, regional and local advertisers is basically an urban business. Its standardized panels are erected on high-traffic arteries in urban areas. Its messages are aimed at people on the move. If you have a large amount of explaining to do about your product you better not use outdoor exclusively. Use short messages, good bold type, short words, copy that makes the point quickly and clearly, and an attention-getting illustration.

Although the majority of outdoor advertising is done by national advertisers, a printer can purchase space to concentrate his advertising within his small neighborhood area or market. A sign on your own building is also considered outdoor advertising, so every printer should do some outdoor advertising. Be sure your company-owned signs conform to the many neighborhood and state laws that have been passed in the last few years.

"Standardized" outdoor is a 12'x25' panel with copy area measuring 10'5"x22'8". Painted bulletins or boards run a little larger. There are about 270,000 signs owned, operated and controlled by members of the Outdoor Advertising Association of America. Eighty percent of the nation's 600-plus outdoor plant operators belong to the association. The OAAA has a strict code of good principles and it makes suggestions as to construction illumination and placement standards as well as copy acceptability. The association has been using a figure of 26¢ per thousand exposures as its costs for standardized boards.

Since circulation or audience figures are necessary for a printer to evaluate the worth of outdoor advertising to his company, he should request these figures before purchasing outdoor panels. The Traffic Audit

Bureau, sponsored jointly by advertisers, agencies and the outdoor industry, publishes circulation figures on a market-by-market basis. They have actual counts of traffic. Likewise, they evaluate the board's visibility based on length of unobstructed approach, speed and travel, the angle of the panel to the road and the relation of the panel to others nearby. All of this information is available from your local Outdoor business.

Packaging

We have included this subject only because it is an advertising medium. It would rarely apply to printers. When they stopped selling things in bulk from a barrel or large box and decided to put almost everything in attractive packages with the manufacturer's trademark and trade name featured, then packaging became advertising. Many advertising campaigns are built around a new package. Look on a grocery shelf and discover why packaging has become an advertising medium.

Printers' packaging should not be neglected. It is surprising to discover that some printers don't bother to wrap their products neatly. It has even been necessary for some buyers to specify that the job must be wrapped and labeled. If you are proud of your printing, advertise the fact with a nice label. Or, better yet, use a special label to announce that "This package contains fine printing from Jones Printing Company," or some other statement of fact.

Program, Ticket and Charity Promotion

There are one or two legitimate theater programs in the country that have a large enough circulation to business men to possibly be of some benefit to a printer who wishes to advertise.

This is also true of a few sports programs. However, don't consider school plays, amateur theatrical events, high school sports, kermises or church-event programs as good advertising mediums. It also goes for the backs of tickets for any of those events as well as Little League booster sheets or cards.

If you want to help a cause or a charity, please do so, but do not charge it to the advertising budget. It can be argued that it is building good will; therefore, it is good advertising. Weigh your judgement carefully. Be sure that good will can be purchased by an advertisement in a program, on the back of a ticket or on a booster card. There are too many printers doing this form of charity work and calling it advertising. These same printers are also saying that their advertising hasn't been successful; therefore, it isn't any good for their businesses.

Promotion

The word is defined as "the act of furthering the growth or development of something." One of the definitions of a promoter is "a substance that in very small amounts is able to increase the activity of a catalyst." We will accept both of these definitions to define promotion advertising.

Printers' promotion would include exhibits, fairs, some business meetings, sampling, contests, coupons for price-offs, audio-visual units for the sales force to use in presenting the printer's story, awards, trophies, an open house—almost anything that would increase the public's knowledge of the printer's services.

If a printer's business is localized and he depends on small orders to keep the plant going, exhibits and fairs can be profitable. The company's booth can be a show place for the many things the printer can do. For instance: church bulletins, school programs, personal stationery, invitations and scratch pads can be displayed. Contacts for this type of printing can be made.

Some printers who sell specialized printing, such as business stationery, have used price-off coupons with success. The coupon can be the thing that obtains the first order. After that it is up to the salesman and those in the service department to keep the new customer. The coupons are distributed in the printer's catalog or in special direct mail pieces featuring a certain product.

If you are not sure what your salesmen are telling your customers and prospects, an audio-visual presentation is almost a must. If your salesmen are inexperienced, an audio-visual program can be very helpful. This is not the least expensive form of promotion but it assures management that the story and the facts that they want to get across to the public are being told. Incidentally, this film may be shown in exhibit booths with success. Audio-visual production companies may be found in almost every major city and they can be of assistance in writing and producing a printer's story.

Awards and trophies can be used by printers to increase the acceptance or use of a specific type of printing. For instance, annual reports were glamorized by giving awards to those judged to be the finest. Annual reports were at one time four pages, black and white. Bigger and better instruction sheets could be promoted with awards. Catalogs, safety booklets for employees, employees' manuals, newsletters, many things that are now mediocre or just plain could be interesting, exciting and could provide an expanding market for printers if awards were used. Promotion, creativity and hard work are also entailed.

An open house any time can be an excellent promotion for a printer. If a printer is moving into a new location, he has a fine excuse for an open house. However, anyone with a little imagination can find a reason for showing customers and prospects the plant. There are all the holidays, birthdays, anniversaries, recognition of an old employee, new equipment installations, winning an award, surpassing a sales volume goal, introducing a new officer—or simply being proud of your plant and wanting to show it off.

If you can afford it, invite the secretaries are well as the executives of your customers and prospects. It is surprising how often a good word from a secretary will help. If there is some interesting promotion before the open house, a good crowd of interested people can be expected.

People enjoy watching machines operate, so don't have a static pressroom, type department or bindery. Have things moving and try to explain what is happening.

There's another dividend that you receive from an open house. The plant and machinery get cleaned and put into good order. Employees get into the spirit of the thing. Machines get oiled and shined, soiled calendars and posters are finally removed and even the windows may be washed. An open house is not only a good promotion, it is a good morale builder.

Promotion is finally being recognized by marketing executives. Advertising agencies are setting up promotion departments. Printers can make good use of its many facets. If there is a large sales force of 25 or more, a printer should study the sales promotion aspects, of which there are many.

Public Relations

Public relations is a management function that is developed to communicate with the public and earn its good will.

Unless a printer has a very large operation, public relations can be very expensive. It should be handled by a professional PR man. Public relations covers a vast range of promotional, counseling and communications tasks. Product publicity, press relations, speech writing, financial announcements, social issues (consumerism and environmental problems), are all the tasks of public relations personnel. The small to medium size printer should join one of the printing associations such as the National Association of Printers and Lithographers or the Printing Industries of America Inc., and let them handle the public relations function for the printing industry.

In no way do we want to imply that public relations aren't necessary. Public relations is one of the important tools of informing the public. It is one of the great expanding professions. The problems of industry and the complexities of society grow greater every year. For the printing industry, it has to be handled by one of the associations that is staffed to do the job or is financially able to hire one of the large PR agencies. There are approximately 40 agencies in the United States. There are over 4,000 PR companies but many are one-man shops. A small individual printer can not afford to handle the many tasks and problems.

A company's or industry's relations with the public can be established and improved by many good deeds. However, if the public doesn't know about the good deeds, the company or industry may have a poor image. Therefore, a public relations effort is necessary and important. A company's image should be guarded zealously at all times. One poor move or situation can break down everything that has been built for years. An example is the gasoline companies in 1973-1974. Millions of dollars were spent for advertising and public relations and building a good image. It was all wasted when the gasoline shortage appeared and good customers had to wait in long lines for a few gallons of their precious product. Regardless of whose fault it was, the gasoline companies were blamed. They lost their good image.

Publicity

Product publicity and some speech writing can often be handled by the person assigned to the printer's advertising work. Of course, this depends on the person's ability. Product publicity is nothing but writing the facts about your product in understandable form. Embellishing with flowery advertising slogans and descriptions will accomplish nothing because an editor worth that title will recognize the puffery and eliminate it or refuse to run the entire announcement or news release.

It is not uncommon for printers to expect publicity support from the various advertising media that they are using. Appeals of this nature offend most editors or newsmen. They feel that publicity and advertising are two entirely different things and they don't want to be compromised. They believe, and rightfully, so, that their readers or listeners expect and depend on them for newsworthy material. If you have a truly newsworthy item it should be, and almost always will be, accepted by the media in which you advertise. However, don't demand its acceptance. There is no legitimate contract for acceptance of publicity items.

Speeches can be effective public relations for any printer who has the ability to talk before a group. It gives him an opportunity to explain his work, his craftsmanship and the problems of the industry. It helps him to inform his public.

Speech writing is a difficult task for the inexperienced. There are few people available who can write a technical speech for a printer. If the speech is to cover generalities or community life or something other than printing, perhaps a professional speech writer could be found. However, if the speech is about printing, at will be more acceptable if the speech maker will dictate or write his own thoughts, gather his own facts and give the material to a professional to add the humor or nice phrases.

Radio

Radio is a mass medium hooked into more than 64,000,000 homes. The stations insist that it is a selective medium as well, with individual stations programmed into about 11 basic formats to appeal to specific interests of people in various ethnic, age and sex categories. At this time, the formats seem to be popular music, classical music, middle-of-the-road music, country-western music, rock and progressive rock music, rhythm and blues music, gospel music, information, religion and news. Different stations attract different audiences and the time determines who is listening and the number who are listening.

Radio was once a national advertising medium with many half-hour programs. Now it is a locally oriented medium offering tailored shows to a certain group of people. Another change has been FM radio, which has been altering its style to AM programming. Howcvcr, FM is still more music oriented, while AM tends to be more service oriented.

Radio is used by retail and service businesses and national consumer goods advertisers. Some printers have used it with some success. Advertising researchers estimate an average net radio minute in a 13-week contract for morning drive-time ranges from $1,200 to $1,600. Weekend minutes range from $1,200 to $1,400. Please note, these figures are average, so they may be quite different in your town or city.

One of the main considerations a printer has to answer is whether or not his product can be sold better by the human voice or with printed advertising. There is no doubt that the human voice can establish a friendly feeling with listeners. It can be more convincing than type. Another consideration is the cost. One minute for one time will not be enough. People must have their sets on and tuned to the station you are using to hear the message. That is why you hear the same message on so many stations at different times. They are trying to catch their prospects.

The script must be short, colorful and descriptive. There are no pictures to demonstrate what is being sold. In scheduling radio advertising, the printer will have difficulty. There are a number of terms that are confusing. Careful study should be given to rate cards as well as radio-station salesmen statements. Be sure you understand the language.

Another thing that must be considered is the geographical coverage of a station. A small local-channel station may seem like the proper place for your advertising. However, a large 50,000-watt clear-channel station may reach more of the people you wish to sell. In comparing costs, you may find that you seem to be paying for a great number of listeners whom you can't properly service, but your real prospects are listening to this big station. Your cost per 1,000 prospects may still be less for the 50,000-watt station.

Ask to see surveys. Because a station broadcasts in an area with 10,000 sets does not necessarily mean that 10,000 persons or families are listening to the radio when your announcement is being made. The sets have to be turned on and people have to be listening. Privately owned research companies measure radio reach. If you aren't offered a survey to study, beware. If you do have surveys to study, be sure you understand them.

Good time slots and programs that are desirable are quite often not available. Broadcast time is limited. The national advertisers as well as the old local advertisers have contracts for the best time. There may be a long wait for a desirable spot. It is not unusual for stations to suggest that you accept poor time schedules in order to get in line for a better schedule. Your judgement will have to prevail on taking a poor schedule or going to another medium.

We should again caution the buyer that he must try to discover what type of program is preferred by his customers or prospects. Do not make your selection based on the type of program you like.

Soundsheets

Since 1962, there has been an advertising medium available that printers may be able to use for their own advertising. However, we have been unable to find a printer who has used the medium. So, if you want to be different, investigate Soundsheets. Every printer should know about Soundsheets. When they are used they are almost always tied in with printing.

Soundsheets are thin, flexible, vinyl high-fidelity sound recordings that can be used effectively to communicate any type of message. They have been used for advertising, promotion, public relations, instructions, employee communications and premiums by some of the largest companies in the United States.

They can be mailed in envelopes. They weigh about one-quarter of an ounce for a six-mils sheet. They may be tipped or inserted into printed matter, bound into books, catalogs, magazines, folders, albums or almost anything. People can read your printed message and then listen to the Soundsheet. So, you can tell them and then tell them again—a great plus in advertising.

This effective communication—time-saving communication—communication on a one-to-one basis, is easily affordable. Five hundred Soundsheets with six-and-a-half minutes of sound can be tested for as little as $147. One thousand custom-made Soundsheets cost $200; 5,000 for $447.50. All they need is your reel-to-reel tape recording and camera-ready pasteup art for center imprint of the Soundsheet.

The company that markets Soundsheets provides an excellent idea kit which enables almost anyone to get started. There are a price list, sample Soundsheets, a dummy for your art department's use, and suggestions for the use of sound in your advertising or promotional effort. The company's name is Eva-Tone Soundsheets. Additional information is available by writing or calling: Larry McKnight, Eva-Tone Soundsheets, 2051 Waukegan Road, Deerfield, Illinois 60015; 312-945-5600.

Television

Television is an excellent medium for national and large local advertisers. At the present time it seems quite expensive for any but the large printers selling books or other specialized items. It is limited to large marketing areas. There may be bargain rates for the new station, but there are few of them and the rates won't last for long.

Since television combines sound and sight it is perhaps the closest advertising to personal selling. Your company's personality can be shown as well as your product. The product can be placed in natural settings and used.

Planning television advertising is similar to radio, so we won't go into the details. You still must reach your prospects by finding the station that they use. The preparation of your message is different from that for radio because there is sight as well as sound. The preparation is also more expensive.

Theater Screen

So many of the older generation think of theater screen advertising as the slides they used to use in the movie houses between features, or when they broke the film or changed a reel. But there is theater screen advertising today. About 80% of the nation's theaters have agreements with the Motion Picture Advertising Corp. A few theaters take care of their own bookings.

It is said that the motion picture theater audience in the U.S. is about 40 million people. Most printers are not interested in the national audience. However, the neighborhood audience could have interest.s That, of course, reaches into the drive-in theater where film advertising is shown before the start of each main feature.

The commercial films are from 20 to 60 seconds in length. They may be inexpensive slide type film or color and sound motion pictures. Rates are based on theater attendance. Showings can be booked by the week or contracts can be made for 13 weeks or longer. No competing products are shown in the same week. The number of advertisers accepted are mostly limited to five per show.

Movie goers are a captive audience. It is difficult or, at least, inconvenient to escape the advertising message. A printer must weigh how many in the theater audience can be influenced by his advertisement. If he is selling personal stationery, calling cards, calendars and other items that almost everyone can use, then the theater screen could be a good medium.

Transit

Transit advertising, as its name implies, appears inside and outside of buses, subway cars, commuter trains, subway stations, train and airline terminals. There are cards that measure 11" high x 28", 42" or 56" wide. The outside displays or posters for transit vehicles measure 21" high x 44" wide or 30" high x 88" wide or 30" high x 144" wide. In terms of dollar volume, exterior units account for approximately 78% of the total with inside car cards for 22%.

Transit Advertising Association research indicates that advertisers pay an average of between 15¢ and 20¢ per thousand for inside car exposures. Outside posters, on the basis of average cost per thousand exposures, are said to be 7¢.

Advertisers are able to buy advertising in individual markets or in any combination of the 380 urban markets available. Advertisers customarily make buys for 30-day periods and get discounts for 90-day, 6-month and 12-month contracts. Space is usually sold on the basis of a showing—full, half or quarter showings—which means one card in all the vehicles or one half or one fourth of the vehicles in a given fleet. There are a number of special deals that can be worked out such as dimensional product identification, take-one cards, and optical effects. An advertiser may buy all the advertising space on the outside and inside of a vehicle. He may use all one color to create a mood or get special attention. In other words, creativity is not stifled.

Cards or posters in volume for each campaign are provided by the advertiser and at the advertiser's expense. Circulation, which every printer will want to study, refers to the number of individuals who have a chance to observe a transit display during a stated interval. As in choosing any medium, ask the representative to assist you in determining its value, and be sure you understand all the figures and research information he gives you.

Word of Mouth

One never sees word-of-mouth advertising listed as one of the many media. We have included it because we feel it is important and quite effective.

Many activities that printers do not associate with advertising are a form of "calling public attention." One of these activities is word-of-mouth communications. Printers should make a strong effort to use such activities to help increase their businesses.

For instance, the printer to whom we referred in the chapter headed "Why Advertise?" said that his plant received enough business right through the front door and so they didn't have to advertise. That printer happens to be a "joiner." He belongs to the Masonic order. He is an active Rotarian. He belongs to the Y.M.C.A. He is on the board of a hospital and he is an active church member. He enjoys being around people. He doesn't realize that he is advertising when he quickly gets acquainted with people and somehow or other they learn that he is a printer. He sincerely believes that business just comes in the front door. He is using word-of-mouth advertising when he is attending all of these meetings and being a hale fellow well met. He is advertising but he doesn't know it.

Even if a printer does advertise in the usual media, we suggest that if it is possible, and if he can sincerely participate in neighborhood or national civic activities, that he do so. When he does participate, we suggest, for the good of his company, that he doesn't hide his light under a bushel but lets people know that he is a printer.

Some, we believe, fear that informing people of their occupation will do nothing but increase the number of gratis jobs they are requested to do. This can be easily and quickly handled by acting like a professional businessman. A simple statement with a smile will most always take care of the situation. For instance, he may say, "Our company (not you, personally) would like to produce that job and it can handle such a piece in fine style. We will give you a quotation in a few days. I, personally, would like to do it without charge, but the company gets so many requests of this nature from so many good causes that we do not know how to discriminate. We would go out of business if we honored all the requests for free printing. I am sure you doctors, attorneys, insurance men, engineers (or whoever is in the group) will understand that. We will send you a quotation in a few days." There are many other ways to handle the situation. The main thing is to be prepared with a pleasant reply. However, keep telling people about your company. Use word-of-mouth advertising.

Not only should the executives of a company get exposure in civic affairs but all employees should be encouraged to participate. Their participation is good for the community and the company. Management should suggest that employees tell friends and neighbors where they work and what they do. An employee who is proud of his work and his company is a great advertising medium. Word-of-mouth advertising can be very effective.

CHAPTER 4
DIRECT MAIL HINTS

"Hide not your talents,
they for use were made:
What's a Sun Dial in the shade?"

—Benjamin Franklin

As most printers know, there are really just three methods of sales and advertising communication that are personal and effective. They are a personal meeting, a telephone call, or a letter. When everyone has a standard tape recorder, a cassette will probably be added to that list.

These three methods, working together, bring great results. The face-to-face meeting is, of course, the most personal and effective form of sales communication. There is one "if"—if the important part of the message is written or printed for future reference.

The telephone call is also personal and effective and, again, if the important part of the message is written or printed for future reference.

Then comes the letter which can be personal, can illustrate the product through the inclusion of pictures and is written or printed for future reference. So, when you consider the three methods, the letter is not far behind the spoken-voice methods. In other words, the mail can be an excellent method of sales and advertising communication. Considering the cost of a personal visit, or the cost of a telephone call involving a salesman, a mailed piece of information is relatively inexpensive.

Since most printers have a good idea of who their prospects are and where they are located, it seems quite logical that they should use direct mail, the advertising medium that can be directed to those prospects without waste. If the mailing list is a correct one, there will be no waste circulation. There will not be the name of anyone who can't or doesn't buy printing. There is no other advertising medium with such a direct approach. Therefore, we are devoting one chapter of this book to cover some of the many details of direct mail advertising. The subjects will be many and will be in no particular order. They will apply to a general printer's advertising and, therefore, some of these hints may not apply to a printer who is specializing in a particular product. The index may help you to find a subject in which you are interested.

Costs

If you try to break down direct mail costs per piece you will find it is, perhaps, the most expensive advertising medium. If you consider it on its circulation value it is, perhaps, the least expensive. Direct mail is sent to bonafide prospects. With any other medium, you may contact your prospects but you will also pay to contact children, housewives, libraries, institutions and many, many people and places that cannot influence an order for printing. With direct mail advertising, the printer has control of its distribution.

The least expensive direct mail advertising piece to prepare is, no doubt, the postal card. Although this size mailing seems small and inadequate, it can be very effective for the small printer if it is used consistently. Copy should be interesting and informative. At the time this is written, if you were making regular mailings of over 200 pieces, the bulk rate postage would be the least expensive. With so many rule changes and frequent postage rate changes, we suggest you consult with the customer services department of your local post office before planning your mailings.

Consideration should be given to using third-class bulk rate mail. If your message does not have to be in your prospect's hands on a certain day, we would advise third-class, bulk rate, postage-metered mail. If it is local mail, it is rarely held at the post office for any great length of time. It is less expensive than first class even though you must sort and bundle the mail by zip codes. With the use of the postage meter indicia, it looks like first-class mail on the face of the envelope. Close inspection will indicate that the words "bulk rate" are shown in the indicia but it seems that many people do not inspect it that closely. If you do not have a postage meter machine nor a bulk rate permit, then perhaps this would not be the most economical method because you cannot purchase fractions-of-a-cent stamps. Again, we warn you to check with your post office. Rates and rules change.

26 Ways Direct Mail Advertising Can be Used By Printers

We believe that every book ever written about direct mail has contained a check list of direct mail uses. Over the years these check lists have been helpful to many people in being reminded of things they should do with direct mail. So, this chapter will also contain a check list. Some of the ideas are original but most of the points have been borrowed or taken from many sources. Our 26 ways or uses are limited to printers' requirements.

1. Image Building

Almost every printer of any size must deal with the problem of public acceptance at many levels. Fundamentally, continuous support must come from current customers. A need for understanding with the people of the community in which the plant is located is necessary. There is need for rapport between management and public officials at local, state and national levels of legislative policy-making. Of course, and perhaps of most importance, there is need to influence the opinion of bankers or potential sources of financial support. And there is the need for acceptance from employees and the members of their families. The list can grow in accordance with a printer's special needs or local situation. Direct mail is an ideal public relations tool for sending your particular message to all these groups. A printer may find that such a public relations activity may prove to be a better growth and sales endeavor in the long run than a slam-bang, sophisticated type of sales promotion.

In planning direct mail or any advertising, one should understand the side effects of advertising. A sales objective may be the primary reason for advertising. However, any communication, whether designed to produce a sales lead, an inquiry or just to announce something, will inevitably influence the recipient in a favorable or unfavorable manner toward the company that sent it. So often, we forget that fact. We have all seen it happen.

A printer cannot afford to send to every "Post Office Patron" a single sheet of newsprint, poorly printed in a fire sale red with wooden type and misspelled words, an announcement of a gigantic sale of scratch pads for ten cents each and then in the next few months try to sell his ability to design and print brochures or annual reports. All of your advertising must reflect the quality of your product. You cannot build an image of nobility by dressing and acting like an outcast. This factor is widely ignored in the preparation of advertising.

If you wish to create a favorable image for your company, work hard on such small things as paper stock; type; color; spelling; clear, concise copy; illustrations and overall style. Plan and design your direct mail piece so that it will achieve its marketing objective but will also give your company a good image.

2. Securing Inquiries for Salesmen

This is one of the big features of direct mail. It will bring back inquiries. You can quickly ascertain if your advertising was a success or a failure. The inquiries are from live, qualified prospects who are interested and are waiting for your organization to contact them. There is nothing in business quite so heart-warming as a handful of inquiry cards returned from a direct advertising mailing.

3. Paving the Way for Salesmen

Direct mail sent before the salesman calls will help to introduce the salesman. It will eliminate the time the salesman would have to take on a cold call to tell the prospect about your company, its history and its products. Consistent advertising will help to open doors for salesmen. Prospects, after receiving your advertising, will feel that they are acquainted with the company and are ready to be sold.

4. Registering the Salesman's Sales Points After a Call

Your salesman can tell a customer or prospect some real facts. The prospect may believe it or mark it up to a salesman's zealous pitch. However, if the same sales points are sent to him a few days later and they are illustrated and printed in black and white with the company's name signed, they become believable and acceptable. A direct mail piece can back up a salesman.

5. Creating a Demand for Your Product

Consistently used, direct mail advertising can stimulate a demand for your kind of creativity and printing on annual reports, booklets, package inserts, catalogs or whatever you want to feature.

6. Reminding Prospects of All Your Services

Most printers are able to do many things that their customers or prospects do not know are available to them through their printer. Direct mail pieces can help to educate your customers. Do they realize that you can collate sheets, emboss, punch odd-sized holes, die cut, rule lines, bind booklets in many ways, fold intricate folds, pad paper, print personalized identification badges, do layout and design work and perform many other services that are rarely sold by most printers?

7. Announcing Something New

If it is new equipment, a new salesman, a new address or telephone number, a new addition to your building or even a new delivery truck, it can be told quickly and effectively through direct mail. A letter or announcement sent through the mail on the day of the happening will register your message quickly.

8. Winning Back Inactive Customers

An inactive customer indicates a wasted investment because you had to invest money in acquiring that customer. A series of direct mail messages can often revive his interest. At least, you may discover what went wrong and then can make the necessary adjustments so you don't continue to lose customers.

9. Keeping Contact with Customers Between Orders

Direct Mail advertising to customers between orders or salesmen's calls will help to convince them that they made the correct decision when they purchased printing from you. It will also keep your name and services in their minds for future business.

10. Building Good Will

One thing that direct mail can do so well is to create warmth and friendship through a program of beautifully printed poems, mottoes, excerpts from outstanding speeches, pictures and kindly thoughts. The low-key sell of your copy, the friendly tone of your regular advertising message can all contribute to cementing good business relationships.

11. Making Sales Points

Prospective customers can be educated by planned, factual mailings. If you have three or four sales points that you want to be sure your prospects understand, prepare three or four letters or mailings and feature one of the points in each piece. Make the design or layout interesting, give the facts, back them with proof if that is possible to do in a printed piece, and mail them to your prospects. This enables you to get the same story to each prospect and it can be referred to from time to time by your salesmen. The information is authenticated by your company's signature, and if you have developed a good image it will be believed.

12. Building Morale of Employees

A single sheet or four-pager published regularly (at least four times a year) communicating company policies, plans, growth and ideals, promoting safety and efficiency, encouraging thrift, stimulating ambition and giving recognition for jobs well done will help to increase loyalty, teamwork and knowledge. It doesn't have to be expensive. Typewritten and multi-lithed will do the job. Be sure to mail it to the employee's home so the family becomes involved.

13. Welcoming New Customers

Everyone enjoys being recognized. A letter welcoming a new customer will help to cement a closer friendship. If you have a list of good customers who are recognized in the community, let them know about the good company you keep. It will confirm the wise choice they made.

14. Distribution of Samples

We don't know of a better way for a printer to show what he can do than to show samples of his actual work. Direct mail can be effectively used to mail samples and explanations of your work to prospects. Some printers call these mailings "The Job Of The Month." Good samples not only impress prospects but also compliment the customer whose work you use to promote your company.

15. Bringing Buyers to Plant

Announcements, letters and invitations will help to bring customers and prospects to your offices and plant to see how you are equipped and how various jobs are accomplished. An open house, anniversary or any special occasion makes an excellent excuse for becoming better acquainted.

16. Developing Sales Among Specified Groups

Direct Mail can assist you in developing more catalog business, or annual report business or whatever you wish to push. Develop a series of mailings directed specifically to those companies that use catalogs in selling their products or annual reports for their stockholders. Be sure your mailing list includes just those companies that will buy your particular product.

17. Acknowledging Orders or Payments

So few companies acknowledge an order or a prompt payment of an invoice that such a gesture will be looked upon with great favor. An interesting note, folder or card with a personal touch will develop good will for anyone who will take the time to use them.

18. Securing Direct Orders

Printers to the trade have built profitable businesses through orders secured only with the help of direct mail. Price sheets and production details have been explained through mailing pieces. Of course, specialized printing, such as stationery, calling cards and business forms may also be sold by mail without the help of salesmen.

19. Collecting Accounts

An interesting, diplomatic series of collection letters will help to keep accounts up to date. They can be written so they won't offend, and will leave the recipients in a friendly mood. It isn't easy but it has been done.

20. Developing New Sales Territories

If you are not sure of the sales potential in a distant territory, mail a series of tested letters or advertising pieces into the territory to see what inquiries you can obtain. The mailings should be pieces that have obtained results in other territories. Be prepared to answer the inquiries by some method. It is very difficult to repair the damage done by an unanswered inquiry. Word-of-mouth "advertising" can travel fast and for hundreds of miles.

21. Making Advertising in Other Media More Effective

Billboards, Transit Advertising and Broadcasting Advertising are limited by space and time. However, your advertising in these media can be explained, detailed and enhanced by direct mail. Reprint the short message exactly as it was in the other media, then go into detail and explain your sales points.

22. Following Inquiries Received From Other Advertising Media

Inquiries developed through broadcasting, newspaper, magazine, or any of the many advertising media may be quickly answered by a series of messages describing your organization and facilities. This series can be a holding action until the salesman can make a phone or personal call upon the prospect. It shows interest on your part and further develops the prospect's interest. However, don't ever delay acknowledging an inquiry for more than two weeks. That is about as long as anyone will let you get away with inattention.

23. Researching for New Ideas and Suggestions

Mail can be used to find marketing facts, new printing requirements, image valuation, sales effectiveness and many other informational tools that will help your organization to do a better job.

24. Selling Your Company to Financial Institutions

Letters reporting company progress, and also enclosing outstanding or new printing jobs just completed, will impress financial institutions as well as prospects and customers. Enclosures reporting progress with your interest payments, dividend checks, employees' wages and other direct messages will help to inform your financial backer as well as your employees. If, in the letter or advertising pieces, it is suggested that the recipient tell friends, such communications can increase sales through word-of-mouth advertising.

25. Securing Data from Employees

Letters sent to the employees' homes asking for opinions of new equipment or procedures help to create a common interest in the business. Requests for suggestions to improve efficiency or some solution to a difficult problem will often bring back good ideas and practical answers. Don't use this suggestion if you aren't prepared to answer every return you receive. Your employees will cooperate only once if their answers are not acknowledged with interest.

26. Correcting Mailing Lists

You can keep your mailing list up to date by using the mails to secure names of prospective customers. Mailings to present customers, employees, suppliers, associations and friends, asking them for names of people or companies who can use printing, will often bring good results. People enjoy doing favors when properly asked. Of course, the obvious use of direct mail for correcting lists is to ask those on your mailing lists if you have spelled their names correctly, if their addresses are right and the zip codes correct. This can be done along with a regular advertising mailing.

Showmanship

It seems that every year more companies discover that direct mail is a fine advertising medium. Therefore, more advertising mail is crossing prospects' desks. The problem of getting attention to your advertising message grows greater every year. Gimmicks (we prefer the word showmanship) can help to get attention. Be cautious in their use. Never let showmanship become the main point of your mailing piece. The best type of showmanship gets attention and dramatizes your sales point or points. It helps to lead the reader into the sales story.

Never put something into the mail that just attracts attention for attention's sake. Have a reason for using the extra added attraction or don't use it. Showmanship can make your mailings attractive, different and effective, but use it with good common sense and never forget what you are really selling.

Simple Copy

Effective copy is simple copy. Why do so many of us have to show our education when writing advertising copy? If you want to confuse your own sophisticated, blasé Park Avenue world affairs discussion group with ten syllable words, go ahead and have fun. But in advertising, where some of the kind souls who read your material haven't had your wonderful education, keep your words down to two or three syllables. There may be some people in your audience who can't quickly understand what you are trying to say. In this day of speed, you better tell them quickly, or they won't get your message.

The correct use of grammar and language changes daily. The right pronunciation of a word is the way people pronounce it in your locality. You have all discovered how the words creek, oil and water sound 1,000 miles from your home. Rules for grammar were made by men who were describing usage in their day. They are not necessarily related to the way words are used today. Getting people to take action is the purpose of direct mail copy. When proper English interferes with communication of your sales message, it is time to forget the rule book.

Try to write using the same phrasing and expressions that the majority of people use when they talk. If you don't know how they talk, you better ride the bus to work instead of driving. Eat lunch at a cafeteria instead of the swank Athletic Club. Attend some church functions. Drink in a saloon instead of a cocktail lounge. Go where you will meet the majority and learn the language. Split an infinitive now and then. End a sentence in a preposition. Don't use a long word if you can find a couple of small ones to do the job. Tenth-grade education or better has been attained by only 30% of those over 25 years.

There is one thing certain about simple language. Even the highly educated college professor can understand it.

Clichés are O.K.

A cliché is a group of words used so often that people are familiar with them. Most people know the meaning they convey. Therefore, a cliché is useful in advertising copy. The easier it is to understand your copy, the more people will read it. The meaning is understood much faster when using a cliché than when using an involved unfamiliar group of words to express the same thought.

Don't Advertise in July and August

Who started that popular fallacy? It is especially *not* true for printers' advertising. Sales managers plan their fall and winter programs in July and August. They will need printing. Many people now take their vacations in the winter months and work right through the summer. Don't slow up your advertising in any season. Keep it consistent. Some direct mail people think you should not mail anything from November 15 until December 15, because of the Christmas mail. If you are mailing directly to homes, this could be true. If you are mailing to business addresses, we haven't found any difference. Business activity is good in December. Even third-class mail seems to get through.

Dare to Be Different

One of the many virtues of direct mail advertising is the opportunity it gives you to be different. You are not restricted to a 7x10 space. At this writing, pieces weighing 70 pounds, with a width and girth of 100", may be mailed. Third-class mail can be used for pieces weighing less than a pound and three inches wide or more by four and one-quarter inches in length or more. You should check your post office in case of a change in these rules. These dimensions give anyone a wide range of creativity. Your imagination can run rampant. A special fold, a paste-on of some sort, large type, small type—almost anything can be used. Dare to mail a postal card using small six-point type to tell a long but interesting story. Send a letter, typed one word to a line. The message must necessarily be short but it will get attention because it is different. Print your message, roll the sheet into a ball and mail it in a bag. Send a piece of cake or a cookie in a box. Dare to be different. Of course, use good taste and be sure to tie in your product with whatever you do. Always remember—you are selling printing.

Idea Starters

Sometimes we just need a hint to get our creativity started. Listed below are 14 things that may help you to create a new or different piece of direct mail advertising.

1. Take every opportunity to personalize your advertising. If you can use the person's name, use it—even if you can afford only to put it on the mailing envelope.

2. Get the recipient to act. Have the person do something even if it is just checking off a block. Have him assist you. Ask him to do something for you.

3. Magnify the mailing piece by making it larger than the usual pieces of advertising. Everybody uses 8½"x11". Be different.

4. Reduce the size. Make it a miniature of the usual pieces of advertising.

5. Add fun to the mailing. Everyone, even in business, enjoys something foolish, humorous, cute or corny as long as it is in good taste.

6. Adapt someone else's design or idea for your purpose. There's nothing new under the sun. Change the copy for your product. Use different colors. Reverse the layout.

7. Add a color to bring out your main point or enhance the illustration. Split fountains to get unusual color effects. Use colored stock.

8. Add a third dimension by using a fold or pasted-on piece.

9. Add another element to the mailing, such as a piece of fruit a pencil, a thumb tack, a piece of chalk or almost anything to add showmanship and get attention.

10. Add another use to the mailing so the receiver will keep your message. Print some of your message on a ruler or towel or eraser or pencil or calendar. Use almost anything that your prospect will keep around for a while.

11. Use teasers. Don't give your prospect the entire story in the first mailing. Break up your sales story into five or six parts and mail separately. Send jigsaw puzzles, a piece at a time. Send a brochure, one page at a time.

12. Use unusual folds. Oftentimes the folds must be made by hand. The extra expense may be worth the attention it will get.

13. Change the order of things. Place the headline at the bottom of the page or some other change that will attract.

14. Use old-fashioned type or layout to make a point—or an ultra modern theme that seems impossible. Be sure you illustrate a sales point in using these techniques.

Believable Copy

Persuasion in advertising copy is important. A small amount of exaggeration is expected by the reader. However, don't go beyond what is believable. It is a very thin line between believability and downright exaggeration, or putting it more bluntly, untruth! Don't think for one minute that the reader won't catch you. Keep on the soft sell side of your sales story. Qualify your statements. Don't use, "Our deliveries are always made when promised and we are working to improve that 2%." The last portion of that statement is believable. No experienced printing production man will believe the first one.

Recognize Your Customers

People have a need to be recognized as important. They like to be set aside from the majority. Anything you can do to make your customers feel that they are in an exclusive group when they purchase printing from your company is a plus. If you have some well known customers with fine reputations, let your prospects know. Perhaps you could even go so far as to organize a mythical or real club for those who do business with you.

Samples

Use samples of your work to advertise your product. It you don't have time to prepare your own advertising brochure, use samples of work you have done for your customers. Attach a small tab with a handwritten note, if possible—a printed one will suffice—asking the prospect to inspect this job right off the press. Always enclose a reply card in case he wants to see a salesman. You not only compliment your customer whose work you use but you can put the mailing together quickly and it can be effective.

Tests

To be sure of the effectiveness of your mailings, test them. With small mailing lists this is expensive because you must print a small quantity. If you don't get good results you have to try something else. In order to conduct an authentic test, test only one thing at a time. For instance, if you wish to discover whether or not your prospects will respond better to a plain envelope than to an envelope with some mention of the enclosure on the outside, then test only that much. Don't change the color of the envelope, the enclosure, the offer, or even the way the enclosure is placed in the envelope.

The test mailing list should be representative of your total list. Select every n-th name such as every 6th, 12th, 15th name. Or, select samples from all parts of the list at random. Mail one hundred, or as many as you think will givc you a good test (see chart), in a plain envelope. Then on the same day, mail the same number in an envelope with an outside message such as, "New Printing Process Described Inside." Do not change the inside contents except for an initial or number on the business reply card. By referring to the code number on the cards returned, you will be able to determine if your prospects respond better to the plain envelope or the envelope with a message. Remember, this gives you the answer only for those people on your mailing list who are interested in printing. Don't think for one minute that this result will apply to a plumbing supplier's mailing or to a different offer you may have. Testing results change, so don't take anything for granted.

The size of the test mailing, not the size of the list being tested, governs the reliability of the test results.

This is a very short description of testing. There are entire books written on the subject. If you wish to go into a detailed program, we suggest that you visit your public library and study their books on advertising research.

Law of Probability as Applied to Evaluation of the Results of Test Mailings

If- the size of the test mailing is:	**and-** the return on the test mailing is:	**then** 95 chances out of 100, the return on the identical mailing to the whole list will be between	**If-** the size of the test mailing is:	**and-** the return on the test mailing is:	**then** 95 chances out of 100, the return on the identical mailing to the whole list will be between
100	1%	0 & 2.99%	250	1%	0 & 2.26%
100	2%	0 & 4.80%	250	2%	.23% & 3.77%
100	3%	0 & 6.41%	250	3%	.84% & 5.16%
100	4%	.08% & 7.92%	250	4%	1.52% & 6.48%
100	5%	.64% & 9.36%	250	5%	2.24% & 7.76%
100	10%	4.00% & 16.00%	250	10%	6.20% & 13.80%
100	20%	12.00% & 28.00%	250	20%	14.94% & 25.00%
500	1%	.11% & 1.89%	1,000	1%	.37% & 1.63%
500	2%	.75% & 3.25%	1,000	2%	1.12% & 2.88%
500	3%	1.48% & 4.52%	1,000	3%	1.92% & 4.08%
500	4%	2.25% & 5.75%	1,000	4%	2.76% & 5.24%
500	5%	3.05% & 6.95%	1,000	5%	3.62% & 6.38%
500	10%	7.32% & 12.68%	1,000	10%	8.10% & 11.90%
500	20%	16.42% & 23.58%	1,000	20%	17.48% & 22.52%
2,000	1%	.55% & 1.45%	5,000	1%	.72% & 1.28%
2,000	2%	1.37% & 2.63%	5,000	2%	1.60% & 2.40%
2,000	3%	2.24% & 3.76%	5,000	3%	2.52% & 3.48%
2,000	4%	3.12% & 4.88%	5,000	4%	3.45% & 4.55%
2,000	5%	4.03% & 5.97%	5,000	5%	4.38% & 5.62%
2,000	10%	8.66% & 11.34%	5,000	10%	9.15% & 10.85%
2,000	20%	18.21% & 21.79%	5,000	20%	18.87% & 21.13%
10,000	1%	.80% & 1.20%	100,000	1%	.94% & 1.06%
10,000	2%	1.72% & 2.28%	100,000	2%	1.91% & 2.09%
10,000	3%	2.66% & 3.34%	100,000	3%	2.89% & 3.11%
10,000	4%	3.61% & 4.39%	100,000	4%	3.88% & 4.12%
10,000	5%	4.56% & 5.44%	100,000	5%	4.86% & 5.14%
10,000	10%	9.40% & 10.60%	100,000	10%	9.81% & 10.19%
10,000	20%	19.20% & 20.80%	100,000	20%	19.75% & 20.25%

Ask for Prospects' Names

You have heard people bragging about their new cars, fishing rods, boats, lawn mowers and favorite restaurants. They often do this to convince themselves that they have made a wise choice and to induce others to make the same choices. So, now and then, on a business reply card, ask your customers to give you the names and addresses of friends or business associates who also buy printing. You will be surprised at how many good prospects you will receive. If your customer is not willing to assist you, we suggest that you take a look at your product or your service.

Keep Customers

Send your advertising to customers as well as to prospects. Keep them sold. We can't understand why so many companies work so long and spend so much money to convince a prospect that he should buy from the company, and as soon as he becomes a customer he is forgotten.

There is something wrong with our marketing philosophy when we think a prospect we are trying to sell is worth two or three of the customers we already have. Why does a customer's value drop when he places an order with us? Many companies immediately take the new customer off the mailing list and rarely is he sent a "thanks" for the order. A "thank you" note is direct mail advertising. It also shows your good manners. Many printers do very little to keep their customers from becoming first-rate prospects for others.

Tell the Truth

If you are unable to produce high-quality printing in your plant, don't try to sell it as high quality. Customers have become educated. They know what hickies look like. They don't like broken type. All the grand and glorious words in the world will not sell poor printing a second time. You can get the first order with copy that lies, but you won't get repeat orders.

The honest copy is the best copy in direct mail. If you are able to give your advertising people good printing to sell, they can describe it with beautiful copy that will convince almost anyone. When you have to lie about the product, that is when you get into trouble.

We all see or hear obvious falsehoods in various types of advertising but we don't believe the message is meant for us. We believe it is for the person who isn't as educated as we are. We rarely take the general advertising falsehoods personally. But with direct mail, it is different. Direct mail is mostly sent to one individual. We believe the writer is addressing the message to us—one individual. If the message is a lie and we know it, the writer is assuming that we are dumb. None of us like that. It won't pay off in direct mail advertising.

Printers' Jargon

When writing advertising, be careful that you don't mystify your readers by using words that are not familiar to them. Printers communicate among themselves with some words that the average person couldn't possibly understand. Alterations, ascender, backbone, widow, bleed, blanket, chase, crop, flush left, gutter—and we could keep on going—are words that may not be understood in printers' advertising copy. Be sure that everyone can understand your copy.

People of Influence

Don't neglect people of influence when mailing your advertising. These are difficult names to obtain but they can be important to you. They will probably never actually buy printing. However, they are in important positions, and if they like what they see coming from your company, they can help you.

As we have said before, word-of-mouth comments, if they are good, are very valuable. If the comments come from people who have no obvious interest in your printing business, that is powerful advertising. Results from people of influence are difficult to trace but don't overlook these people.

Watch the Time Element

If you mention a season in your copy be sure you send it out before or during that season. For instance, "Summer is the time to think about ordering calendars." Don't send such a statement in the fall.

Don't brag about your speedy printing service and then send the January issue of your newsletter in February.

Don't send a sample piece of printing with a 1974 date next to the form number and mention that it just came off the press when your mailing was sent in April, 1975. Your prospects are dubious. Don't give them an opportunity to catch you cheating.

Don't mention, "Prices Are Falling," on the same day that there is an article in the newspaper about paper costs going sky high. Statements such as that are not believable even if you are cutting prices.

Sex!

We think it is a great thing but be very careful of its use in your advertising. You can turn off some prospects. If you are selling nightgowns, of course, you have to show pretty girls in nightgowns, but they aren't necessary in printing. Just because you like spicy copy or an off-color joke is not a good reason for using them in your advertising. Bathing beauties on folders selling a summer resort will be acceptable but on a printer's folder selling office forms it just doesn't work. It gets attention the same way a con artist at a country fair does. You are insulting the intelligence of your reader when you use such material.

Qualify Inquiries

Almost anyone can double or triple the number of inquiries he will get from a direct mail piece. The question is, do you want these kinds of inquiries? To greatly increase your inquiries, offer a gift if the recipient returns the reply card. The fancier the gift the more inquiries you will receive. Such inquiries are mostly worthless and they surely damage the respect a sales force will have for future inquiries. Salesmen will waste their valuable time in following inquiries obtained in this manner.

Try to qualify your inquiries by asking what particular type of printing they are interested in. Let them know a salesman will call. Ask what day is the best to visit. Any question that will indicate the sender's interest will help qualify the inquirer.

Persistence

We have said it once or twice in this book, so once more won't hurt. Consistent advertising will pay off. If you keep telling your prospects that you are ready, willing and able to do their printing and show them what you can do, you will increase your business.

Once a month is not too often to remind your prospects that you are out there waiting to help them. Set a deadline for getting your monthly mailing in the mail. Make it the most important thing your plant does. You will find it really is the most important thing you can do because it will keep you in business.

Free

Watch how you use the word "free." The Federal Trade Commission may be at your doorstep if you aren't careful. They believe, and rightfully so, that nothing is free if the buyer actually pays for it through certain requirements attached to the offer. Inflating the price to accommodate the "free" item is out of order. A one-cent sale, or two for the price of one is safe, provided the price charged for the item is the regular price. For instance, if a book costs $4.00, and a small booklet would add another dollar, you couldn't sell the book for $5.00 and offer a free booklet.

Testimonials

If they are believable, testimonials can be used successfully. Your prospects may question a statement made by your company but will go along with the statement if made by an outsider. The testimonial should be truthful and believable. Customers can be so pleased with your printing or service that they may make statements that most people won't believe. For instance, "They are fabulous. They could even print on water, and they deliver your job before you ask for it." Well, we have seen demonstrations of printing on water by screen printers but it was just for fun and they couldn't possibly deliver the job. As for delivery before the customer asks for it, buyers of printing know that it rarely happens. The statement isn't believable and so it isn't effective, even though your enthusiastic customer thought he was telling the truth.

Be sure to get a release from the person giving you the testimonial. Never use statements unless you have a release authorizing their use in advertising. Be sure to keep the original testimonial. Someone, including the Federal Trade Commission, may wish to see it. Many years ago the FTC set down some rules for the mail order insurance industry. We imagine they are still checking on testimonials in about the same way. The rule for the insurance industry read, "No testimonial, appraisal or analysis shall be used in any advertisement which is not genuine, does not represent the current opinion of the author, does not accurately describe the facts, does not correctly reflect the present practices of an insurer, is not applicable to the policy of insurer advertised or is not accurately reproduced."

Make It Easy to Reply

Anything you can do to make it easy for your prospects to reply to your mailing, to get into your mailing, to understand your sales proposition, will benefit your advertising effort.

A business reply card with the prospect's name and address typed on it will help. Boxes for his check mark to indicate his interest will make it easy to reply. Offer him a free collect telephone call. Be sure your reply cards or envelopes can be mailed postage-free.

Don't use staples to tie a self-mailer shut. They are too difficult to pry loose. They break finger nails. They may ruin a nice illustration. Shoppers and cheap forms of advertising contain staples, so don't get into that class.

Go over your sales message before you print. Be sure it is simple and easily understood. Don't use printers' terms. Take some time and space to describe what you are selling. Everyone doesn't know what an eight-page folder, three-color bleed pages, saddle stitched, hand-set heads, 12-point machine body copy and accordian folded for a number five envelope will look like.

Knock-It-Out

Some retailers, tire shops, discount houses have had excellent results with cheap-looking direct mail advertising. Some products have to look cheap to sell. Grocery store ads mostly shout at us. Newspaper tire ads that aren't corny don't sell. However, printers' direct mail cannot be "knocked out." It must be of good design, colorful, in good taste and have a professional look.

Once a year, if you want to demonstrate that you can produce a quick and dirty job, then go ahead and really shock them. Perhaps some of your prospects can use that kind of advertising. Be sure to tell your prospects how quickly it was done because that is a sales point in doing that type of work. A job of that type sent from a printer who has been using beautiful printing for his advertising has a good shock value. However, under no circumstance use fire sale advertising to sell high-quality printing.

What Were the Results?

Never be too busy to take the time to keep a record of the results of your advertising. When you buy a new press you check the number of saleable impressions you get from the machine. You want to know if you are getting your money's worth. The same should hold true of the money you spend for advertising–any kind of advertising.

If you mail a calendar or keepsake piece, it is nice to know how many requests you get for additional copies, but the important thing is how many requests you received asking for a salesman to visit. Or, better yet, requests asking for someone to quote or pick up a job. Good advertising can bring in such requests and you should know if you are producing good advertising.

Letters from friends saying they enjoyed your last advertising piece do not increase your business. You should look for letters or calls from total strangers. They are the ones you have to impress. Keep records of your advertising results. Be sure you are producing advertising that is effective for your company.

The Cranks

As you increase the size of your mailing list and the area your advertising covers, you may receive some anonymous or crank letters. Read them with an open mind and if you believe the thoughts expressed are based on fact, then and only then should you pay any attention to them. You will find that most of these letters are written by chronic complainers. Or, they are written by fanatics of an unpopular cause. Some just do not like direct mail advertising. When you find that to be the case and you are able to obtain their names, remove the names from your mailing list. You can also give them the name and address of the Direct Mail Advertising Association. They, in turn, will help to have their names removed from many lists.

Don't let one or two uncomplimentary crank letters affect your advertising campaign. If they are anonymous, they could come from a competitor! Be sure your campaign is in good taste and then go right ahead.

Using odors in mailings will sometimes bring negative responses from a few. Some men do not like the smell of a volatile perfume in their offices. A limburger cheese smell is not popular. We have had a few complaints when we used a smell of smoke. But at the same time, these mailings receive attention and illustrate a sales point. We used odors for three mailings to announce a direct mail day for the Cleveland Ad Club. We received two complaints, but in that year we had the largest turnout ever for a speaker at the Club. John Yeck, of Dayton, was the man. He is great, but so were our promotional pieces.

Pictures

We all know that pictures help to illustrate or explain almost anything. Pictures of your employees, head and shoulder "mug shots," are effective. Politicians found that out years ago. Your prospects want to buy from people, not a company. So, any time that you can put your picture in your advertising, do it.

CHAPTER 5
HOW TO BUILD A MAILING LIST

To advertise and then neglect inquiries is to buy ill will for cash.

This is the most important chapter in this book. It is a subject that is ignored by most professional advertising men. It seems to be below their dignity to be concerned about such a mundane thing as a mailing list. You can plan, research, set goals, create a great idea, write inspired copy and sweat over art and production, but if the advertising isn't directed to the correct people it is useless.

There could and probably should be a subtitle to this chapter. It would be "How To Build A Calling List." A calling list which should also be a mailing list is often the weak link in an excellent marketing program. It is surprising, almost unbelievable, how many supposedly well-managed companies do not even have an official customer's list, not to mention a calling list for their salesmen. Of course, they say they can put one together in a few days. Their salesmen all have their own personal lists. However, there is no place in the company where there is an up-to-date complete file with chief executives' names and correct company names and addresses of all the present customers; nor is there a list of companies that haven't given them an order for over a year; nor is there a list of prospects to whom they want to sell.

How can a company do a good job of communicating if it doesn't even have a correct list of its present customers? The answer is that it can't do a good job of communicating. It rarely tells its customers anything. It lets the salesmen tell the customers about the new services, the new equipment. It hopes the salesmen won't forget and that they all have the same information and same message.

Mailing Lists are Expensive

Before you start, you may as well make up your mind that it is going to cost more than you thought to compile a good, effective list. A good list does not come cheaply. However, a list gathered together through invoices, salesmen, executives, employees and friends can be of immeasurable worth. It should be kept under lock and key and never sold to anyone in the same business. Many of your competitors will want your list. Some will go to unusual lengths to obtain it. Guard your list jealously!

Assign One Person

Building a mailing list—a calling list—is a difficult task. The work should be assigned to one intelligent, interested, devoted person who is well paid for handling a tedious, frustrating, monotonous, wearisome job. Everyone cannot work on a mailing list. So few people have the patience and the tender loving care that is necessary. You, no doubt, will have to make three or four false starts before you find the one person who can accept the responsibility and have the intelligence to build a good list. In a small organization it may be necessary for the top executive and his secretary to compile the list. Even in a large organization it may be necessary.

In one large organization, the president, vice president in charge of sales, the comptroller and the writer compiled, after working hours, its first list of prospects. We are certain this would be called a poor management practice. However, these men were vitally interested. We were not going to advertise or send our salesmen to call upon companies that didn't have the credit or the volume of business to purchase our equipment. We purchased Dun and Bradstreet reports on almost every prospect and then evaluated them before placing their names on our list. It was a valuable list of 19 thousand names. One young, dedicated girl kept the list up-to-date after we established it. The salesmen were properly put in their places by the vice president in charge of sales if they failed to give the mailing list supervisor any changes in that list. The president would call the young lady into his office and ask questions about the list. She knew, and everyone in the company knew, that she had an important assignment.

The average clerk or little old lady who works in the bindery and also runs the addressography machine cannot handle a mailing list efficiently. It takes a certain kind of person who enjoys a challenging task. The task should also have the interest and blessing of the top executives. Through their interest and attention they should let the person who is responsible for the mailing list know of its importance. The list is the heart of successful selling and advertising. Please go back and read that last sentence again.

A Perfect List—Never

The mailing list will never be perfect. It should be as good as it is humanly possible to make it. It should be continually brought up-to-date, not once a year, but every month.

Your success with communication will greatly depend upon your ability to keep up with the changes of your customers and prospects. There are all kinds of percentages quoted for the annual rate of changes of a mailing list of manufacturing companies. The figures run from 20% to 75%. If your mailing list includes a person's name and title and is filed by net worth or number of employees or some other changing qualification, then the list should go into the 75% rate of change. If the list includes only the company name and address, then, no doubt, the 20% figure will apply.

List Specifications

Here is that word again—plan. It will be difficult to obtain a mailing list without a plan. Just as for a printing job, you will need a specification.

If you are specializing in one or two forms of printing, you will need an entirely different list from the commercial printer. No doubt, your market will also be larger. You may want to purchase a list from one of the many compilers of lists. But first, you must know what you want.

Here are some of the things you will have to decide in order to write a specification for your mailing list:

Where is your market? Is it 25 miles from your plant? Is it in one or two counties? Is it in a corridor 10 miles wide between two cities? Is it the entire United States? The answers all depend on the type of printing you are doing and the salesmen you have to cover the territory. Or, perhaps you intend to sell by mail. Then your advertising takes on a mail-order approach. A common mistake is to set a market area that is larger than the organization can handle. For instance, if you set a market within a radius of 100 miles of the plant, you must be prepared to send a salesman to the edge of that radius in any direction in any day. It never fails that when a prospect wants a salesman 100 miles to the north there will be a call for a salesman 100 miles to the south on that very same day. If you aren't prepared to take care of that type of request then you can't live up to your advertising claims of prompt service.

Whom do you want to sell? A criterion should be established. There is not much sense in advertising or trying to sell a company that has a poor credit rating. A one- or two-man company is not going to purchase much printing. When salesmen's calls are valued at $50.00 or over, you don't want to send your salesmen to the very small companies. A refuse or garbage collection service employing 300 men is a large organization but hardly one that would require much printing. Therefore, many criteria must be considered and judgments made so that someone preparing a mailing list will know who should be on the list.

How many lists will you need? You will surely need a customer list—perhaps a list of customers who haven't purchased anything for over a year. Then a prospect list is necessary. Should it be divided into two or three categories? For instance, do you want a list of prospects that should be converted into customers within the year? Then a list of those who will perhaps take longer to sell? Then a list of those on the fringes? Perhaps you want to try specialization. If you want to print nursery or seed catalogs, then you should have a list of nursery or seed companies. Such lists can be purchased. Or, perhaps you want to work only with advertising agencies, or automobile dealers or banks. Those lists can also be purchased or compiled.

Do you want to address your advertising to a certain man? Do you want your salesmen to talk to the top executive of the company? Or, should your advertising and salesmen be directed to the man who influences printing or the purchasing agent? Or, should the top executive, the buying influence and the purchasing agent all be included on your list? All of these considerations must be discussed and decided. Sometimes costs enter into the decision and at other times it can be the organization or personalities in a company.

Some companies will not use names on their mailing lists because people change positions so often. They address their mail to titles only, such as President, Advertising Manager, Sales Manager, Purchasing Agent. If you are mailing to 50 thousand or more and your advertising message is of a general nature, then mailing to a title is the economical thing to do. However, if you want the recipient to believe that you are talking to him, personally, then you better address him with his name and initials. We believe a small to medium size printer should use the man's name on the mailing or calling list. His list will not be so large that he cannot afford to make the changes when they occur. We believe that a large amount of advertising is wasted when it is just addressed to the company. Very few mailroom employees know whom you want to read your advertising. If your prospect is a small company and you know the owner opens the mail, then only the company's name will suffice, but even then it will be more effective if it is personally addressed to the owner.

In what form do you want your list? Will 8½" x 11" sheets of paper be satisfactory? Are you going to make Addressograph plates, and will that file be enough? Can you work from galley sheets? Mailing list houses prefer to send you galleys or computer sheets. We prefer 3 x 5 cards that can be easily alphabetized, filed by city or zip code or territory and then shuffled into some other category if need be.

Compiling the Mailing List

After you have written your mailing list specifications you have to find a method of obtaining the list. If you aren't doing specialized printing and your list will be less than 10 thousand companies in a local area we would suggest that you compile your own list. Mailing list companies are not too interested in selling such a small list and the cost may be quite high, depending on your specifications. Most mailing list houses have a minimum fee. However, you might wish to investigate the possibilities of purchasing your list. You will find a few names of mailing list sources in the back of this book. The yellow pages of your telephone book will also provide you with local company names.

You may rent lists from list owners, magazine publishers, trade associations or list brokers. List brokers are paid by list owners so their services in most cases are free to you. The list is rented on a one-mailing basis and you agree not to copy the list if they send it to you. The general procedure is to ship your mailing pieces to the list owner along with a check for the postage. The list owner addresses the pieces and mails them from his post office or ships them to your post office for mailing. The list owner maintains the list and will guarantee its accuracy within a certain percentage. If the returns are over that percentage, he will refund the postage cost.

Specialized printers should investigate the possibilities, depending on their specialities, for obtaining lists through trade associations, convention registrations, labor organizations, religious groups, automobile registration lists, magazine publishers, alumni lists and trade directories.

Commercial printers can compile their lists from many sources. Here are a few of them. Don't fail to take into consideration that almost any source is out of date the minute it is published. However, you must start somewhere so we suggest a visit to the local library where there are many sources. Also, your regional U.S. Department of Commerce office may be willing to assist you. Then there are the telephone yellow pages, city directories, Thomas's Register, MacRae's Blue Book, various industry buyers' guides, Dun & Bradstreet's directories, Chamber of Commerce directories and lists available through local mailing list houses.

If you have decided to use individuals' names on your mailing list, you have another problem. The mailing list you compile from directories will rarely have individuals' names. If they do show names they probably won't be the names you want. So, you must find methods of getting these names. One method is to make a mailing to each company's mailroom and ask for the names. You may get a 20- to 30-percent reply. If you offer a booklet, scratch pad, pencil or something of that nature for the information you will increase the response and also the expense.

Enclose a postage-paid business reply card for them to return with the information you wish. Be sure to fill in on the card as much information as you have, such as company name, address, zip code, and request that they check that information for accuracy. Make it as easy as possible for them to give you the information. Don't make the error that has been made so often. Companies have requested the name of the president or sales manager and have enclosed a card for that information to be returned, but have not identified the company in any way. The company asking for the information receives hundreds of cards with persons' names on them but they don't know where they work! The company wasn't identified.

Another method is to hire two or three housewives who can work at home. Get them to call each company and obtain the correct name of each person you want on your list. In most cases the telephone operators can give them the information. If it is a large company with a busy switchboard then ask for the personnel department, the mailroom, or the secretary of the advertising man, sales manager or whoever you wish to add to your list.

A much slower method, also more expensive, is to assign your salesmen to the task. Direct them to make calls on every prospect company and then obtain the names of the persons who should be called upon and who should receive your advertising.

Mailing List Maintenance

Compiling or buying a mailing list is a costly proposition. To neglect the list after you have it is ridiculous. Many executives believe that once you have the list then it is smooth sailing. To people who do not wish to worry about details, this is an easy assumption. However, lists must be maintained to be of any value. Someone must keep after them continually.

Whatever you do, don't permit employees to make mailing list corrections by phone or by sending scraps of paper to the mailing list supervisor. If a customer or prospect phones in to make a correction, of course you have to accept it. The person who receives the correction should then place it on a mailing list change form.

There are thousands of different mailing list forms being used. There are no set patterns. Make yours as simple as possible. Here are some of the necessities:

1. Legible writing or printing.

2. Dates—when the correction was submitted and when the correction was made on the list.

3. Boxes to indicate the action necessary—Add, Drop, Correct, Change Category.

4. The name and complete address as it is on the present list—codes and incorrect spelling included.

5. The correct name and correct address.

6. Name of the person submitting the mailing list form.

7. A line to indicate where the name should be placed on the list—what category, Customer, Prospect, Inactive Customer, etc.

The main point is to keep the form simple so no one will resent filling it in. If it is complicated, employees will "neglect" the task. There can be a place on the form for remarks and type of business, number of employees and much detail, but you will find that no one will want to use the form and, therefore, mailing list changes are not made.

It will also be necessary for you to set a date for house cleaning your list. It should be done at least once a year. At this time you go back to the library or list sources and check for new names. The world keeps moving and there are always new companies and also new employees in old companies. This is a good time to include a return reply card in a mailing asking for any corrections to your mailing list. This is the time to alphabetically file all your lists together to be sure you haven't any duplications. A prospect may have become a customer and you may have the name in two places.

Perhaps, if your list has been neglected, this is the time to get the outside ladies to make telephone calls again and obtain the necessary information directly from the companies.

Messages may be placed on envelopes asking for corrections and suggesting that they return the face of the envelope to you. You will not receive many replies but everyone received is a plus. Using a double postal card and placing the name and address as you have it on a business reply card with the simple query, "Is your name and address correct?" will sometimes get good results.

Using a special mailing just to ask for corrections to your list will get results provided the mailing is creative and out of the ordinary. Of course, there should be a postage-paid business reply card provided for the answer.

The postal services can help you to correct your lists, especially if you use third- or fourth-class mail. We will not go into detail about the many ways your list can be checked by the post offices. They change the rules, forms and fees and what may be true today will not be true tomorrow. We suggest you go to the main post office in your city and ask to talk to an expert who can tell you of the many ways you can correct your list. Ask about the following services. If they have been changed, or are not in existence, you will quickly get the correct substitute or information.

1. Using "Form 3547 Requested"

2. "Forwarding Postage Guaranteed"

3. Submitting your mailing list on cards and having the postal services check them.

4. Using certified mail and asking for a return receipt in order to get a correct address.

Of course, everyone in your organization should be aware of the mailing list revision and should assist in adding and correcting names. The men on the firing line, the salesmen, should be vitally interested in the procedure and in assisting. Your list, even after companies who have gone out of business have been removed, should grow each year, provided, of course, that you wish to increase your business each year.

Mailing lists - calling lists are the heart of successful selling and advertising. They are expensive to obtain. You should assign one devoted person to the task of keeping the list up-to-date. You will never have a 100% perfect list. You should have a written specification for your list. Maintaining the list is just as important as compiling it. Once a year, a complete revision should be made. Always remember, everyone loves to see his or her name, especially if it is spelled correctly.

CHAPTER 6
PRINTERS' ADVERTISING

"This amount of repetition to some
will probably appear to be tedious,
but only by varied iteration
can alien conceptions
be forced on reluctant minds."

—Herbert Spencer

This chapter is what this book is all about. It is the longest in the book. It is primarily written to give printers ideas for their advertising. We hope the descriptions of the advertising of others will give to those who have not used advertising enough creative impetus to generate some productive advertising of their own. We will try to describe the various forms of advertising used by printers in the past 25 years. One may wonder why we have gone back so far. We believe the same fundamentals of selling that were used 50 years ago apply today. The marketing ideas are still valid. The art and type faces have changed but the selling points remain the same. All of the pieces have been tested in the market place and the printers who have used them have been pleased with the results. At least, if they didn't know the results, they said they were happy that they advertised.

It is a very difficult undertaking to try to describe a printed piece in a few words. In describing some, we, perhaps, have gone into too many production details. In other descriptions we probably haven't given enough details to make them clear. We have done our best, and if you can't understand some details, perhaps you can write to the company and ask to see a copy. All of the printers whose work is described here have been very cooperative. There were only two individuals who didn't want to give us any information about their advertising. The one company's advertising is missing from these descriptions. The other company's president was pleased to cooperate.

Points that we made in past chapters are often repeated in this chapter. We found many illustrations of what we said constituted good advertising in other chapters. We were taught by some very talented advertising professionals that you have to tell them once, then again and again before people get your point. So, at the risk of being too repetitive, we have tried to show things that made the advertisements effective.

We have used or quoted a large amount of the copy in describing the pieces. We want to show techniques of writing that any printer can use. We don't believe professional writers need to be hired to write copy for printers who know their business and love their work. We also hope that this copy will give ideas to printers about how to sell their services.

A printer can get many ideas for his own advertising if he reads every paragraph of this chapter. He will find things that he can adapt to his own business. However, if he has one type of advertising in mind, such as a capabilities book or an open house invitation, or how to advertise form printing, then, perhaps, he should use the index and cull out the paragraphs that have no interest to him at this time. We believe the reader will get the most from this chapter if it is read to help spark ideas and to convince himself that if others can have success with advertising, so can he.

We have arranged these paragraphs alphabetically according to company names. We may start by describing a company's calendar and finish by writing about its direct mail campaign. Don't let some of the paragraph headings confuse you. There may be more ammunition further along. The index should help you refer to companies, personalities and forms of advertising.

Advertisers Associates

Merchandising Awards

Advertisers Associates, Inc., Pittsburgh, Pa., knows how to prepare eye-catching direct mail pieces for its customers, so they do the same thing for themselves. Oh, how they do it! They won two awards in the Annual Exhibition of Western Pennsylvania Printing and their announcements were the best we have ever seen. They had real showmanship.

One announcement came in a 12½"x14½", Grandee Seville Orange Cover stock envelope. The flap was printed in a dark red ink with the company name and address. There was a printed panel for placement of an address label on the front. In a three-inch panel going down the left hand side of the envelope were three well drawn line illustrations of ancient warriors. The words between the three drawings read, "Veni," "Vidi," "Vici." They were set in about 48-point type.

The folder inside was printed in two colors, a dark red and a silver. The stock was a heavy duplex sheet, one side Valencia Red, the other Seaville Orange. The sheet size was 12"x38", scored and folded three times to make a 12"x14" folded piece. The cover page and page two were 9½" wide; page three was 14" wide; page four, 9½" wide and pages five and six a bit short of 5" wide. Pages five and six folded back on page seven, which was the reverse side of page four. That is quite complicated!

The cover page folded over to expose a 4½"-wide panel of page seven, where there was a line drawing of a statue of a warrior standing 11" tall printed in silver. On page one was repeated the art panel that appeared on the cover. This art also appeared on the narrow page five inside.

As one folded the broad expanse of paper, the first thing found was an 8"x10" full color photograph of four boxes containing chess figures, molded as classic Roman warriors. These boxes were covered with excellent art and printed in four colors. There was a box for the Roman soldiers, gladiators, Roman army and charioteers. Standing beside the boxes were folders captioned, "The Glory of Rome."

Then on page three was tipped-on a letter from Carl N. Neuman, executive vice president of Advertisers Associates, Inc. The letter was

personalized to the recipient and was well written. The salutation pleased this writer because he doesn't believe in calling men "Dear Joe" or "Dear Mr. Glick." Girls are "dears" but not men! Mr. Neuman's salutation was, "Nothing well done comes easy, Joe." The letter went on to explain that he thought USS Chemicals Division of United States Steel Corporation made the right move when it selected Advertisers Associates to handle the mailing of a five-part chess set. Two paragraphs told of the problems, one paragraph about the award and there were two paragraphs of sell. On page three was also another copy in dark red of the Roman statuette and a listing giving the sequence of the mailings.

On page four was another full color photograph of the complete chess set in two boxes and the accompanying folder. The award certificate was included in this photograph.

The colorful folder and the way the mailers were shown and explained in the letter leaves nothing to be desired. All bases were covered. Even on the reverse side of th folder you could find the company name and address.

The second announcement was contained in a large, narrow, heavy Grandee Valencia Red cover stock envelope, 9½"x19½". There was no printing on the envelope.

The 9"x19" four-page folder inside was printed on a duplex Valencia Red and Seville Orange sheet, the red on the outside. On the first page, in at least 48-point type, were the words, "We're proud . . ." Then, mounted in a slit in the cover, was an actual peacock feather—a beautiful one—14" long.

On page three was another letter, personalized, from Mr. Neuman, telling of the awards given to them for a four-color promotion piece for Aluminum Company of America. The piece was best in its category and best of show. The letter was friendly and well written. It mentioned that they were proud to do business with the recipient, a nice gesture. This page also had a tipped-on 9"x10" photograph of the prize winning piece and the award certificates.

These two mailings exemplified advertising showmanship at its best. The question remains: How can we get more printers to go and do likewise? So few, who do excellent work and win awards, bother to tell customers and friends that they do good work and can do it for them.

Ahrendt Inc.

Consistent Advertising

For years we have been telling printers that consistent advertising is the only type of advertising that will work. We even suggested that they put their own advertising in the production schedule. If it is time to mail or produce their own advertising, they must forget the customers' jobs and put their own on the press.

You can imagine how popular that suggestion was. We quite often lost our audience after a statement like that. But advertising that produces new customers and keeps the old ones interested must be consistent.

We've now found a gentleman who long ago put our suggestion to practice. In fact, his secretary, who watches the sales figures and helps send out the invoices, gets quite upset. He orders his advertising put on the presses at the end of the month when she is interested in getting out jobs and billing to try to break some sales record or, at least, keep even with the preceding month.

Herbert R. Ahrendt, president of Ahrendt Inc., New York, is our man. And what a man he is. He knows that advertising works. He knows that it has to be consistent. He turns it out in volume and he enjoys the work.

His company has been advertising regularly since 1930, when Herbie took over the company from his father. His father pioneered what was then called embossographing. The modern version is called thermography. Webster's dictionary describes it as "a raised-printing process in which matter printed by letterpress is dusted with powder and heated to make the lettering rise." Webster has not bothered to define the difference between the raised printing that is first printed by letterpress or that printed by offset. However, Herbie says the letterpress print is called thermoprint and the offset is thermolith.

Ahrendt Inc. primarily prints by thermography or thermoprint. It also does letterpress printing. It prints a large volume of trade work as well as society printing (wedding invitations, formal announcements) and a line of Christmas cards sold through sample books known as the Pioneer, Thomas and Burgoyne lines. Herbie has a small offset press and experiments with it as a hobby but does not sell offset. There are 12 to 15 employees, and the plant occupies about 8000 square feet.

They spend one to two percent of their sales volume on advertising. Their mailing list has 3000 names which are on Elliot stencils—white stencils for prospects and blue stencils when they become customers.

Many printers wonder where they can get ideas for advertising. Herbie says he gets some of his best ideas for advertising, as well as plant management, between three and four o'clock in the morning. He has a scratch pad and a ball point pen with a light on it at the side of his bed. He awakens with an idea and jots it down. In the morning he finds some real good thoughts that make the rest of the day quite productive.

Herbie has a love of, or interest in, mottoes, wise sayings, short poems and proverbs. He keeps scrap books of this type of material and his advertising pieces are built around such keepsakes. Most of his advertising is 8½" x 11", 3⅞" x 9", 3¼" x 5½", or 2" x 3½". In other words, anything that will go into a No. 10 envelope. He uses many colors of stock and sometimes prints lithographic backgrounds using his hobby press. He often prints slogans on the envelopes.

Here are a few of the Ahrendt masterpieces: "Please Drive Carefully, Daddy. We Need You!" on a 2" x 3½" card. On a 3¼" x 5½" card with a nice border is this: "Our Business Is Always Good - It's Partly Your Fault." "Show Us No Mercy . . . Send More Orders" on a 4" x 9" card, and on another of the same size: "He who works with his hands is a Laborer. He who works with his hands and his head is a Craftsman. He who works with his hands, head and heart is an Artist. He who works with his hands and his head and his heart and his feet is a Salesman."

On 8½" x 11" sheets appear such wise sayings as these: "Whistle While You Work - It Will Drive Everyone Nuts."

"When in Charge, Ponder. When in Trouble, Delegate. When in Doubt, Mumble."

"We believe everyone should work - especially those who have jobs."

"The sure sign of the little man is the big head."

"Do Something - Either Lead, Follow Or Get The Devil Out Of The Way!"

"Now we know what's wrong with the world. If You Let The Bars Down, First Thing You Know, The Cattle Are Running All Over The Lot."

"The reason a dollar won't do as much as it once did is because people won't do as much for a dollar right now."

"Anger is one letter short of Danger."

"Bargain Sale - Today We Cut Our Prices - Tomorrow We Cut Our Throats."

"Every Successful Firm Must Have An Incentive Plan - Work Harder Or Get Fired."

"Do It Tomorrow - You Made Enough Mistakes Today."

"Fight Poverty The American Way - Work!"

"Youth Is An Icicle, Once Melted It Is Gone Forever."

"Do Right and Fear No Man - Don't Write and Fear No Woman."

"You ain't learnin' nothin' when you're busy talkin' "

"Don't lend money to friends . . . It gives them amnesia."

There are hundreds of similar proverbs. Here is one we assume Herbie uses when it is time to print his own advertising: "Notice - There's A Rush Job I'd Like You To Rush Out Before That Rush Job You're Rushing Now."

Herbie Ahrendt has a calling card that he uses for fun and to get attention. It has a plastic rifle pasted on it. Neatly arranged around the card are these words: Used Cars - Land - Whiskey - Fertilizer - Nails - Dry Goods - Fly Swatters - Racing Forms - Bongo Drums - Computers - Franchises - Fires Arranged - Uprisings Quelled - Revolutions Started - Assassinations Plotted - Wars Fought - Rugs Hooked - Bars Emptied - Market Advice.

If you are a regular customer you get the full treatment. Invoices are sent in No. 10 envelopes and the postage is never wasted. They have a very accurate postage scale and the latest pieces of advertising are inserted into the envelope until the maximum weight for the postage required is reached.

A recipient of Ahrendt Inc. advertising will rarely throw it away. The motto or proverb, if it isn't something you want to post on your bulletin board, is something you want to send to a friend or take home to the children. Rarely is there more than the company name, address and telephone number in small print. Sometimes there is an offer to frame one of the mottoes for a dollar or two. We have over 200 different pieces in our file and just five of them have a direct sales story for the Christmas card line. Of course, to put a blatant sales message on the piece would ruin its keepsake value.

Ahrendt Inc. does something else right. It merchandises its public notices and publicity. When the company or Herbie gets a good notice in a newspaper, magazine or industry newsletter, it is reprinted and passed around to customers or to those who may not have seen it. We wrote an article about Ahrendt Inc. for *Printing Impressions* magazine. About a month after it was published, we discovered that they had reprinted the article in a small 3½" x 5", 16-page booklet. The booklet had an embossed and gold stamped, thermoprinted cover with a pasted inter leaf. Three colors were used on the inside pages. It was a beautiful job and was almost a keepsake item as one wouldn't want to throw it away. They merchandised or publicized their own publicity and with the extra effort they obtained some extra publicity.

The company has won many awards for its consistent advertising. However, more important than awards, does the advertising bring in new customers? We asked Herbie that question and his answer was, "Definitely." There was no doubt in his mind that his form of advertising pays. He also knows that it develops repeat business. He is positive that his advertising is being read because of the letters he receives asking for extra copies. Some pieces have had to be re-run and he has distrbuted as high as 20,000 copies of one proverb.

Herbie is quite interested in various graphic arts groups, especially the Craftsmen and Salesmen's Guild. He makes a few speeches around the country discussing tricks of the printing trade. During these visits he is continually reminded of his advertising by people who come to him and remark about this or that wise saying. Sometimes they recall cards that were mailed many years ago.

And finally, let us give you the real proof of the worth of Ahrendt advertising: The company has no salesmen. Prospects are found and developed by advertising. You will find that it pays to put your own advertising job right in your production schedule and, if necessary, print it before a customer's job. Consistent advertising pays.

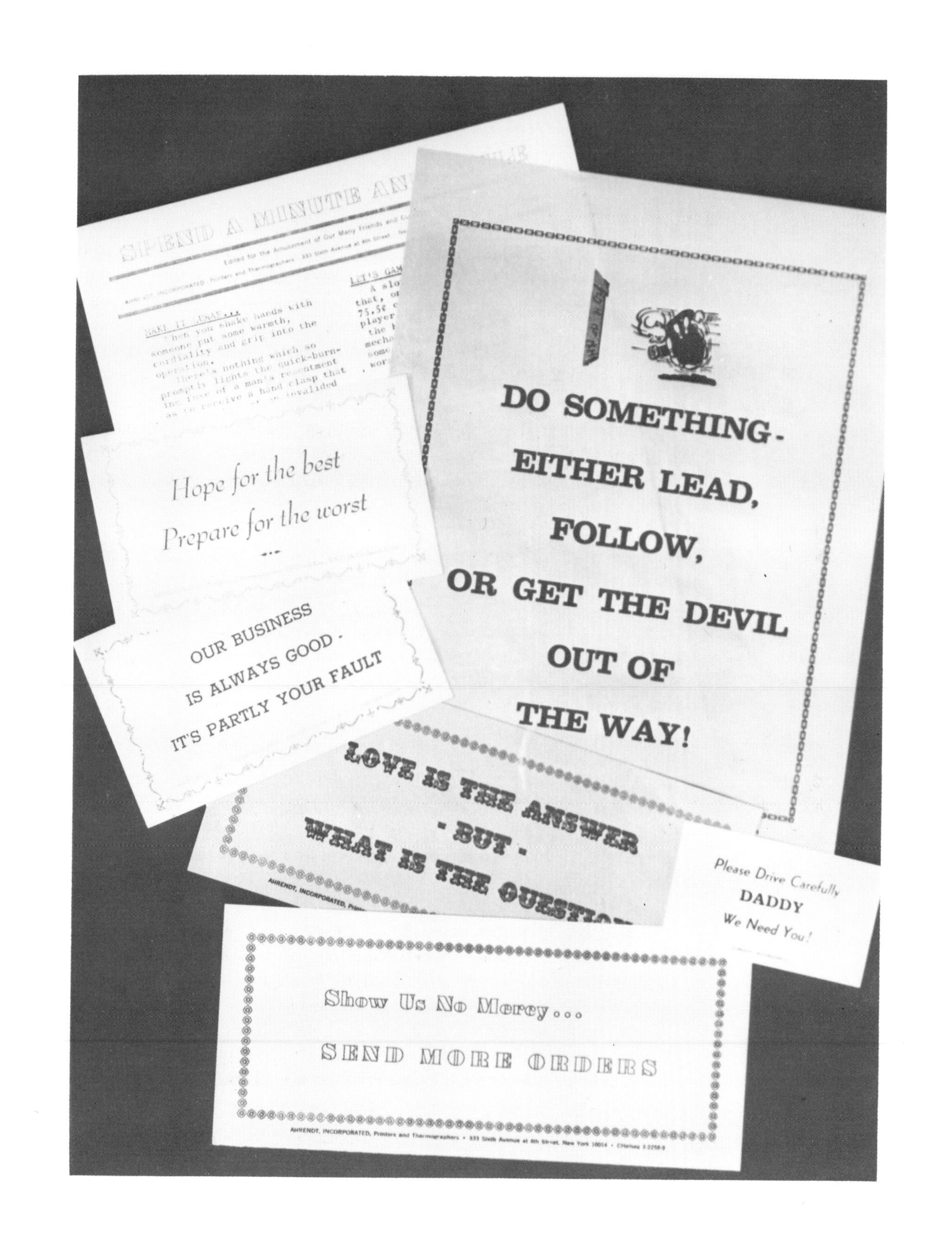
SPEND A MINUTE AN
Hope for the best
Prepare for the worst
OUR BUSINESS
IS ALWAYS GOOD -
IT'S PARTLY YOUR FAULT
DO SOMETHING -
EITHER LEAD,
FOLLOW,
OR GET THE DEVIL
OUT OF
THE WAY!
LOVE IS THE ANSWER
- BUT -
WHAT IS THE QUESTION
Please Drive Carefully
DADDY
We Need You!
Show Us No Mercy . . .
SEND MORE ORDERS

American Printers and Lithographers, Inc.

Image Building

American Printers and Lithographers, Inc., Chicago, Illinois, wanted to continuously build its image. One of its efforts was a planned direct mail program of four 8½" x 11" four-page folders. Each folder was lithographed in four colors of 80# Champion Wedgwood Coated Offset and enclosed in a 9" x 12" white envelope of 70# All Purpose Litho. The mailings were sent third-class bulk to approximately 5,000 prospects.

The envelopes were designed for this series of mailings. On the flap side of the envelope was a large 9" x 11½" four-color process photo of the well landscaped driveway and entrance to the offices and plant. American Printers and Lithographers employs 230 persons and has 17 sheetfed offset presses and five letterpresses. Annual sales are in the 13 million dollar range. On the address side of the envelope was printed an octagon-shaped half-tone in four colors showing a sunset over a lake. Below the octagon were the words, "Horizons of Quality for Offset Lithography Issue #3." Below that was a panel, 1" x 4½", that continued the horizon scene. To the right was this quotation: ". . . we should chart our course to capitalize most on what tomorrow offers." Where the address should appear was a small 1½" x 3½" die-cut window.

The addresses were placed on an 8½" x 11" sheet of 65# Sand, antique finish Carnival cover, which was not only used as a stiffener for the mailing but as a large postage-paid business reply card.

In a four-inch wide column down the left hand side of the card, "capability" was defined. Twenty-two examples of folders and promotion pieces were shown as examples of their creative capabilities. There is also a place on the card for requesting a representative to call, for a tour of the plant or additional copies of "Horizons of Quality." Since the card has the recipient's adress on it, all that is necessary is his signature, and it is ready for mailing.

The four-page folders reflect the quality of the printing plant. The four-color illustrations on the covers are in good taste and well printed. The company trade mark, AP&L, with four primary color dots, is used at the top of each cover. The illustrations are 8" x 8½" with a one-inch white band cut through the bottom half. In the white band is printed the subject of the folder, such as "Electronic Color Register" and below that line "Another PLUS from AP&L." They have surely illustrated their ability to print in register by running a 12-pt reverse line of type through the top of each picture. The inside pages are devoted to an explanation of color register, or moisture and ink control, or film plastic packaging, or a general description of "the house that Quality built."

The folders, without a doubt, help to build a quality image for American Printers and Lithographers. They believe that the folders created three new customers and 14 good prospects, with a $123,000 increase in business.

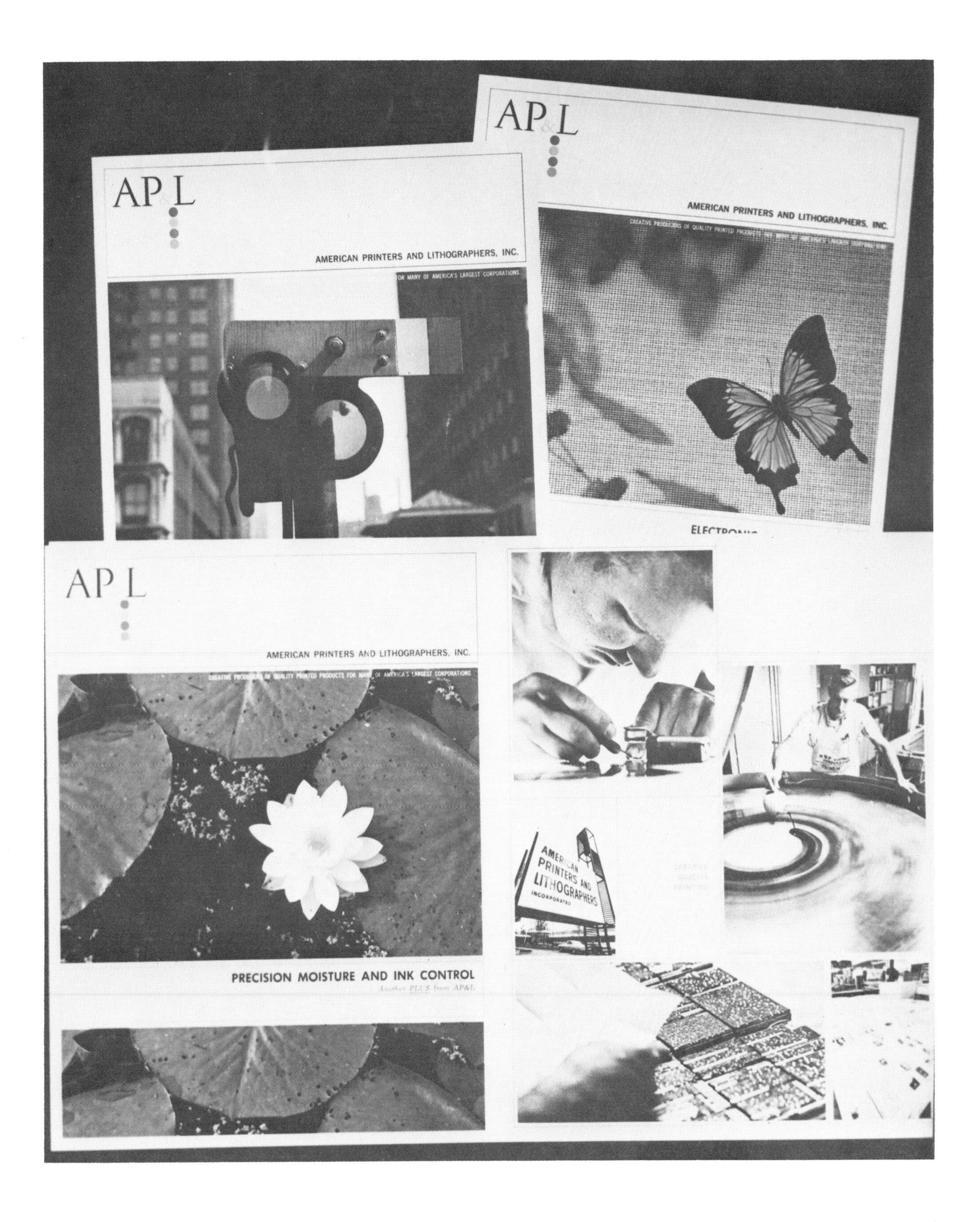
AP&L
AMERICAN PRINTERS AND LITHOGRAPHERS, INC.
FOR MANY OF AMERICA'S LARGEST CORPORATIONS
AP&L
AMERICAN PRINTERS AND LITHOGRAPHERS, INC.
AP&L
AMERICAN PRINTERS AND LITHOGRAPHERS, INC.
CREATIVE PRODUCERS OF QUALITY PRINTED PRODUCTS FOR MANY OF AMERICA'S LARGEST CORPORATIONS
PRECISION MOISTURE AND INK CONTROL
AMERICAN PRINTERS AND LITHOGRAPHERS INCORPORATED

AP&L also has a very elaborate and complete 40-page brochure which is distributed to new prospects. The cover and envelope are a dark brown 80# Peninsular Snoweave and are embossed with an AP&L on the envelope and the words "the house that Quality built" on the cover. The flyleaf, a 20# American Translucent stock, has been printed in four colors and shows the entrance to the offices and plant. The inside pages are 9" x 11½" bound on the 9" side. The stock is 100# Consolidated Blade/Coated White Poloma Offset. Before each white sheet is a brown embossed half-page introducing the copy on the white sheet with a suitable illustration and a line of type. Left-hand bleed pages show excellent acrylic-vinyl paintings of craftsmen at work. The copy on the white right-hand pages describes the functions of various departments. It is well written and beautifully set.

Mr. George W. Schnitzius, Vice President-Sales and Marketing, says, "The brochure is most effective when the salesman has to 'close' the sale. It is the small edge that can get the order for us."

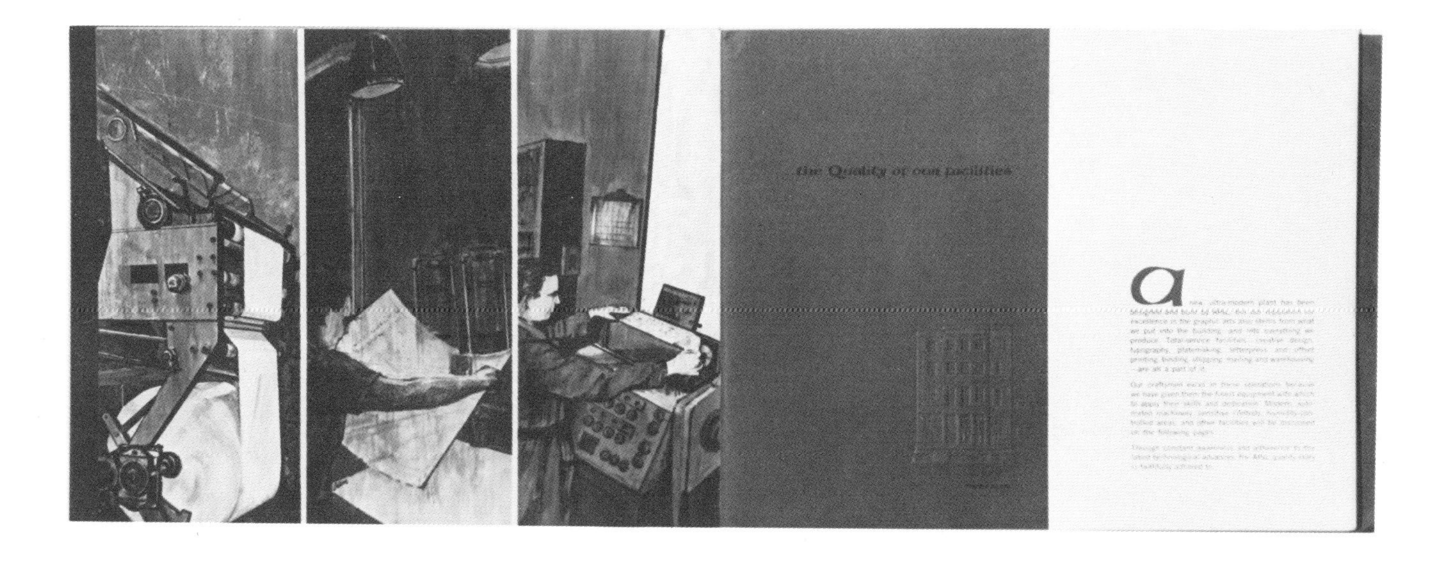

American Printing Company

Anniversaries

If you can't find a theme for your advertising there are always anniversaries you can talk about. If you think you don't have time to complete a real advertising campaign, the least you can do is to create a piece once a year to announce that you have another year's experience in the printing business.

American Printing Company, Washington, D.C., has approximately 13 employees. They do very little advertising but won an award for a four-page folder, 6" x 9", that announced they had been in business for 44 years.

The green cover was printed with a large red foil "44". A die-cut circle in the left-hand corner of the cover let another "44" show through from page three. The inside pages were printed with blue ink on a blue background. The copy established that they had been in business 44 years, "certainly a long time to be in any business." The copy also stated, "When your business is serving people, you remain in business 44 years only by delivering quality printing at a fair price." They assured the reader that they were not so old that they couldn't help them. They suggested returning a postage-paid reply card that was tipped on to page two. The card had space for writing in the date and time the customer would like to see a sales representative.

The folder was enclosed in an envelope and made a very nice appearance. They received compliments from customers and felt they had at least said "hello" to some prospects they hadn't seen for a while.

Apex Die and Paper Box Company

Work File Folder

Printers have many different ways to demonstrate their products. One of the best is the use of a file folder containing samples of work produced for customers. Apex Die and Paper Box Co., Inc., San Carlos, California, used this means to demonstrate its ability. They employ 16 people and have just one person selling. They have eight letterpresses and three die cutters. Annual sales amount to approximately $375,000. The assistance of an advertising consultant was obtained to help with the copy and layout of their spectacular file folder.

Apex used a heavy Torino Duo, charcoal-white cover stock for its 9" x 12½" file folder. The charcoal side was used for pages one and four and was folded inside to make the pockets. On the right-hand inside pocket, complete production notes were given which greatly help the customer to understand how this exceptionally fine job was produced.

The front cover was flat stamped with a heavy impression using photo-etched magnesium dies. Although there was no embossing, the selection of colors and art makes it appear embossed. The illustration is a mechanically stylized platen press. Eight passes through the press were necessary to apply the eight roll leaf colors, which included a pearl white, wood grain and black. The black was laid down last to cover all the seams between colors.

The page two pocket was die cut to hold a calling card. Incidentally, the rounded-corners calling card is of heavy brown stock. It is embossed and bright blue foil stamped with the words "Apex Die" approximately one inch high. The man's name, as well as the company name, is printed in black on the card. It is a very striking card.

On the page three pocket, the words "Apex Die" are again embossed and gold foil stamped with a hand tooled brass combination die. On this pocket is a list of every type of foil stamping, embossing, die cutting, scoring, perforating, sheet mounting, easeling, eyeletting, drilling, hand finishing, folding and gluing that this company can produce. It is a helpful list for any buyer of printing but such a list is often forgotten by most printers when producing their advertising. There is also the company name, address and phone number, along with the production notes mentioned before.

On page four, the same press shown on the cover page has been blind embossed with hand tooled brass embossing dies.

This piece won a PIA award and is used constantly by Apex to show samples, enclose proposals or quotations and to generally demonstrate their work. Several designers have designed jobs using some of the techniques used on the Apex folder. New customers have also been acquired through the use of it.

One sheet enclosed in the folder is a "Capabilities Listing" with a date so that it can be updated as new equipment is added. On this sheet is listed the presses that are available and a column to indicate if they can be used for die cutting, embossing or foil stamping. There is a list of miscellaneous equipment. They also mention their steel rule die shop and hand folding, gluing and fabrication departments. In other words, nothing is left to the imagination. Prospects and customers know what Apex Die can do. From the samples we have seen in the pockets they do beautiful work.

Arts & Crafts Press

Capabilities File

There are many types of capabilities folders or booklets. We believe Arts & Crafts Press, San Diego, California, has one of the better ones. When the 12" x 26¾" sheet is folded twice into thirds, it measures 9" x 12". The front side (three pages) is printed in four colors and is laminated. The cover page uses ten AC trade marks to illustrate the various screens from a 100% solid to 20%. They have used five horizontal bars of the same screens to add to the design. The company name is printed in red on the bottom 100% black bar.

On the reverse side of the center fold is printed eight ⅞" high AC trademarks on a jet black background showing how the trademarks can be reversed or printed with process colors, or overprinted on the black background.

On the back cover page are many color bars showing how various screens and colors appear when overprinted or combined. There are also six halftones of the same illustration showing process colors and various types of duotones. These three pages would be very helpful to the designer or purchaser of printing who wasn't quite sure of what tones he wanted to specify for his work.

Two of the inside pages listed the company's capabilities in terms of equipment. These pages were printed in two colors. The information was quite detailed and, no doubt, of great value to a customer. The third page on the inside contained a foldover pocket so samples could be inserted.

The folder that we received contained a very well printed annual report of Intermark, an organization of many companies all based in California. Arts & Crafts Press happened to be one of the companies. The annual report was a beautiful job of four-color printing, embossing, fine typography and good use of white space. The left hand page in the 8½" x 11" report (bound on the 8½" side) were covered by four-color process illustrations.

What made the annual report so interesting for buyers of printing was a small booklet of 24 pages, 4⅜" x 5⅝", bound in the same cover stock as the annual report. The booklet contained the annual report story of how the illustrations were taken by the photographer, Kenneth Robert Shearer. Some photos were taken 48 times in order to get the right one. Others had clouds sandwiched over the original negative. Various filters were used. In one photo the sky looked better upside down so they printed the sky that way. On the inside cover were production details for the booklet, and on page 24 a story about the photographer.

This small booklet could be another source of business to those printers who print elaborate annual reports. Many recipients of annual reports would enjoy reading how the report was put together. The time, effort, craftsmanship and planning that are put into so many reports would be interesting to many. Why not sell an extra—the annual report story.

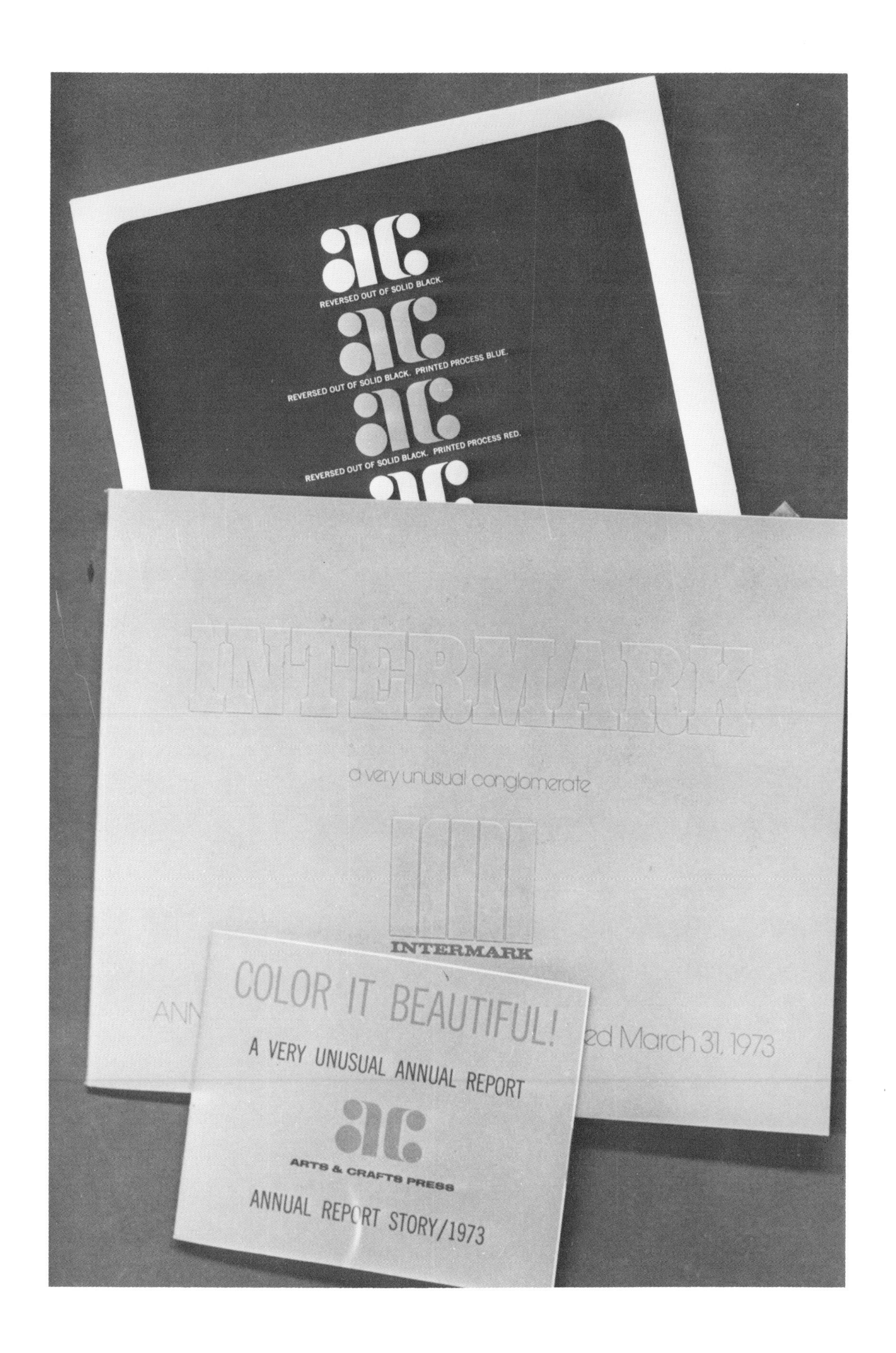
REVERSED OUT OF SOLID BLACK.
REVERSED OUT OF SOLID BLACK. PRINTED PROCESS BLUE.
REVERSED OUT OF SOLID BLACK. PRINTED PROCESS RED.
INTERMARK
a very unusual conglomerate
INTERMARK
COLOR IT BEAUTIFUL!
A VERY UNUSUAL ANNUAL REPORT
ARTS & CRAFTS PRESS
ANNUAL REPORT STORY/1973

Blair Graphics Group

Capabilities Folders

"The Power Of The Presses" is the caption for two 13" x 31⅜" sheets folded three times to 9" x 13" that we have recently seen from the Blair Graphics Group. The Group is comprised of Alden Press and American Printers & Lithographers, in Chicago, and Meehan-Tooker, New York. Volume One of their folders covered press equipment. Volume Two was headed "The Before and After." Volume Three, which we haven't seen, is to tell about the people who make the Blair Graphics operation a success.

The folders are printed on a heavy coated stock. The last fold, which makes a 4⅜" x 13" panel, contains a perforated business reply card so those interested can request a 16" x 20" poster of one of the illustrations shown in the folder. The folders are enclosed in large envelopes produced from sheets with an overall background of process yellow for Volume One and magenta for Volume Two. There is a panel of white left for the address. The free poster offer is mentioned on the envelope and a small reproduction of the poster in four process colors is also used. The mailings are sent bulk rate.

The folders adequately describe the capabilities of the Group and the individual companies. Thirty-eight presses, web and sheet fed, are listed in Volume One to illustrate the companies' versatility. They also list their many clients and show 31 pieces of printing for some of these clients. One of the pages is used to show an unusual angle of a web going through the press.

Volume Two also uses a full-color bleed page. This one is a photograph of their paper storage taken at an unusual angle. There is a page of ten photographs illustrating the various steps in producing a printed piece.

The copy is interesting and covers "The Before and After" of a printing job. They make a good sales point of their ability to cover the many steps preceding and following the actual press run. Everything can be done in-house. "How To? and How Much?" is another heading for a paragraph. Then follows: "Production Coordination," "On Camera," "Separating the Yellow from the Magenta," "A Dot Can Make The Difference," "Getting It All Together," "Turning One Image Into A Hundred," "On Press," "A Stitch in Time" (covering bindery) and "En Route."

These folders describe a large organization's capabilities but there is no reason why similar folders couldn't be produced for a small organization. If you don't have all the departments, you can describe how you handle this work and what controls you have. Capabilities booklets or folders are almost a must in any good advertising campaign. How do buyers of printing know what you can do if you don't tell them?

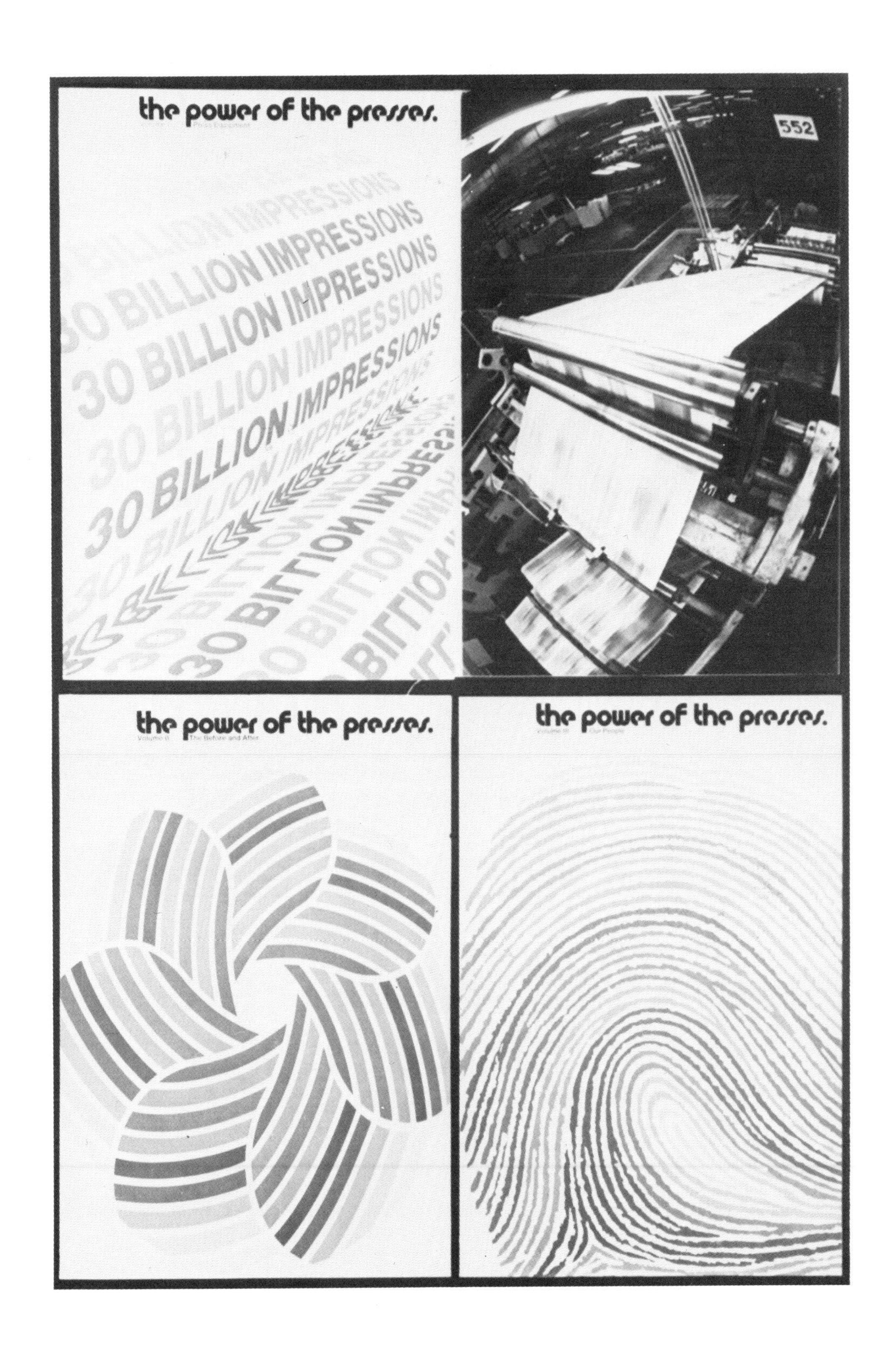
the power of the presses.
30 BILLION IMPRESSIONS
552
the power of the presses.
the power of the presses.

California Printing Company

Fun Contest

Advertising that works doesn't always have to be formal and serious. In fact, some pieces that have been very successful have been real fun things. For instance, the Hubba Hubba contest used by California Printing Co. of San Francisco. This contest, or a similar one, could be adapted and adopted by any printer located a thousand miles from San Francisco.

California Printing is a medium sized plant with approximately 55 employees. It does all types of printing except form work.

The fun all started when Ernest Haskin, CP's president, talked to Jack Jannes of Dancer-Fitzgerald-Sample Advertising Agency about an idea for its quarterly campaign. California Printing tries to advertise each quarter. Jack Jannes came up with a fantastic prize to give away to some lucky person—a genuine, vintage 1949, Rock-Ola jukebox.

Wally Wenner, the California Printing art director, was told about someone seeing a jukebox in a funky old shop on Valencia Street in San Francisco. Wally went off on the hunt, found the shop and hauled the jukebox off to the plant.

After the box was there about two weeks, George Edwards, of Premier Cutting & Mounting Co., saw it. He asked if he could take it home and refurbish it. His hobby was electronics. He repaired the box, rewired the circuitry, removed a bee's nest and put the lights back in place, polished the chrome and woodwork and the juke box looked beautiful. Some of the old records came from another friend who is in the pinball and jukebox business. Even Mrs. Haskin got into the act, for she typed the tune titles and made them fit into place.

A striking 11" square french folder was produced from a 22" x 22"-plus-bleed enameled sheet. The front and back cover background was black. Yellow, blue and magenta inks were also used on pages one and four. The words "Hubba Hubba" were emblazoned in neon lettering on the front cover.

The background on the two inside pages was printed with a tan ink. Two four-color photos were used, one of an old record, "Drop Another Nickel In The Jukebox," and the other a beautiful photo of "Marvelous Marilyn" leaning wistfully on the top of the Rock-Ola. The copy was excellent. It read:

"Save Your 78's, We're Rafflin' a Rock-Ola. Want to make this schmaltzy office of yours really zing? Then fill out and mail in the enclosed raffle ticket. You just might win a gen-u-ine 1949 Rock-Ola Jukebox. Complete with five-foot high gold glowing tubes and swinging boogie woogie sounds: 'Rum and Coca-Cola' by the Andrews Sisters. 'Prisoner of Love' by Perry Como. 'String of Pearls' by Glenn Miller. And More. What's the occasion? You're holding it, man. It's another high quality piece by the Proud Princes of Printing at California Printing. We can give you the same kind of work, with our ultra modern Four-Color Fifty Press, our snazzy Two-Color Fifty Press and our famous killer diller craftsmanship. Remember us next time you have a classy job to do. And send in your raffle ticket now. The Rock-Ola would go perfectly with your pleated pants and two-tone shoes. A hubba hubba hubba. California Printing Co. The Proud Princes of Printing."

With the folder was a card to be filled out and returned to make the contestant eligible for the drawing.

The first mailing was followed by a 22-inch long, mysterious glossy black mailing tube, three inches in diameter. On the tube was a large two-color label with the words "Hubba Hubba" and the usual address. The tube carried a 35" x 49" four color poster, bearing a full-length photograph printed in four glossy colors of the Rock-Ola with Marilyn revealed in all her 1949 authenticity—pompadour hairdo, sloppy Joe sweater, bobby sox and all. Incidentally, Marilyn was a model and came dressed for the photograph in perfect 1949 garb with the exception of her red knee sox. The crisis was met by the photographer who took off his sweat socks and put them on Marilyn. She just had to have bobby sox to portray a 1949-vintage young lady. A second entry card was enclosed. Both of these pieces were beautifully printed. Everything was in excellent register and there were no hickies on any of the heavily covered backgrounds.

Timed to ride the crest of the nostalgia boom, the contest owed much of its success to its exciting graphics and the excellence of its presentation. Both the first folder and the poster were printed on Fotolith II Gloss, 80-lb. stock, run on California Printing's four-color Miehle 38 x 50, then varnished on the single-color 60" press.

The mailings, pure nostalgia from the bright "Hubba Hubba" labels through the final "Daddy-O" on the contest cards, went to a mailing list of 1,287. This list included customers, prospects and members of the communications industries throughout San Francisco and southern California.

Was this campaign successful? Almost immediately the cards came back—many in artistically designed envelopes and some with nostalgic messages of memories of those bygone days.

"We had a better than 83-percent return from the cards we mailed," said Marv Rossi, vice president and sales manager for California Printing. "The mail didn't stop when the contest ended. Every week we hear from people who want a copy of our poster, or who ask to be added to the mailing list for the next contest. Most of them assume we're planning to make Hubba Hubba an annual event!"

According to Dick Evans, marketing director, the contest opened up six new accounts and brought in numerous additional requests for presentations and quotes. He said doors definitely opened more easily. Salesmen were greeted with such comments as, "Oh, you're with the guys with the jukebox." There is now an easy-going rapport between the prospects and the sales staff because the company is identified as a place with a spirit of fun. The impact of seeing the quality of the poster was tremendous.

Anyone knowing anything at all about printing recognizes what a job it was to produce something of that size with that quality—so, seeing the sample was most effective. Even after the contest ended, the poster was still hanging in many offices and some radio stations.

KFRC-FM, a local radio station, purchased 2,000 posters and had a sales message silk-screened across the top and bottom. A local TV station went to the office of the winner of the jukebox to film the box in action.

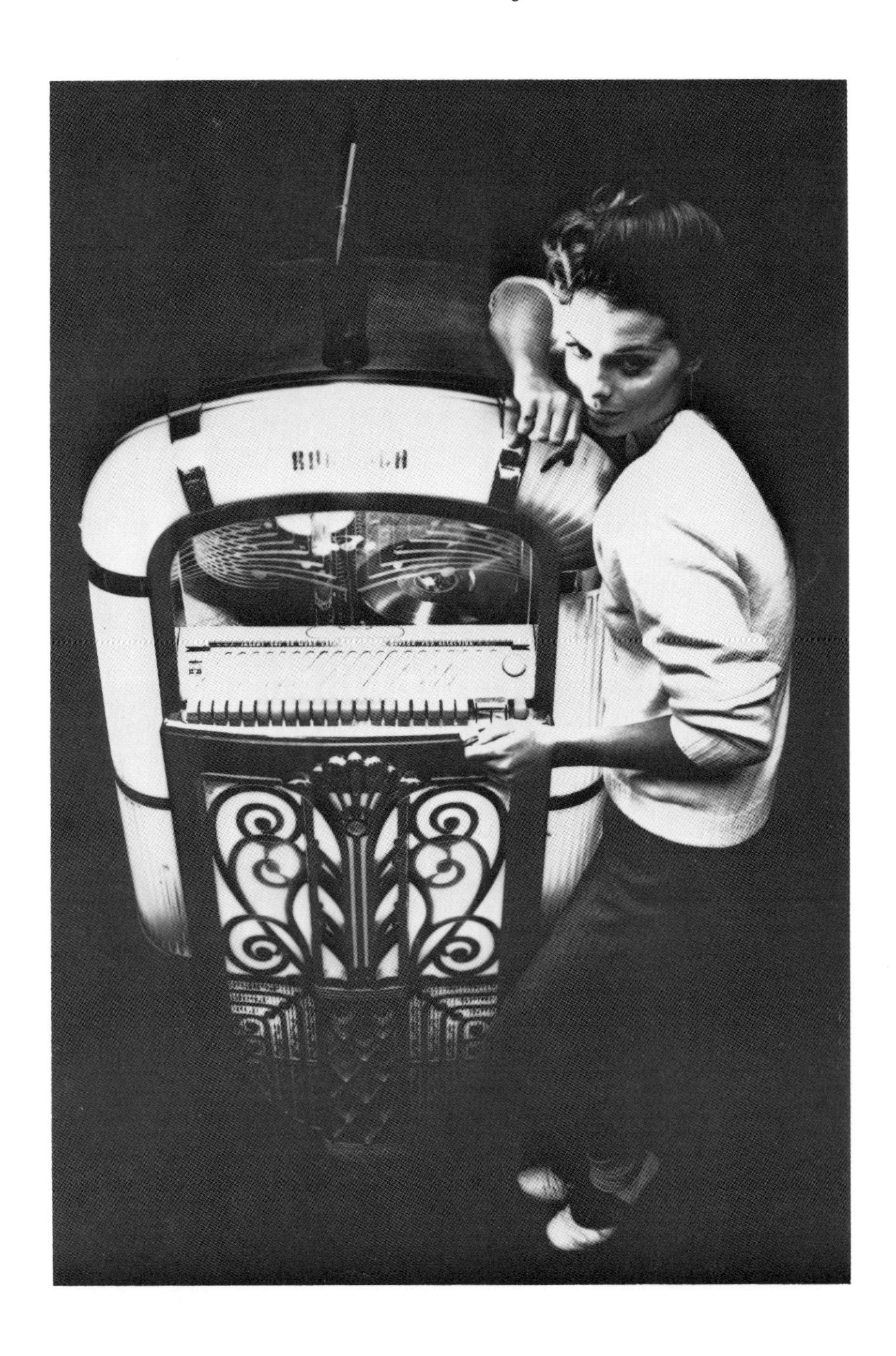

Interest in the contest outcome was so high that a follow-up mailer was prepared by Wally Wenner, art director of California Printing, announcing the name of the winner—Lee M. Smith, D'Arcy MacManus & Masius, a San Francisco advertising agency. The six-page folder was printed on a Carnival Kraft yellow stock in two colors, green and red. Duotones and tone line conversions from the original Kodachrome of the jukebox were used. It was printed on a single-color Miehle 29.

The follow-up folder gave the entrants another glimpse of the Rock-Ola and the cute Marilyn. It showed a photo of the proud winner standing beside the jukebox. The runner-up won the Hubba Hubba neon sign and installed it in his office as a beacon, he says, to assist persons wishing to locate him.

We understand that the winner, Lee Smith, keeps changing the records in the jukebox because California Printing Co.'s competitors try to get into the act by supplying him with records. Occasionally he will call marketing man Dick Evans, put a nickel in the machine and serenade Dick with his favorite song: "Frenesi."

The entire campaign, exclusive of the jukebox (which cost $350 to buy and $150 to put into fine condition) but including the model and art, was approximately $6,000.

California Printing had the same problem as many printers do. It had trouble getting its own advertising on the press because of customers' work. In fact, the drawing for the jukebox had to be postponed a month because they wanted to get the follow-up piece in the mail after the drawing and they didn't have any available press time. Of course, it is this writer's contention that you have to put your own advertising in the regular production schedule and you don't let anyone pull it out, or you will never get it done.

Advertising that works can also be fun. Try something crazy—something out of this world—and see what happens.

Calendar

California Printing Company has a calendar that it has been printing for eight years. The 1975 calendar was distributed to "3,000 customers, suppliers and a growing list of friends."

California Printing Company's calendar has always been printed in four colors on a 12" x 18" sheet and scored and folded once. The calendars have been mailed two in an envelope. The 1975 calendar was printed on Quintessence Dull Cover - 100#.

A beautiful full-color photograph of San Francisco's fishing fleet, taken by Loren Smith of San Francisco, occupies the vertical left half of the sheet. The calendar months are printed down the right side in two vertical banks. The type is clean, of a sans serif variety, with a nice use of white space to separate the months. The calendar month occupies a space 1⅝" x 2½". Sundays and holidays are printed with a process blue ink.

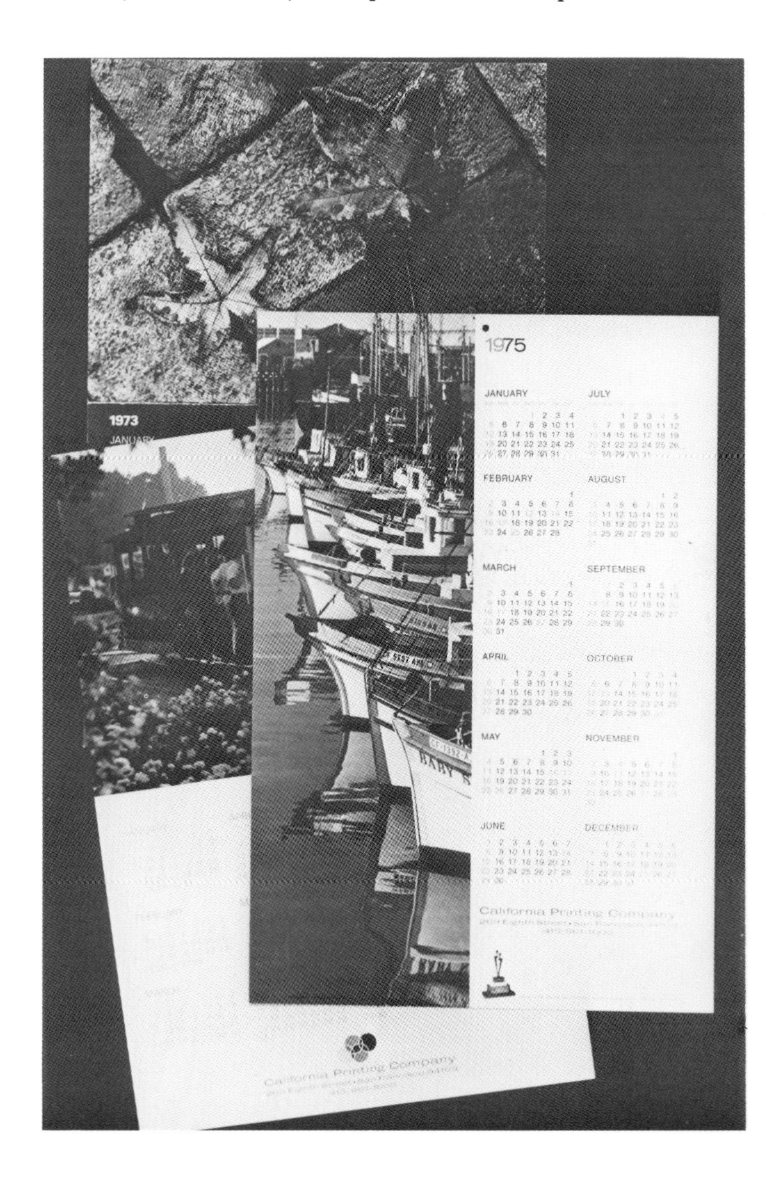

The company name, address and phone number occupy the lower 2½" of the calendar. In this area is a small full color reproduction of the Addy trophy, presented to California Printing by the American Advertising Federation for its "Hubba-Hubba" direct mail campaign.

The 1974 calendar featured a San Francisco cable car photograph taken by Loren Smith. It occupied the top horizontal half of the sheet. The 1973 sheet was laid out in the same manner, using a large photograph of two fall leaves on a brick pavement. The calendar months were reversed out of a black background; the Sunday and holiday dates were screened and were just a bit too dark for good legibility at a distance. The 1972, 1971 and 1970 calendars were printed on a linen finish sheet that was very attractive. The top horizontal half was taken up with a Golden Gate Bridge photo by Tom Tracy in 1972. Three Tracy photos were used in the 1971 calendar. Four San Francisco Convention and Visitors' Bureau photos were used in 1970. In these three years the monthly calendars were printed on white backgrounds.

California Printing Co. executives state, "Over the years our calendar has become a fixture in many offices. Since it has always been the same size and shape, many recipients have reserved the same spot on the wall for the calendar year after year. Others have lined their office or shop walls with them to prolong their enjoyment of the San Francisco scenes. Every year the request list grows longer."

In 1975, California Printing used three elaborate mailings to promote its printing. It commissioned three young, relatively unknown artists to design the pieces and thereby demonstrate their talents. Jack Jannes, who conceived the Hubba Hubba campaign, provided the concept for this series also. Each brochure was lithographed on 10-point Kromekote in four colors, and was contained in a handsome Kromecote folder sealed with a silver seal. The sheet size was 8" x 24", folded and scored twice to produce a six-page folder.

The first folder described the circumstances of the award of the coveted Blue Max to Baron Manfred von Richthoven. There was a stylized cartoon of the Baron on page three, and another cartoon on page five. On page four was copy promising a replica of the Blue Max if the reader would listen to a few of California Printings' war stories. The copy went on to tell of its winning of various awards. After the company signature, there is a six-point line which reads, "The most decorated color lithographer in the area." On page six appeared the company signature, address and telephone number along with some credit lines. Mark Matsuno drew the illustrations. Omnicomp did the typography which was very good.

Three days after the first piece was mailed, another folder was sent telling the story of Deacon Ewry, who, in 1926, won five Olympic gold medals, bringing his career total to 10 individual gold medals. There were two pages of drawings by Patrick Chapin. Copy again promised a medal for examining California Printing's track record.

Three days later they mailed another folder describing the shortest war on record, which concluded with the awarding of the Brilliant Star of Zanzibar to Admiral Harry Holdsworth Rawson. Again, there were two pages of illustrations by Lars Melander. The copy promised another award if the recipient would look at some of the California Printing's award winning work.

There were no return cards in the mailing. The prospect had to telephone and then he was given a promise to "send one of our foot soldiers over with some colorful samples and your very own award. After all, it takes courage to willingly let a printing salesman into your office. But never fear. He won't bombard you for hours. In fact, his visit will be much shorter than some wars."

Each salesman, when answering the calls, delivered first a 3½" x 7" heavy stock folder, the fold on the 7" side, which read on the first page, "For courage in the face of printing house salesmen and other adversities." On page two, "Please rise." On page 3, "California Printing hereby awards you the Brilliant Star of Zanzibar (First Class), the Blue Max and an Olympic Gold Medal. Punch them out and use them to impress relatives, sweethearts and casual acquaintances at cocktail parties. And please, when your next big printing job rolls around, remember us, the most decorated color lithographer in the area." California Printing's name was also on page three, as well as on page four, with its address.

The medals were printed in three colors and gold leaf, hot embossed and die cut on 8" x 8" Kromecote sheets. The printing of all the pieces was beautiful. Kromecote luster was used to good advantage and it all spells quality. There is no doubt that this campaign will be remembered by California's prospects and customers.

On January 16, 1917 he received
the Blue Max, Imperial
Germany's highest award for
individual gallantry.
Pour le Mérite
F
Blue Max
CITIUS ALTIUS FORTIUS
These victories brought
his career total to an all-time
Olympic record of 10 individual
gold medals.

Case-Hoyt

Response

They started a serious self-advertising program in late 1966. Their sales were around $17,000,000 then. Today, their sales are about $40,000,000. With a business as large as that, Case-Hoyt, of Rochester, N.Y., must be doing a number of things right. Although they do some beautiful self-advertising, we are sure that advertising alone has not been the cause or the reason for their success. They are quality printers and there are no ands, ifs or buts about that. Their advertising reflects the quality of their product. If your advertising can do that you have accomplished an excellent bit of communication.

Case-Hoyt is like the winning football team that is in the last five minutes of the last quarter and the score is 28 to 0. They can afford to try some complicated plays and do some fun things. Case-Hoyt produces some self-advertising that must be a joy to plan and print. It is expensive and it is unusual and, of course, it gets attention. It enhances their image. It works.

Dick Stites, their Creative Director, states, "Our self-advertising program's primary purpose is to establish a good selling environment for our salesmen to both new and old accounts. The fact that our business has continued to grow steadily is at least some measure of proof that the program is working." They have won so many awards for their self-advertising and printing that they must feel that awards are pretty old hat.

Response is the name of a publication produced by Case-Hoyt to advertise and demonstrate their printing capabilities. *Response* is a registered trademark of the company. It seems to have no set format or publishing cycle. Each issue has one thing in common: beautiful type, illustration and quality printing.

Let us try to describe *Response 6* and *Response 7*. *Response 6* is a 10½" x 12", 12-page, saddle stitched booklet. The cover has a fold-over page, making four pages. The cover is CelestraKote 75. We will print the copy used on page four of the inside cover, so you can see its simplicity but discern the information that has been given to a buyer of printing.

"The paper used for this cover is something else—it's plastic.

"Case-Hoyt used CelestraKote, a new kind of printing sheet. Its surface is so smooth it defies instruments measuring irregularities.

"It has no fibers or grain direction.

"It remains stable even when the relative humidity does not.

"It scores and folds well.

"It has an extremely white but dull finish with almost no glare at normal reading angle and distance, although the printing appears glossy.

"Its unique coating takes 4-color inks beautifully, doesn't absorb them. Note how well the solid is laying on the inside back cover.

"Cost? About double Kromekote's price.

"We've printed on both sides of the cover so you can judge the plastic printing sheet's qualities—and Case-Hoyt's—for yourself.

"Case-Hoyt is interested in anything that makes printing better, because that's what our customers are looking for.

"You can't always tell a book by its cover. But you can always tell a printer by his printing. *Response 6* is ours.

"If you're interested in CelestraKote, write Crown Zellerback, One Bush Street, San Francisco, Calif. 94119. If you're interested in printing, write Case-Hoyt at 800 St. Paul Street, Rochester, N.Y. 14601.

"Production Data:

"Printed sheet fed offset on a 25" x 38" five-color Miller press.

"The 6-page cover is CelestraKote 75 (caliper .0075)

"The text is 100# Mead Black and White Gloss

"The other side of this sheet has been press varnished over-all.

"This side has not been varnished.

"*Response* is a registered trademark of the Case-Hoyt Corporation."

That is all the copy in the entire booklet with the exception of captions for the beautiful halftones and 42 words about Case-Hoyt Packaging Corp., along with a tipped-on flat of a small package especially designed for the publication. The flat was gold stamped as well as printed in four colors and varnished.

The cover illustration, as well as all the other large four-color halftones, one must assume, are illustrations taken from various things Case-Hoyt has printed. Each illustration is a beautiful example of printing craftsmanship. It makes one proud of the printing professions.

On the inside back cover they have tipped on a 4" x 6" Xograph sample. The back cover shows another small but beautiful photograph with a complete listing of their sales offices, a signature slug and a line "The People Responsible For Response." The Direct Mail Trademark is also shown.

Response 7 is eight pages, 17½" x 23", with cover and inside fly leaf. White space is used lavishly and the small amount of copy is so good that we are going to print it here so you can read it and, perhaps, profit from its example.

"It is man's nature to live free from artificiality. He responds to the natural state of unspoiled beauty, the real color he sees and touches and feels. This issue of *Response*, like all others before it, is a collection of subjects reproduced in their natural colors. Free from artificiality.

"We call this color Case-Hoyt Color because no other printer has it. Without it, the butterflies in the center spread wouldn't be real butterflies. And Case-Hoyt wouldn't by Case-Hoyt.

"Production data: Printed sheet-fed offset on a 25" x 38" four-color Harris press.

"Front and back cover silk-screened on 60-lb. Champion Colorcast Litho mounted on both sides of 60-lb. cover stock.

"Inside front and inside back covers printed offset.

"Inside pages 10-point Kromekote. Page size 17½" x 23"

"*Response 7* was designed by Dominic Arbitrio of Page, Arbitrio & Resen, Ltd.

"*Response* is a registered trademark of Case-Hoyt Corporation."

That is the entire copy, the entire selling message, with the exception of 39 words describing five tip-ins of folding cartons and labels produced by Case-Hoyt Packaging Corp. All the illustrations are captioned and credit is given to the photographer and client. There is one short line describing a "Painting with a Camera" technique used in the background of one of the photographs.

The illustrations are four-color photographs of statuary, gears and machinery, an automobile, a fashion model, a soft drink, food and an unusual set of 34 butterfly photographs on the center spread. The superb printing, the beautiful use of white space and the large size of this piece make it something that one just can not throw away.

response

Awards Booklet

Case-Hoyt does other forms of self-advertising and again, it is of the highest quality. In 1969 and 1970, the company won 65 different awards for its advertising or printing for customers, so it produced an eight-page 7½" square booklet. It was printed in six colors. The cover was a drawing of Benjamin Franklin's head, printed in black over a purple background, with the words, "Well done is better than well said," overprinted in orange.

Page two was printed in a mustard yellow with a fine black border and the words, "We took the words right out of Ben's mouth," overprinted in black. Page three was an orange background with "Because We Still Believe in Them" reversed so the white showed through. This was a beautiful hand-lettered script page. They used a magenta background for page four. The words, "A good example is the best sermon," were printed in blue. Some more hand lettering stated, "You Can Say That Again." Page five showed the 1969 and 1970 First Award-Campaign Benjamin Franklin statuettes. They were printed in four colors on a light tinted olive-gray background.

Pages six and seven used a black background to display a gold seal with the words, "A good example is the best sermon." Dropping below the gold seal was a wide red ribbon on which were listed the many awards, ending with a predictable prediction, "Good printing does more than win awards. It wins good customers. And you can win 'em all." The Case-Hoyt signature, address and phone number followed. Page eight was blank.

Color Folder

Another fun piece was entitled, "case-hoyt color." It was printed on a sheet 8" x 51", scored and folded page over page to an 8" x 6½" 15-page folder. It was printed in three process colors and a black. Page one just had the words "case-hoyt color" in lower case with an attractive design on a black background. Then as the folder was unfolded, each left-hand page had a suitable process halftone to illustrate the words on the right-hand page. As the pages opened they stated, "it's go—mango," "it's original," "it looks good enough to eat," "it's doing your own thing right," "it makes trees beautiful again," "it's the real thing." On the last inside page was this copy. Please note how readable it is. This is copy with a smile.

"You spend good money to create a unique corporate identity.

"Special logo, special typeface, special color. You shoot the works.

"Then you give everything to a printer (the low bidder?) and tell him to produce exact copies of the original.

"And you cross your fingers.

"This is where we come into the picture.

"We can make copies—thousands or millions—look like the original.

"Because we have something no other printer has.

"Case-Hoyt Color is as unique as your own corporate face and complexion.

"Compare our work with any other printer and see for yourself. Web or sheet fed.

"Last year, more than 50 major corporations put their annual reports in our hands.

"And hundreds more gave us brochures, booklets, broadsides, catalogs, inserts, campaigns, the works. All because we could give them what they wanted: Color that's right on.

"And the Printing Industries of America gave us 24 awards for excellence in 1971. That made us No. 1.

"Case-Hoyt Color. If you buy printing, it can make you look good."

Case-Hoyt advertising is quality stuff. They do a great job. They tell us it works for them.

Catalog HQ, Inc.

Shocker

"Your best salesman is a BUM! . . . compared to a simple easy-to-read CATALOG!" What would you think if you opened an envelope and read that headline on a small 3¾" x 8⅞" folder? I'm sure it would shock you a bit. Of course, that is what Harry King, president of Catalog HQ, Inc., New York, wanted to do. The folder is printed on a heavy weight white stock in four colors with glossy inks. Every page except the reply card page has a solid black background.

This is not a pretty piece. The illustration on each page except the reply card page consists of a scratch pen and ink characterization of a bum. He sits on a green bench in a bright blue suit with yellow patches and a bright red shirt with a chocolate brown hat and shoes. There are many panels and blocks of copy with red, blue and yellow backgrounds.

The first page, which is 3¾" x 7¼", is short, so a large red arrow points to the reply card that is perforated and on the last page of the three pages. (The 3¾" x 23⅜" sheet is scored and folded twice.) The bum smoking a cigar is on page one. His mouth is wide open and the headline is at the right. The first line is printed in yellow with the word "Bum!" in red. The second line is in blue. The third line, which reads " . . . and CATALOGS are our business . . . OUR ONLY BUSINESS!" is printed in red, the capital letters in yellow. I'm going into this detail because I want to impress you with the fact that this is not a pleasing piece. It is purposely designed to get attention.

The company has used this folder for five years and Mr. King says he wouldn't change it for the world. We understand that Catalog HQ, Inc., was sued by Greater New York Salesmen's Association for using the headline phrase. The judge threw the case out of court. On the top of page two there is this note: "Our apologies for the use of the word 'Bum.' It was selected to illustrate our point with impact. There is no intent to offend salesmen for whom we have the highest regard and respect."

The copy on pages two and three is concise and hard selling. You quickly find that Catalog HQ, Inc. produces, under one roof, catalogs, self-mailers, brochures, stuffers and price lists. They give you a complete cost breakdown before they start and there's no extra cost. Their prices are surprisingly competitive for a finished catalog because of their "Systemated" organization. They will handle your complete catalog from start to finish or even take over in the middle.

Probably the most convincing copy is in a yellow panel on the reverse side of the folder. It reads, "When you inquire about a catalog, we don't send a 'Bum,' we send you the president of the company.

"That's right! The President, because the last thing you need is a 'BUM'S' counsel to help you decide the kind of catalog you need. It's too big an investment.

"Our President will answer any questions you may have. He'll discuss format, design, photography as against illustrations, kind of paper, quantity, type, price . . . anything . . . right then and there.

"And he'll answer you 'straight.' No pressure, no selling. Call or drop us a line . . . let's discuss it!"

"Results have been so powerful (would you believe 20 leads out of a thousand?) that I don't go out anymore unless it sounds like a big deal," says Mr. King. They employ 20 people. Twelve are paste-up specialists. Gross sales volume is a bit less than one million dollars. Very few jobs are under $5,000. Their customers are in the one- to five-million dollar sales volume range.

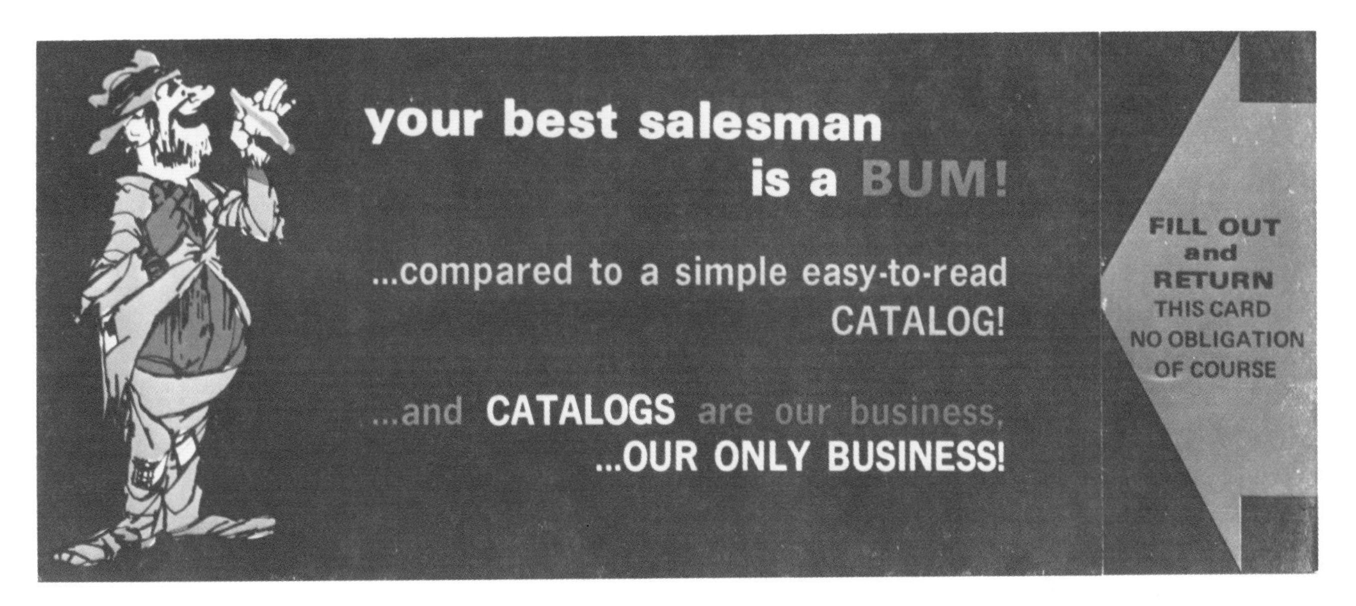

Collins, Miller & Hutchings

Magazine Ads

Collins, Miller & Hutchings, Chicago, Illinois, are not printers but photo-engravers for letterpress, gravure and offset. They have approximately 250 employees and their annual sales volume is around $7 million. Over the years, they have consistently advertised in trade papers directed to the advertising industry. Their four-color process ads, as well as black and white, have been eye-catching and quite often provocative. Each ad was in itself a complete selling message aimed at specific production problems.

They have won many awards for their advertising and, because of the volume of awards displayed in the reception area and in the main office, visitors and customers are continually reminded of their capabilities for getting results. The ads and the awards have established their reputation for quality. Collins, Miller & Hutchings have always been believers in self-advertising as an effective medium for selling and re-selling customers, both old and new.

One series of ads that were interesting and won a P.I.A. award, and also drew letters of praise and commendation, along with at least five new customers, consisted of four large photographs which took up almost the entire page. One photograph (all were in full color) of a queen of diamonds playing card, was not tied into the copy. The queen had a china face and hand. The headdress and clothes were cleverly made of a patchwork of silks and satins bound together with braids, ribbons, jeweled binding and rickrack. The copy referred to things that made their company different from other engravers.

Another photograph showed the corner of a sculptor's studio with chips of stone all around. There is a large mass of stone on a pedestal that has been roughly cut away. From the back and top of this stone a classic, muscular, nude man, seeming to emerge from the piece of sculpture, is found using a chisel and mallet. The model and stone mass is so arranged that it looks as though the human is chipping away the stone from his own body. It is an eye-catching photograph taken by Victor Skrebneski. Copy relates to art for art's sake. Here are two photographs:

"We go about making a photoengraving or a positive the way you go about making an ad.

"Slowly, carefully refining every detail. Chipping away at the rough edges until things start coming to life."

The third ad in this series is a photograph by Alan Brooks, showing a heavy horse-race jockey on a scale indicating a weight of 210 pounds. An elderly tout in a tweed jacket, binoculars and pad and pencil, is gravely writing down the weight. The copy headline reads, "Sometimes you don't want more for your money."

The fourth ad is another eye catching photograph and the copy is exceptionally good. The photograph by Richard Noble shows the interior of a barber shop with a pensive nude sitting in the chair. A barber stands by. The nude girl is amply covered by long golden blonde tresses that almost fall to the floor. Here is the headline and copy: "Short Cuts Can Be Embarrassing.

"Many times we've been asked, can you take off a little here, can you save a little there.

"Well, we can. But we don't. Short cuts are not our style.

"We make photoengravings and film positives only one way. Step by step. Dot by dot.

"Actually, we've been doing it this way so long that we save you money just by doing it right.

"Which is better. Because if you make just one wrong cut, it shows."

That ad just had to get attention and the copy fits perfectly.

You may wonder why we have included this photoengraver's advertising in a book primarily written for printers. We believe this type of advertising can be used by printers and directed to advertisers. The copy, the illustrations could quickly be adapted for a printer's use.

Colonist Printers Limited

Birthdays

A birthday presents an excellent excuse to advertise. There are many ways to celebrate a birthday or anniversary. It isn't necessary to have a high-level creative session about the subject because almost any celebration is acceptable. The main point is to make a special occasion of the day and advertise your company. There is probably nothing that someone hasn't done about a birthday or anniversary. So, don't worry about copying someone else's idea.

Colonist Printers Limited, Victoria, B.C., Canada, had an excellent idea for its 115th birthday anniversary presentation. It mailed a package of Dore *mélange à gâteau* which was named "Celebration." In case you don't know any more French than we do, that means a gold cake mix. In Canada, you can purchase cake mixes in 5¼" x 7½" moisture proof paper envelopes or bags. The *mode d'emploi,* or directions for mixing, were written in French as well as English. The mailing box was only ¾" deep. It was 6" x 8" printed in red and black on a white background, well covered with the company name and trademark, duplicated many times.

Besides the cake mix, which, incidentally, made an excellent cake, was a white card printed in blue ink and headed "Happy Birthday, Colonist Printers Limited." The words and music of the familiar birthday song followed.

There was also a tan folder printed in brown ink. The first page read, "Thanks for the Birthday present . . ." Then on the inside pages was this message:

"On this happy occasion of our 115th anniversary, we would like to express our thanks by inviting you to join us, in the comfort of your own home, for a piece of birthday cake.

"In fact, such continued loyalty and goodwill as yours deserves the whole cake. That is what you will find in the enclosed package. It is a Robin Hood cake mix.

"So have yourself a party with us. May your birthdays be as many, your friends as true, and your customers as loyal as ours.

"You have helped Colonist Printers Limited to grow with British Columbia from a territory to a province; survive under six monarchs; volunteer for four wars and participate in Victoria's 25th, 50th, 75th and 100th anniversaries and become one of western Canada's leading printing and lithographing plants. We thank you for this very fine 115th birthday present.

"The Staff and Management of Colonist Printers Limited.

"P.S.: While you are eating your cake we will be taking the wrapping off the biggest present of our life—$235,000 worth of new location and equipment, soon to be located at 2840 Nanaimo St., Victoria, B.C. You have an invitation to be the first in line at our official opening."

The mailing was sent to Colonist's extensive mailing list of customers and to a number of old established businesses that had grown up with it.

In the usual reserve and restraint of Canadians, T.A. Barber, the general manager of Colonist, said, "The promotion was received most favorably and earned plaudits by newspaper, television and personal phone calls." Translated into Americanese, that means it was a good mailing. Any time that you can get newspapers and television to even mention a direct mail advertising piece, you have hit the top rung.

Colonist Printers Limited is a division of Ronalds-Federated Limited, having joined that organization in 1972. The total number of employees from coast to coast is approximately 2,500.

As Barber said, "We feel strongly in favor of the sales promotion approach rather than waiting for customers to tell us what their requirements are." However, like so many printers in the United States, it has no scheduled basis for its advertising. We have seen six or seven pieces.

Two Christmas cards were attractively done on magenta cover stock, heavily embossed, and a large amount of foil printing was used. The designs were modern and very attractive. One card had an unusual fold

and all the type and illustration were gold embossed. The other card was printed in black, orange and gold foil. A small folder was enclosed to explain how the card could be folded and hung on the Christmas tree.

For its advertising folders, its art director came up with some cartoon characters. One looks something like Superman. There are also two dogs. The three are called Colin and His Sprinters. If you repeat the name Colonist Printers rapidly, you will discover how they arrived at this play on words. There is also a masked man called Deadly Dull.

The copy is warm and friendly. We believe that if you can sell your product you can write good advertising copy, provided, of course, that you don't go high hat and try to write in a style and with words that you wouldn't be caught using during a sales presentation. Be natural. Read some of these paragraphs from several different Colonist folders:

"This printing business is a volatile, dynamic, ever-changing industry. The journey from the Gutenberg Bible to today's modern multi-color, multi-million impression press was not made in one giant step—rather through a steadily moving parade of progress . . . an ever-changing answer to the question, 'What's new?'

"We at Colonist Printers Limited have learned that what people want most is an honest, enthusiastic sales approach, and service to match. Nothing

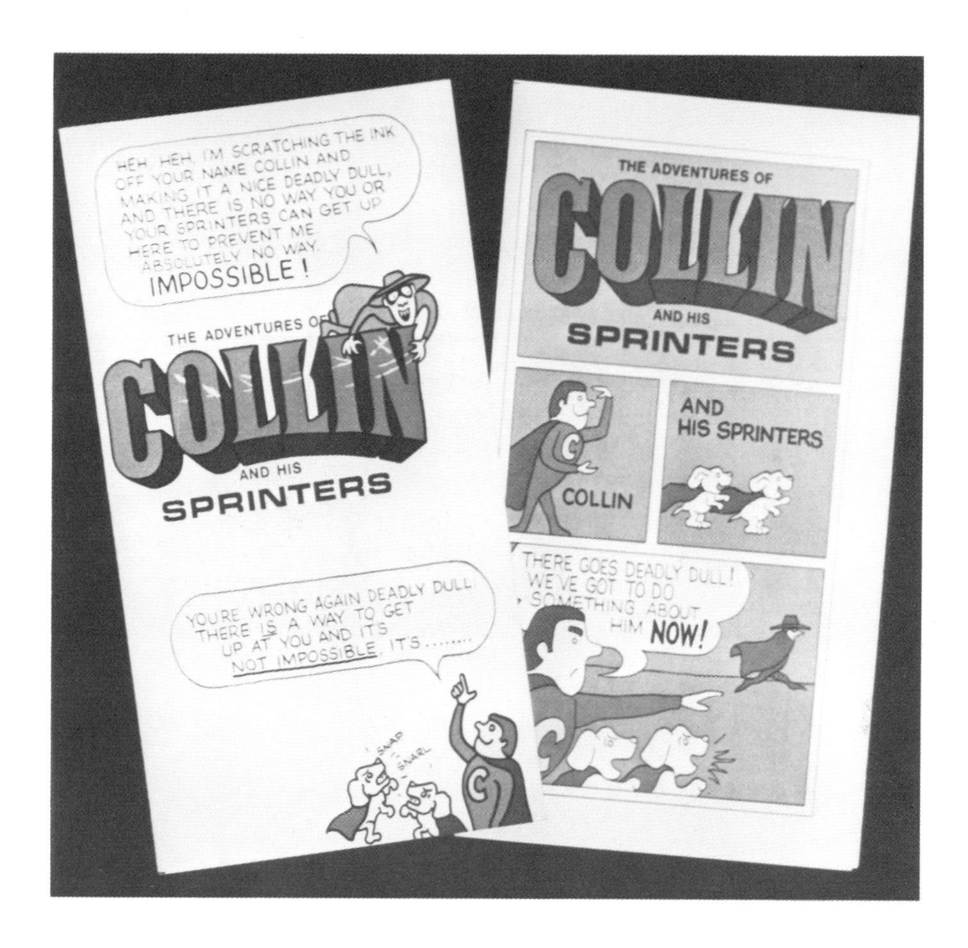

fancy, just truthful enthusiasm for all facets of the job at hand. We love to get orders and we do our best to let it show. We sell service. And we serve.

"Creativity is the prime ingredient of our attitude and approach to customers. We supply paper dummies, even if not asked, provide layouts above and beyond what is requested, and redesign jobs to improve them if the client is receptive to such assistance. We like to start from scratch and create new pieces for our business friends, and ourselves."

"What is new in the printing business? To the beginning printing buyer, just about everything. To the veteran pro it is tomorrow's development. Most important, perhaps, is that any item or process that you have not previously heard about is new and interesting to you.

"Perhaps the most interesting of 'What's new' is the process of embossing, or printing without ink: simple, inexpensive but having a very prestigious look and feel. For information, phone 383-4111. Since our salesman can't knock on the customer's door every day, these mailers serve to keep Colonist Printers Limited and our product in front of you. Why not phone us about Colin and His Printers so that we may do your 'embossable' jobs.

There was an interesting and colorful jigsaw puzzle used. It was 8" x 9" and printed in four-color process. Colin and His Sprinters were featured. Like everyone, we are sure, who received the puzzle, we put it together and were confused by one piece that didn't seem to fit. We didn't read the message balloon on the piece that partly showed the Deadly Dull character until we finally put the puzzle together. The main copy balloon stated, "Call Colin for puzzle-poppin' ideas and printing." One of the Sprinters was asking, "Where is Deadly Dull?" Another Sprinter said, "Deadly Dull just doesn't fit into this scene . . . too much color for him, you know." The piece that didn't fit anywhere had a copy balloon on it that read, "As Deadly Dull, I just don't fit in with this colorful crowd, curses." That was an interesting twist and it really worked.

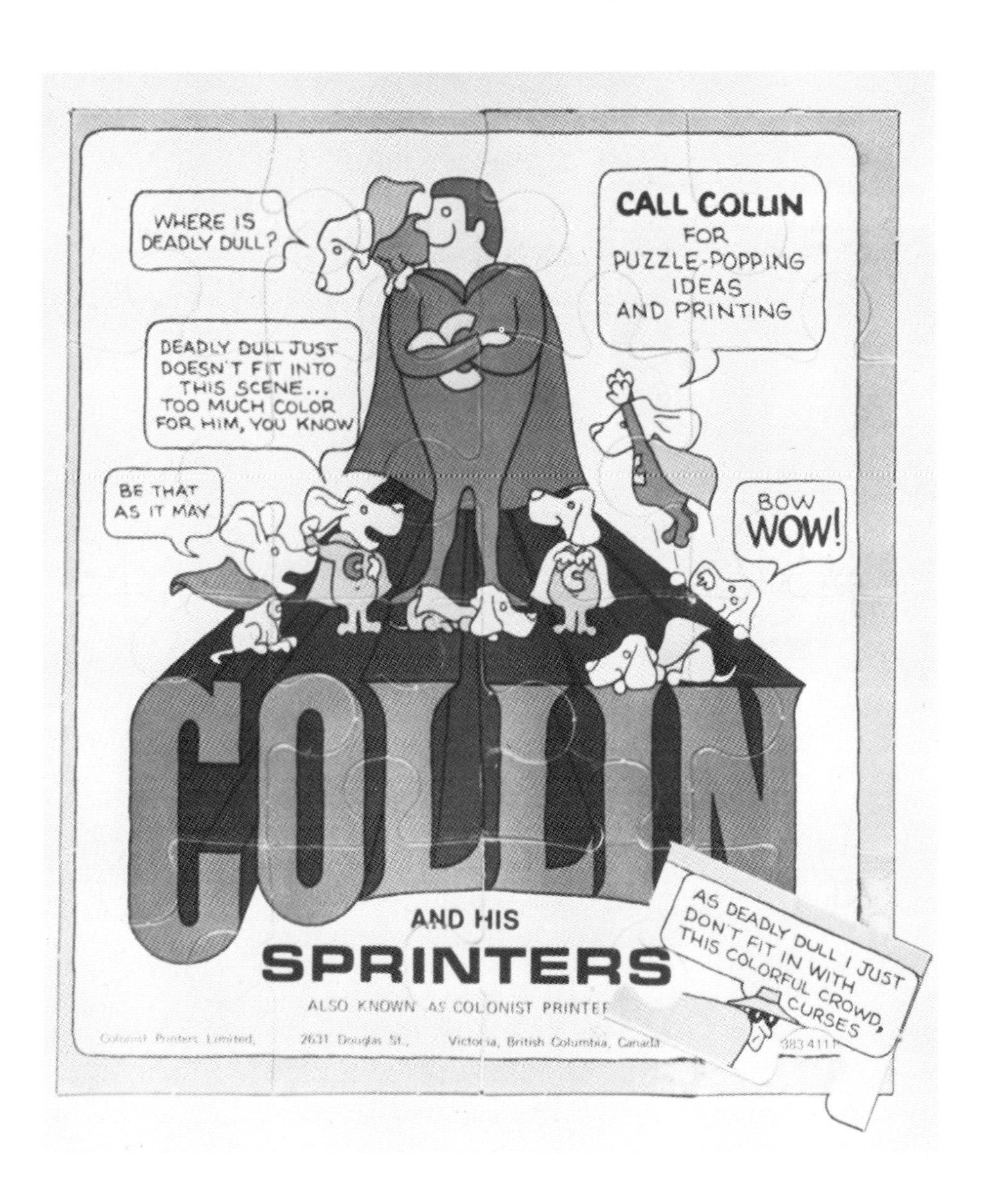

Colonist Printers also used scratch pads with outlines of two faces printed in blue on the pad. There are no eyes, nose or mouth. Below the outlines are two lines of type: One, "Be An Artist." The other is the company's name.

Colonist used a 9⅝" x 19¼" heavy white board stock to make a die-cut easel for its calendar. The monthly pad is 4¾" x 8" and has been attached by staples. Below the pad is the usual name, address and phone number. On the reverse side of the easel is a four-color process print of a Japanese Garden in Victoria. It is a good printing job on that dull-coated board.

There is one other thing that we should mention. Colonist uses a nice, blind-embossed trademark on its letterhead, with the company name printed with red foil. The laid stock is tinted a light green and has a crackle to it. In other words, the company uses a first-class letterhead that reflects the quality of the company.

Few printers use modern, good quality letterheads. It would seem that, being in the printing business, they would use nothing but the best. "Don't do as I do. Do as I say." That is the motto in the printing industry when it comes to advertising, promotion and public relations.

Columbus Bank Note

A Salesman's Direct Mail Program

Here is a description of a well planned campaign that would be approved by any printing salesman. This gives the salesman the type of help he wants. He is the boss of this direct mail effort.

It was planned, conceived and printed by Columbus Bank Note, Dublin, Ohio. Robert G. Kelley, president, tells us, "It took some time to get it into production and run; however, it has been a tremendous success." It has improved their image, kept their name before prospects and helped to get them about a million dollars' worth of other printing.

Columbus Bank Note was founded in 1890. It has 150 employees and does about $4.5 million in sales.

This campaign won them a gold Benny in the P.I.A. contest. Of more importance, they attribute 12 new accounts to this campaign and expect to open many more. They will use the campaign for two years.

First, let us tell you about one of the main features. Salesmen are given forms called "Start Order." The salesmen fill out these forms requesting a direct mail program. There is a place for name, title, company name and address. Then they circle a code letter for the pieces they want sent. There are eight subjects. The salesmen indicate when they want them mailed—twice a week, once a week, once every two weeks, once a month or some special period of time. They also order the starting date and the ending date. Return cards, two types, may be enclosed or left out. It is whatever the salesman wants to do. Also, an equipment list may be enclosed or left out. And business cards can be attached to each mailing if the salesman supplies them. This form is then given to a young lady in the sales promotion department and they take it from there. The salesmen's requests are returned to them so that they can initiate a prompt and appropriate follow-through.

There's a five-page, 8½" x 10½", four-color process folder telling about the plant. It is printed on a heavy cast coated sheet. The first page shows the Columbus Bank Note sign with a background of green trees. The headline reads, "You Can't See The Plant For The Trees." On page five, which is folded in, there is a fish eye lens photograph of the plant. On page two, a beautiful exterior photograph of the offices taken about sundown. In the foreground is a large lake with the reflection of the lighted offices showing in the pool. There are trees all around.

The copy on page five reads, "When you come across a clearing in a forest, you don't expect to find somebody's ultra-modern printing plant. Somehow, there seems to be something mutually exclusive about the velvet glove of Mother Nature and the sweaty hand of man. You don't often find them clasped in friendship."

The balance of the copy is very well written. It mentions the lake and the ducks and geese but it isn't just for the birds. It is a reservoir for the sprinkler system and saves them $30,000 a year in annual fire insurance premiums. They ask the reader to "Visit us soon. Look for the forestewith the sign out front." The copy ends with, "There's a lot more to Bank Note than meets the eye, even if what meets the eye is beautiful."

On pages three and four are 12 halftones of scenes around the grounds and in the plant. Even one in the moonlight. The envelope for this piece is printed with the word "Trees" in 6-pica high type. There is also the Company trademark printed in two colors and the trademark shows the company name. The address and phone numbers are below.

All the folders are the same size and printed on cast coated heavy stock. The second folder is a piece of cross-stitched embroidery headed, "We Never Tell An Off-Color Story." The Bank Note building and ducks are stylized at the top and bottom. Inside this four-pager is plenty of white space with six paragraphs of copy set in 14-point type. The copy refers to critical color match. The trademark and address appear on page three. Page four is blank. The one word on the envelope is "Story," done in cross stitch. The envelope is printed in three colors.

Another folder is about its sales promotion section. The envelope word is "Worms." The cover is used for this copy with a large line cartoon of a man's head and shoulders, "Did you hear them say they were looking for someone to stick with the next special sales promotion can-of-worms?" The copy continues with a cartoon of the same man and a can overflowing with worms. It reads, " . . . and you turned out to be the stuckee?"

Page three states that Bank Note can help get it all sorted out. There are four paragraphs set in 14-point type telling about the new sales promotion section and how they can handle a program. It ends with, "We like being the stuckee."

"We Touch All The Bases" is the subject of another four-page folder. The copy explains that they can handle copy, art, photography, assembly, manufacturing and finish. They can deliver the final product or seal it, address it and put it in the mail. "Bases" is the only word on the envelope beside the corner card, name, address and trademark.

Another four-page folder is headed, "How Do You Turn On A Bank?" Inside copy explains, "Only by offering knowledgable services for a bank's unique needs. We've been doing it for decades." Then the copy goes on to explain the company's many services. Every folder uses the trademark with address and phone number. The envelope uses the words, "Turn On."

The illustrations on another folder are a stylized orange, apple and lemon printed in process color. The copy to the left of each piece of fruit reads, "We may be bidding on oranges. And they may be bidding on apples . . . and you may get a lemon. The inside copy with a lot of good white space refers to the intangibles of printing. The headline is, "There are lots of specs that you just can't put in a quote. Reliability and fine craftsmanship, for instance." One block of copy covers things that you can't really write into a specification, things like, "Experienced craftsmen imbued with a sense of responsibility to the job, availability of diverse special equipment and the imagination to use it effectively, the ability to set up special procedure intelligently, meticulous attention to follow-through, professional sales representatives with the authority to make critical promises . . . and the integrity to keep them." The word "Apples" appears on the envelope.

"Do You Enjoy Shooting Down A Comp Layout?" is the heading for another folder. The copy explains that Bank Note works with the customer knowledgeably and in stages. They ask for the customer's approval at every step, beginning with the original rough concept. In most cases, they believe their way of working eliminates the need for a costly comp. The envelope, printed in three colors, shows the word "Ouch" in six-pica high type.

Another piece which is a sheet, 8½" x 51¾", accordion folded four times, is printed in three process colors and black. The illustration is a rocket and covers four of the folded pages. The headline on page one is, "So What's Wrong With Being Big?" On the fifth page the copy continues, "When you're going to the moon . . . big helps. When you're trying to get a complicated, color-critical print program off the ground . . . let Bank Note help. We're one of the biggies . . . in 10 different ways." Then there are eleven paragraphs set in 14-point type and starting with 10. Big, ultra-modern plant. 9. Big presses. 8. Lots of little presses. 7. Complete Prep Facilities. 6. Peripheral Facilities. 5. Shipping. 4. Mailing Service. 3. IBM Computer Center. 2. Diverse Staff. 1. Little things and 0. Zero Defects. When we launch a printing program, it flies perfectly. Or we don't let it off the pad. The envelope in which this folder is contained has the word "Biggie" printed in 11½ pica high type.

This is an outstanding campaign. Everything is in good taste, copy is excellent, art is interesting and craftsmanship is demonstrated. Every printing salesman should have advertising of this nature to back him up. Our hats are off to Columbus Bank Note.

Cone-Heiden

Capabilities Book

Cone-Heiden, Seattle, Washington, has an interesting capabilities book. It is 8½" x 9", saddle stitched on the 9" side. There are 32 pages, plus fly leaves and cover. The cover and many pages inside are printed in four-color process. The front cover design is a Chinese puzzle called a Tangram. It is composed of five triangles, a square and a rhomboid, each printed in a different color on Kromecote stock. The company name appears in 14-point type at the bottom left of the page. The back cover is embossed with fine lines outlining the Tangram. No printing is used.

There are seven sections to the book: planning, printing, mailing, bindery, personalized letters, mailing lists and special mail services. Each section is preceded by an introductory page using the Tangram design. The first section starts with one triangle; the second section shows that another triangle has been added. This is continued until all seven parts have been put together.

The copy is well written, short and to the point. The photographs of people working in the various departments are interesting. Through layout, design and printing, the reader could acquire a feeling that here is a company that can produce quality work.

Cone-Heiden used the book for over two years in mailings and personal contacts. It won awards and they felt it was an important part of their advertising program.

Crafton Graphic Company

Awards

Crafton Graphic Company, Inc., New York, knows how to make use of the awards they receive. In 1973, they had 14 winners in the Communication Graphics competition sponsored by the American Institute of Graphic Arts. That year, Grafton won more AIGA awards than any other printer in the country. They told their customers and prospects about these awards in a 12-page booklet that measured 3⅞" x 9¼". The booklet was black and white with two halftone illustrations of each prize winning piece per page. They listed the client's name, title of the piece, the designer, art director and artist's name.

The copy was short. Here are the first two paragraphs:

"Three things bring us gratification in this business.

"One, is doing a damn good job. Two, is earning the respect and loyalty of clients. Three, is being able to win the toughest awards."

Crafton has always believed in self-advertising. From the time they went into business in 1934, they tried to stress quality and promoted the fact that they won more awards than most printers.

Craftsman & Met Press

25 Years of Calendars

There are two schools of thought in regard to calendars as well as many others for customers. Now some printers have discontinued their own because they say people accept them but don't hang them. The calendars don't blend in with every fancy office decor. Printers who still use calendars believe they are a great form of advertising and they see their calendars hung everywhere. So, we guess what is really needed is a good survey to determine how many companies or, rather, prospective printing customers permit calendars with advertising messages to be hung on their walls.

There are also two schools of thought in regard to the size of the actual calendar—the months of the year. There are those who seem to design posters or, at least, use large illustrations and just incidentally include the months of the year. Then there are those who think a calendar should be utilitarian and use a calendar that can be easily read and, perhaps, use an attractive illustration. We personally vote for the easily read, no typographic gimmicks calendar, with a small but pleasing illustration. Most of us have been reading calendars for years, with the days reading from left to right, Sunday through Saturday. The weeks have been listed in four or five horizontal lines. Most of us are lazy readers and are happy with a conventional calendar. When the days are set in circles or five days in a row instead of seven, or any other typographical gimmickry, we have difficulty and quickly give up.

With that preamble, let us describe some of the calendars that some printers have found successful. In other words, advertising that works.

A calendar of long standing is the one produced by Craftsman & Met Press, Seattle, Washington. This will be the 25th year in which they have presented the paintings of Northwest artists through the medium of the calendar.

The calendar measures 16½" x 23" and consists of four pages and a top overlay sheet. The 1975 top sheet is largely taken up with a head and shoulder photograph of one of their smiling receptionists. The words, "Happy anniversary to you!" are at the top of this sheet and right below is this striking photograph of Linda Cerezo on a tan background. They have used the same background ink to print a duotone of Linda.

Copy below the 13" x 16½" panel reads, "This is Linda Cerezo, who is one of our receptionists. She's intelligent, attractive and 23 years old. Twenty-five years ago, before Linda's generation was born, we published our first Craftsman calendar which featured paintings of this region by well known Northwest artists. Because of its continued popularity we've maintained the calendar program ever since.

"So, after a happy quarter of a century, we're having a 'Calendar Anniversary' party. To celebrate we're offering to send you, without charge, a set of the four paintings reproduced on this calendar. These fine color reproductions are printed on heavy stock with wide margins suitable for framing.

APRIL

sun	mon	tue	wed	thu	fri	sat
		1	2	3	4	5
6	7	8	9	10	11	12
13	14	15	16	17	18	19
20	21	22	23	24	25	26
27	28	29	30			

MAY

sun	mon	tue	wed	thu	fri	sat
				1	2	3
4	5	6	7	8	9	10
11	12	13	14	15	16	17
18	19	20	21	22	23	24
25	26	27	28	29	30	31

JUNE

sun	mon	tue	wed	thu	fri	sat
1	2	3	4	5	6	7
8	9	10	11	12	13	14
15	16	17	18	19	20	21
22	23	24	25	26	27	28
29	30					

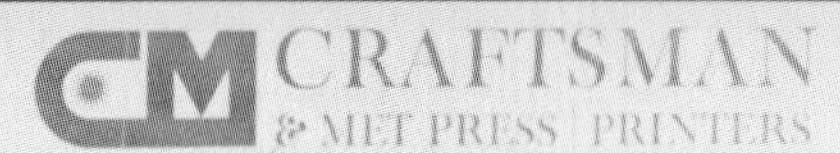

Fairview Avenue North at Valley St., Seattle, Washington 98109 (206) 682-8800 / in Portland (503) 222-2980 / in San Francisco (415) 495-0244 ■ One source for all your printing needs

"Just send a request on your company letterhead to Linda's attention and she'll be glad to mail you a set while the supply lasts (no phone calls, please). There is one stipulation: we cannot honor requests for more than one set of reproductions from any individual. Happy Calendar Anniversary!"

On the reverse side of the top sheet is some interesting copy about the many printing services of Craftsman & Met Press. On the reverse side of each calendar sheet is copy describing the artist and the artist's photograph.

Four artists have their work reproduced on the four calendar sheets. The reproductions measure 12" x 15½". The three-month calendar on each sheet measures 6¾" x 16½". Each sheet has a different color background for the calendar. The calendar is quite legible. The Craftsman & Met Press signature, addresses and phone numbers occupy a bottom two-inch high panel.

The calendar is very attractive and Vice President M.R. Bailey says, "Over the years our calendars have received many P.I.A., advertising and other art awards. They have done much to help us build a reputation as a fine color house and have been a great ice breaker for our salesmen."

The 1974 Craftsman & Met Press calendar was similar to the 1975 calendar in make-up. The top sheet was quite different. It looked like a torn tan window blind. The tear was die cut and the drawing was well done, so it looked as if the blind cloth had curled up on itself. Through the hole in the blind you could see a young boy in his birthday suit. It was part of the reproduction of a painting on the first sheet of a boy about to cross a slippery creek bed. The top sheet caught your eye and the die cut was very effective.

There was no sales story on the 1974 calendar. In our opinion the 1975 calendar was better because it sold Craftsman services.

Pocket Appointment Calendars

Craftsman & Met Press also uses pocket appointment calendars for advertising. These are 7" x 9⅜" sheets of a heavy white enamel stock folded twice to 3-3/16" x 7" to fit in the inside jacket pocket. The outside pages are used for notes and a description of the company's services: "One source for all your printing needs." The cover shows the month, year and a fine reproduction of the paintings used in the calendar. There is also the title of the painting and the artist's name on the cover.

The inside pages are ruled off in 1¼" x 1½" blocks with small numerals in each block to indicate the date. The preceding and succeeding months are shown in one of the blocks. Many business men find these appointment calendars very helpful. If they are used religiously, appointments are one less detail that have to be remembered.

Some companies mail their complete sets of appointment calendars for the year at one time. Craftsman & Met mails six months at a time. Other companies send one out each month with a sales message.

Calendar Promotion

We must tell you of the great promotional program Craftsman & Met Press used to promote their calendars back in the 1950s. The idea was abandoned a few years ago because of the illness of Vice President Merv Bailey, who was the prime mover. We will admit that the program took substantial time, effort and money. But anything that is worth doing is worth doing right and this program was done right.

The company purchased, as they do today, four paintings for its calendar. They obtained the paintings from a company-sponsored art show that was held at a Seattle museum. Announcements of the coming show were sent to artists in the Northwest in January for the show in October. Reminders were also sent to all the artists. News releases were sent to all media and a great amount of public interest was aroused through publicity.

They obtained over 400 entries. There had to be judging for hanging in the exhibit as well as for finding four paintings for the calendar. Because of the publicity, the artists felt it was an unusual chance to show their work. The publicity also made the calendar of great value. Craftsman & Met Press customers were invited to a prevue and this was one of the social events of the year. The company was advancing the arts and they received full credit from many sources. It was truly a public relations and advertising scoop. It was a top rung promotion that could be adapted for other companies' calendars.

Capabilities Booklet

The Craftsman & Met Press capabilities booklet won a P.I.A. award. It is an excellent 32-page, 8½" x 11" book, saddle stitched on the 8½" side. The full color photographs taken by Merv Bailey and Bart Attebery are excellent and were reproduced from 35mm color slides. Many of the slides have been enlarged 1,000%, but are still sharp and without grain.

The C & M Seattle plant is not small. It occupies a city block and the floor space is three acres. Its mechanical payroll numbers more than 200, who work two and three shifts. They feature "one source printing service" and have sales offices in Portland and San Francisco.

The cover of the booklet is quite attractive. It is a bleed page showing a whirling vat of red ink being mixed with some black. The photograph was, no doubt, taken in C & M's own ink department. In the top left hand corner of the cover, in 14-pt. type, are the words, "Welcome to our World." In the bottom right hand corner is a 1½" high trademark reversed so it appears in white.

Each left-hand page of the booklet contains a large bleed photograph of some aspect of the business. The right-hand page contains copy describing the department, and anywhere from one to seven photos of craftsmen at work in that department.

The type work is beautiful, the photos are excellent and they tell the story. The reproductions are clear, with skin tones and colors quite natural. It is an excellent booklet and fully describes the services as well as demonstrates the craftsmanship of Craftsman & Met Press.

Craftsmen Photo Lithographers

Christmas Cards

Craftsmen Photo Lithographers, East Hanover, N.J., produces some very successful Christmas cards that they use each year. It is their way of reminding their customers and prospects that they are still in business. Jerry Schuster, head of the art department, designs these pieces of paper sculpture.

The card is contained in a 7½" x 10½" mailing envelope. Also enclosed is a concise but detailed sheet giving instructions for putting the card together. There are four to six pieces, die cut and scored, to make the Santa, choir boy or some other Christmas character. The face is printed in two or three colors on one of the sheets. The Christmas greeting, as well as the Craftsmen name and trademark, is always shown in some spot on the completed card.

This is a novel idea and Craftsmen receives many compliments about its cards. There is no attempt to sell printing. This is a reminder that Craftsmen Photo Lithographers are still in business. They distribute about 1,000 cards.

Davis-Delaney-Arrow, Inc.

Awards

Many printers produce prize-winning products. They take the time and effort to prepare the entry blanks and samples, and they pay the fees in the various competitions. They win the awards and then don't cash in on them. It's fine to know that your work is good enough to win awards but it is more important to tell your prospects and customers. It doesn't have to be anything pretentious, even a letter will do the job, but do *something* to inform your public.

Davis-Delaney-Arrow, Inc., New York, are quality printers. Although they could afford an elaborate brochure telling the world about their prize-winning achievements, they use small announcements. One we have in hand is 3¾" x 9", four pages, printed on the reverse side of a bright blue cast coated stock, with no printing on pages one and four. Inside, on page two, is a large blue and green D.D.A. trade mark. On page three, they mention the 56 pieces produced and selected for awards in the Printing Industries of Metropolitan New York's Exhibition of Printing. Then the names are listed of the companies whose work they produced and which won awards. There are very few sales points more convincing than a list of prominent companies for which you do work and win awards. That tells quite a story. And why more printers don't use their awards is difficult to understand.

Wm. A. Didier & Sons, Inc.

Announcing New Equipment

Wm. A. Didier & Sons, Inc., Fort Wayne, Indiana, had an instant press party to announce its new equipment. Didier has a medium-sized operation with 30 employees. They produce offset, letterpress and flexographic printing. Their presses range from 10"x15" through 38" two colors. Didier & Sons purchased a new four-color Webtron 650 flexographic press not long ago. It is capable of producing small die cut ½" labels on roll stock. Die cutting, stripping, laminating or individual sheet labels by the millions are no problem.

They wanted to introduce this new piece of equipment in an avant-garde way. There have been many photos of storks and illustrations of equipment in a diaper and headlines about "our new baby." They thought, and rightfully so, that people were tired of this type of announcement. They wanted to do something a bit more creative.

They called in a specialty advertising counselor, a fancy name for a sales representative of a firm selling advertising specialties. You can find such firms in the yellow pages of your telephone directory under "advertising specialties." These "counselors," in most cases, are top grade salesmen. We don't mean that they pressure you, although they will ask for the order. They are creative people who want to help you with advertising or promotional ideas. They have had experience in the field of specialty advertising, so they can come up with some good suggestions.

Didier executives did some planning. They knew what they wanted, which is half the battle, and here is how they developed their program:

1. They defined their specific advertising goal. Having just purchased the new equipment, they wanted to immediately inform and gain new customers while establishing prospects in their market as possible long-range customers.

2. They wanted to develop advertising with a central theme. The announcement had to be appealing, catchy, yet not too juvenile. If possible, it was to be soft sell, and it had to get action which they hoped their salesmen could turn into results—orders.

3. They identified the intended audience. They wished to inform 200 prospects located within a 50-mile radius of Fort Wayne. They had the list.

William A. Didier, Jr., the president, discussed the advertising goal with the counselor and they came up with an announcement that had a theme. In fact, it answered all their requirements. Their announcement was so unique, so successful, that the salesmen wrote 50 new business orders, seven of them from large users who are now customers on a continuing basis. According to Mr. Didier, one customer has done $50,000 worth of label business with them since the announcement.

They started their program by mailing a personalized letter and invitation to a "press party." Please note, this was not a form letter, but a fully hand typed letter. There was a reply card but no mention of a time or date. Calling the party a "press" party tied in well with the new equipment. Since Didier & Sons have five busy salesmen, they did not want a flood of reply cards to come in and not be able to handle them. That showed they had faith in their program! So, they sent the letters and reply cards to ten prospects at a time, leaving an interval between each batch in order to have time to contact those who wanted to attend their "press party."

When the reply cards were received—the return was 45 percent, which is excellent for any advertising piece unless you are giving away dollar bills—they sent the salesmen out with their kits. The kits contained the ingredients for an instant press party which let the recipient hold his own party without ever leaving the office. The box contained liquor, corn chips, an old-fashioned glass, liquor stirrers and an announcement of the new label printing equipment. There was also a card to mail to Didier, asking a salesman to make a call.

The graphics for the invitations, kits and return cards were light, colorful caricatures. Only Didier's trademark, which is modern in design, was imprinted on the glass and on the stirrers. The Didier name was left off these two items. The inside lids of the kits proclaimed that "Didiers takes the headache out of your label business."

Since the kits contained a bottle of liquor, and since the salesman also wanted to talk to the prospect, it was decided that the best way to deliver a kit was in person. The salesman then explained that with the prospect's first order, he would receive seven additional matching glasses to complete a set of eight. Of course, after the party was over, the glassware remained as a constant reminder to the party-goer that the Didier printing plant was there to serve him.

President Didier reported that the response was very gratifying. We heard from another employee, who wasn't so modest, that they had a ball. At first, the prospects were a little dubious, but word got around that Didiers had a real cute presentation going. Then the cards really came back. The salesmen had no trouble getting in to see prospects. In fact, they were all smiles and waiting for their kits.

The long-distance visits were scheduled by phone ahead of time so the salesman wouldn't have to make two or three 50-mile trips. Everyone understood and cooperated. When it was all over they weren't sure that the Didier employees didn't have more fun than the prospects. There were telephone calls acknowledging the party and every day the salesmen had a new story about how the kits were received and how they obtained an order for labels or, at least, a promise.

If you will go back to Didier's planning, you will see that their plan worked. They wanted to immediately gain new customers and establish other prospects in their market. They wanted to develop advertising with a theme. The announcement was appealing, catchy and not juvenile. It was soft sell. They never really asked for the order in the advertising and it did get results. They sent out the invitations and informed 200 prospects. Forty-five percent took action—a wonderful return.

By coupling ingenuity with long-lasting impact, Didier & Sons discovered that printers' advertising can work. Specialty advertising used with some creativity is an excellent promotional medium for generating excitement and the needed business to help new equipment pay for itself.

Frye & Smith, Ltd.

Calendar Sheets

Frye & Smith, Ltd., San Diego, California, uses a series of monthly calendar sheets that measure 12"x18" to advertise its services. They believe that the sheets help to insure their identity with San Diego designers. They want to be known as the creative and design-oriented San Diego printer. That is a good advertising objective and can be accomplished through Frye & Smith's program.

Joel Crockett, sales manager, created this idea which demonstrates how creative printing can be. The monthly sheets are all quality printing jobs, so they also demonstrate how well the company can print. Artists participating in this program are bound to send referral business to the company. Those who aren't particularly interested in design can also see that the company has some craftsmen in their group. Mr. Crockett states, "This calendar has helped us maintain our established image. That was our prime goal with this campaign and we feel we were most successful. Our sales staff has brought back numerous positive reports from the design community stressing their thoughts on how well we were identifying with and supporting them."

Frye & Smith commissions each of 12 local artists to do a calendar page for one month of the year. There are very few rules. The size is definitely 12"x18". They must use four process colors. It must have the calendar dates and days. The design is subject to approval but they let the designer be as dramatic and startling as he pleases. The artists are paid the going commercial rate for their work.

Since the sheets are used to show the creativity of the designer, the calendar is secondary on some sheets and not always easily read. Each month a new sheet is mailed to the Frye & Smith customers and pótential customers. The designs used are attractive and interesting and, no doubt, the recipients are watching to see what will be done next.

One of the most creative calendar sheets was designed and photographed by Philip Kaplan. He used two-inch square photographs of numbers found almost anywhere. It was for the month of February. There were five squares across for five days of the week, and six rows printed in four colors. It was necessary to look below the photograph for the correct day, which was set in eight-point caps. The photographs were such things as, "First" from a bank sign; a number 2 billiard ball; .03 on a cash register; 4th round on a prize fight board; 5 from a five dollar bill; 6 from a parking lot sign; 7 from a 7-Up bottle, etc. It was very clever but a poor calendar if you wished to quickly identify the date of a certain day.

A January sheet was also very interesting but a poor calendar. January first that year was on a Friday, so there was one straight line of consecutive numbers going across the sheet starting with 1. Above each number was an initial identifying the day as Friday, Saturday, Sunday, etc. Since we are not accustomed to reading calendars in that way, it was confusing. The 100-pound Cameo Dull sheet was printed with a bleed black background. There was a large 8"x12" four-color process reproduction placed at the optical center of the sheet. It was a photograph of a man and girl looking quite pensive at each other, perhaps in disagreement over something. They were resting on the trunks of gnarled and twisted trees.

The copy above the picture, in reverse type, was, "The shortest distance between two points is a straight line." Below the picture, all in reverse, was this copy: "A straight line like, 'I need you.' A straight line like, 'You really hurt me.' A straight line like, 'I haven't been honest with you.' A straight line like, "I love you.' Sometimes these words seem so basic that we take them for granted. But think about the things that you wanted to say that were left unsaid. To a parent who is gone. To a lover who walked away. To a child who ran away. Our hope for this year is to leave as little unsaid as we possibly can. And maybe if the words we say can influence the words we write, then the printed word can begin to shorten the distance between the points." The illustration and copy were excellent. There were two small reproductions, 1"x1⅛", at the bottom of the sheet. One photograph showed the couple smiling and united in an embrace. The other photograph was, we assume, the head of Howard Sanders, who designed and did the photography.

Frye & Smith, Ltd., was organized in 1893. There are 75 employees. Seven are salesmen. Their sales volume is approximately $3,000,000. They have four divisions: an art studio, electronic phototypesetting, a group producing small collateral pieces and the main printing plant.

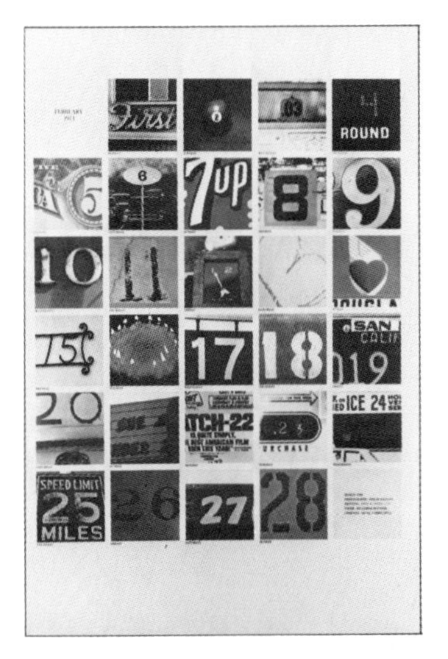

Fiedler Printing Co.

Das Colour Perfectors

Fiedler Printing Co. of St. Louis, recently printed a large 23"x35" piece that could be called a poster, although it had a large amount of copy running half way down the right hand side. The copy was 21 points wide and set in 14-point type.

This poster was unusual because of its large illustration and copy. The photograph, taking up almost the entire sheet, was an enlarged photo of a clenched hand showing the back of the four folded fingers and the front of the thumb sticking up as a sign of approval or good wishes. Every crease, wrinkle and hair on the fingers stands out prominently. The thumbprint can easily be seen. However, over some of the thumbprint is a modern, posterized version of a rainbow including the sun, stars and clouds. This illustration was printed with glossy inks and almost looks as if it is a pasted-on label. The contrast of these colors with the gray of the hand and in the overall background is excellent.

The copy, written by Mary Timmerman, can probably be described as bastardized German. We will copy one paragraph so you will understand our description:

"Once upon eine tyme, in das ancient olde kingdom of Drabsville, there lived ein sad, thin king named Rudolf. Now das reason for all of his rue was that ein monotonous, humdrum hue hung over das kingdom throughout every season. Clouds covered das sky through summer and spring. No rain would dispel das dull grayish cast that hung over trees und turrets, pidgeons und peasants."

The story goes on to explain that the king called on a baker, who had a white thumb, to dispel the dull gray by cooking some of his famous and colorful dishes. But, even the food turned to gray. He tried a gardener, but to no avail. He then saw a rainbow and asked all of his people to try to capture those colors. If one could, he would be given the title of "Das Colour Perfector." One day Printer von Fiedler came and stuck his thumb into the rainbow and when he pulled it out it was "ein process thumb endowed with all of das magical powers of das rainbow." So now, after the Fiedler Printing Co. name, there is a title, "Das Colour Perfectors."

The poster was designed by Zipatoni, Manoli and Thorwegan. It should create a great amount of comment in the St. Louis area.

In most cases, because of their large area, posters surely demonstrate the ink coverage of a printer's press. If they are designed and drawn by an in-house artist, they can also be used to show the staff's artistic abilities. Most recipients will not want to throw a good poster away, so it will have a longevity that less expensive forms of advertising may not have.

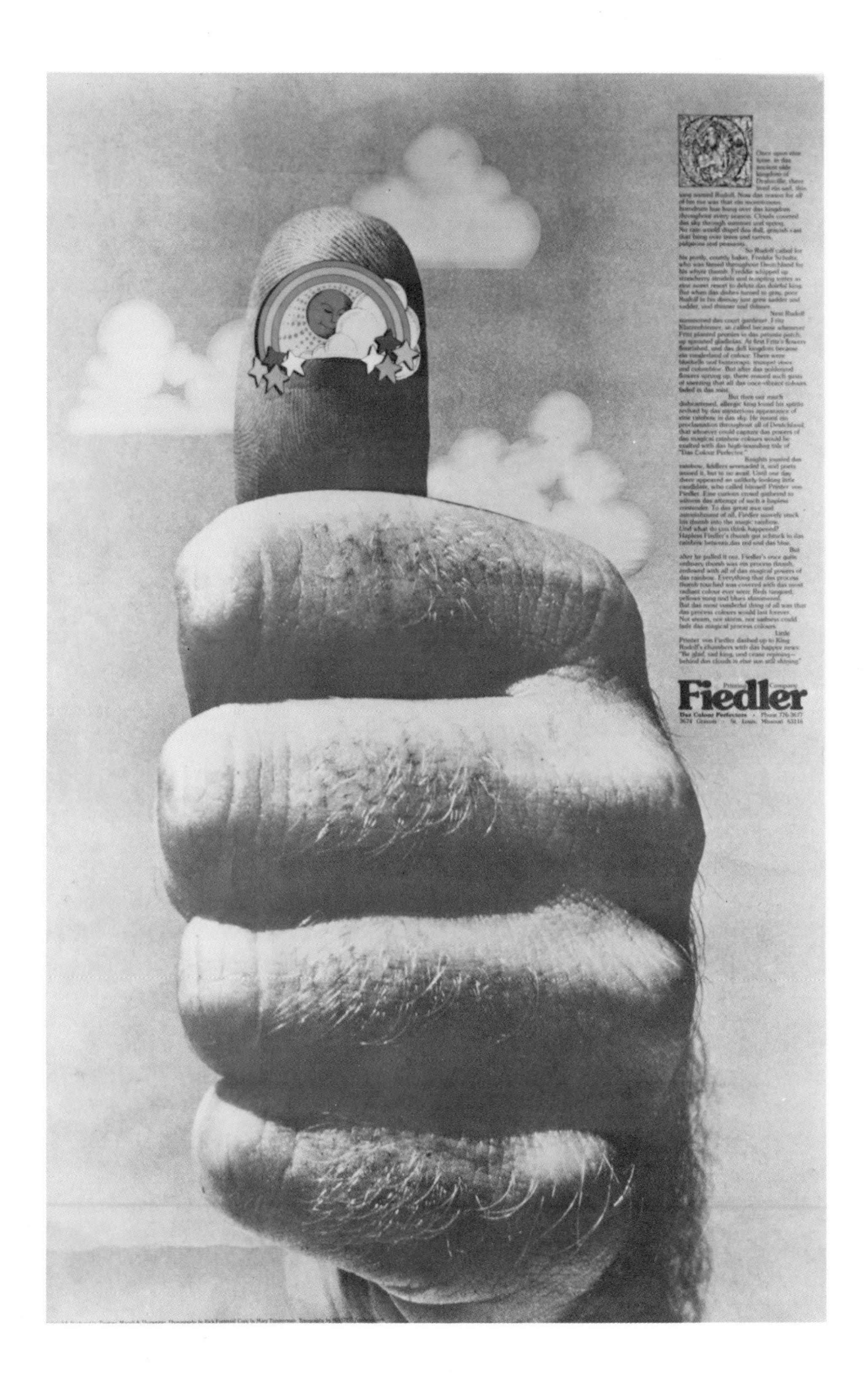
Fiedler

Globe Color Press, Inc.

Concept

Globe Color Press, Inc. Oklahoma City, won a P.I.A. Benny for their advertising campaign, a series of four-page folders headed "Concept." These folders were mailed each month for ten months. A vacation schedule and a Christmas card were also sent during the year. With the help of this campaign, they added 84 new accounts. Mr. Jack White, president, believes that their salesmen have a better reception when they call following a mailing. He believes prospects are more willing to give them an opportunity to make a presentation after they have been on the mailing list for awhile. Globe has been mailing pieces to customers for 15 years. They have 19 employees, three of which are salesmen. They were founded in 1954, and do approximately $700,000 in sales.

Each of the pieces was designed to stand on its own. An outside consultant helped with copy and layout. We will try to describe one or two of the folders: They all measure 8½"x11", and are printed in four colors on a heavy-weight, textured white enamel stock. The fourth page is blank on each folder. There is a reproduction of a color photograph on each cover. Page two is taken with copy, and page three is used for a reproduction of some type of artwork. The word "Concept" is on every cover, as is a line at the bottom in 8-pt. type, "Another In A Series Of Globe's Concept Of Quality."

On the cover of one folder is a beautiful photograph of a stack of pancakes and a pitcher of maple syrup sitting on some old pieces of weathered, worn wood from a wheelbarrow. The colors are perfect, and the butter topped pancakes look delicious.

On page three is a drawing in color of an American Indian in an old felt hat. It has been painted on burlap and the burlap forms a bleed border for the page.

On page two is the copy set in four paragraphs of 12-pt. type. The headline, set in all caps, reads, "Selling Is A Matter Of Moods." Here is the copy. "When you get a man in the mood to buy, your selling job is half done. You've made the sale when you make him want your product or service more than the money it takes to buy it.

"Whether you're selling food, cigars, a place to sleep or a vacation in some far off land, you can accomplish both halves of your selling job with quality color printing.

"Show your prospect how attractive your product is, and convince him he'll be happier, more successful or more comfortable when he buys it. The best way we know to show him is to put it down in colorful illustrations and persuasive words. Give it to him so he can read it again and again. Even a cigar store Indian would be cheered by the result.

Your Globe representative can show you the most convincing way to tell your story. He's a specialist in graphic communication."

We think that is using some "persuasive words." The four-color Globe trademark, name and address also appear on page two. It is large, so no one will have to hunt for it. The telephone number is missing. That would make it a bit easier for a prospect to call.

The illustrations on the folders run from pretty girls to men hunting and fishing, to children, to airplanes, to a modern rendition of a lion's head. They are all beautifully printed and the copy ties in with the illustration. It is quite obvious why Globe won a P.I.A. award and why the advertising makes it easier for the salesmen to call.

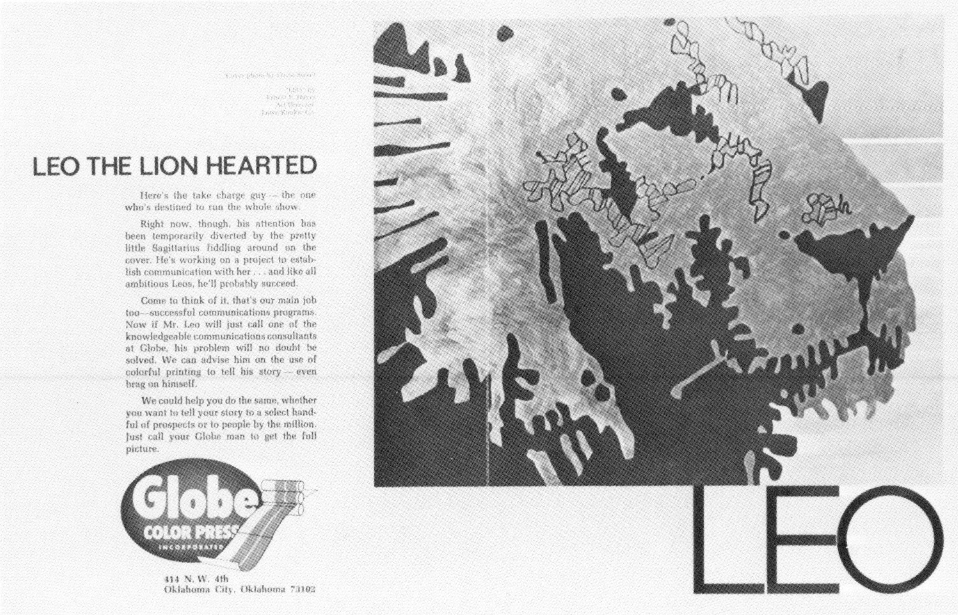

Graphic Arts Center

Corporate Brochure

Graphic Arts Center, Portland, Oregon, won a P.I.A. award for its corporate brochure or facilities booklet. G.A.C. has five divisions: Farwest/Acme, Seattle; Graphic Arts Center of Seattle, Typographers; Lincoln & Allen Book Manufacturers, Portland; Paul O. Giesey/Adcrafters, Portland; Shelton-Turnbull, Inc., Eugene, Oregon. Their booklet describes all these divisions.

G.A.C. has 250 employees and its annual sales are around $8 million. They specialize in business literature and financial printing. The 8½"x11" booklet was a kick-off piece for a series of advertising. They also used it as a piece for their salesmen to leave with prospects. It was enclosed in a clear plastic envelope. They engaged an outsider to help them with copy and layout.

The booklet is printed on white stock with every one of the 16 bleed pages completely printed with gloss inks and varnished. The background for the reverse type and beautiful photographs is a dark blue. The photographs are dramatically lit. Five pages are printed with large montage photographic compositions of various printing equipment.

The copy is concise and interesting. Here are the first four paragraphs:

"The media is print, first in putting across strong messages for keeps.

"The printer is Graphic Arts Center, printers with imagination.

"Graphic Arts Center is the one organization equipped to carry out virtually every step of your graphic communications requirements.

"From layout to copy, when required. Typography. Color separations. Presswork. Folding. Stitching. Hardbound and perfect bookbinding."

Throughout the booklet there are terse quotations placed at the top left-hand corner of the left hand pages that add interest and are a type of sales point. For instance, "It's easier to deliver excellence than alibis." "You've got to have organization to do it well." "Keen people make automation work." "Without good pressmen, the best press isn't worth the paper it prints on." "The only thing our binder can't cover up is a mistake." "Our type faces please some pretty literate designers." "You've seen it all in print."

President of Graphic Arts Center is Robert J. Rickett. He states that this booklet increased his customers by three and uncovered ten very live prospects. Sales were increased by $100,000, and the booklet helped in obtaining a sizeable bank loan. Advertising can help in many roundabout ways.

Graphic Communications Center, Inc.

Graphic Graffiti

Graphic Communications Center, Inc., Appleton, Wisconsin, consists of Badger Printing Division, established in 1922, and five other divisions handling writing and design, hot and cold-type composition, audio-visuals, office supplies and advertising specialties. They advertise, "We've got the whole thing together, under one roof . . . one management and one responsibility."

They have a publication called "Graphic Graffiti" that has great possibilities. We have seen only Volume 1, No. 1. The idea seems to be an excellent one so I will pass it along. "Graphic Graffiti" is 8½"x11", padded on the 8½" side. It has just about everything: news of the plant, mention of services, praise for customers, a sample of their printing and a serviceable scratch pad. It is not an inexpensive piece of advertising. It is novel and useful.

The cover is of a heavy stock and explains the name of the publication. The company name and trademark are also shown. The inside cover is blank. The back cover is also blank and is the backing for the scratch pad.

Page one, inside, shows the masthead and is set in four columns. The first two sheets, or four pages, are on green stock printed in black and a dark green with a glossy ink. The stock has a slight pebble finish. They have two cartoon characters, "Alphie and Ome," who are used to help illustrate columns and to be the spokesman and woman for the publication. They are pleasing characters and the art is well handled.

Many halftones of plant employees are used and articles are short, newsy and well written. One two-column feature is "The Alphie Award" and describes a job they have in the plant that they believe is a winner. There are Personals, a sports column, new faces, a coupon for adding new readers, a copy of a company ad and a short story about an old employee.

After page four, there are two sheets or four pages of a furniture catalog printed beautifully in four colors. This is part of the job that won the Alphie Award. A prospect or customer can quickly see what quality work they can accomplish.

Then comes a 25-page blue-lined scratch pad. Each sheet is printed with the Graphic Communications Center name and trademark. This gives the customer a useful pad which will also be a reminder of the company.

We believe this type of advertising, although expensive, could be adapted by many printers. The size of the piece could be changed to fit the amount of the customer's printing that one wanted to showcase. It furnishes the printer with an excellent communication tool.

a classic keepsake...

VOLUME 1, NO.1.

Why GRAFFITI..?

Why, indeed! As with most things, there's usually a reason for doing the things we do and say . . . including the names we attach to our corporate images and company "house organs," periodicals, newsletters, etc.

Well . . . our "reason" is actually severalfold; one being that "graphic" and "graffiti" have the same first syllable and the same beginning "sound" for the second syllable . . . so the two words blend together fairly well phonetically.

Another, of course, is the meaning of the word. "Graffiti" is the plural of an Italian word meaning to "scratch" or "scribble" (usually on walls, pillars, buildings, etc.) which, in turn, is derived from Latin and Greek words meaning "stylus" and "to write."

The word "graphic" is also derived from the same Latin and Greek words, so, going back far enough, both words on our masthead originate from the same language root.

Probably the two most publicized examples of "graffiti" are the ancient drawings and "scribblings" on cave walls by our prehistoric ancestors, and the well worn phrase, "Kilroy was here," scratched on millions of walls from Podunk Junction to Tokyo during World War II. To this, I guess, we could also add all the "Tom loves Marys" as well as a few million carved hearts on tree trunks all over the world.

Someone also said that graffiti is scribbling one's name here and there for the personal satisfaction of seeing it. Maybe that's where we come in. We think our name and our company should get as much "attention" as we deserve, and so we're putting out our own "graffiti" to make sure that we do! Well, . . . why not? ✽

graphic communications center, inc.

graphic communications center, inc. / VOLUME 1, NO. 1

Meet "ALPHIE and OME"

This is our new hero and heroine, representing all the GCC people. They will be our spokesmen — (spokeswomen?) . . . well, anyway, they will do most of the talking.

Alphie, short for Alpha and Ome, for Omega, (the first and last letters in the Greek alphabet) will represent us . . . in the Forum. They are our characters who will bring out some of the important things we are doing here at GCC. (Well, we can't say how good we are), *so they will!*

Ralph is shown putting a few finishing touches on Alphie and Ome.

The "Tour" Takes Off

Tom Garrigan, our "snow on the roof, but fire in the furnace" Sales Manager tells us that since the audio-visual "Tour" (slide-on-sound program) was developed by our *Video-Print Division,* we have had lots of requests for showing. Tom says, "Most people don't realize how complete our organization is and have really appreciated seeing all of our services." Interested? — contact Tom.

Tom Garrigan

NEW, NEW, NEW

The new IBM SELECTRIC TAPE composition unit is in and operating. This ultra sophisticated cold type section is living up to all that was hoped for. Margie, who is the chief ms., of the operation is setting *Graffiti,* this issue, just to show us how great this unit is. ✽

GRAPHIC GRAFFITI is published by and for the people of Graphic Communications Center, Inc.
217 East Washington Street, Appleton, WI 54911

SALES OFFICES:
MILWAUKEE
CHICAGO
28 East Jackson Blvd.
Chicago, IL 60604

MERV WINS "NAME" AWARD

Merv Farmer receives congratulations from our leader, Marlow Miller, as well as the $25.00 Savings Bond award, for naming "GRAFFITI."

First off, this issue is dedicated to the "name the publication" winner, Merv Farmer, for suggesting "Graphic Graffiti" as the name. Merv, as most of you know, is in our Sale-Service area. He is one of the top fellows who go all out, helping our customers and sales force to *get it down.*

Merv has a broad background in the Graphic Arts, from paper experience to printing and even does a top flight job narrating some of our audio-visual work. (Paul Harvey, watch out.) ✽

Metric System At GCC

Yes, the metric system is coming and as usual, GCC people will be right on top of the situation. We have recently ordered pocket rules which have both the normal inch dimensions on one edge and the metric scale on the other. This should help us all to understand and constantly identify with both measurements. ✽

in this issue...

1

Great Lakes Lithograph Co.

Image Builders

"We believe in the American scene . . ." "We believe in encouraging youth . . ." is the way two of a series of image-building folders started for Great Lakes Lithograph Co., Cleveland, Ohio. We presume the series continued because the first two words, "We believe," had fine possibilities as a continuing theme.

The folders were 14¼" x 19". They were four pages and of heavy pebbled stock. Page three was printed in four colors and consisted of art produced by a Cleveland artist. Approximately 200 of a quantity of 750 were mailed. The balance was hand delivered by six salesmen.

Great Lakes has 70 employees and their sales are a bit over two and a quarter million. They have eight sheetfed offset presses. Copy, layout and design for its folders were handled in their own plant.

On page one were the words, "We believe," which stood 26 picas high. The copy continued in 24-point Bulmer italic. The copy read, " . . . in the American scene. And as we continue our series we will fragment the Big Picture into reproductions suitable for framing. You may not like all our subjects but each has been chosen with great care and respect for youth, beauty, reality and the Country wherein we live."

On page two, the company name, address and phone number appeared with plenty of white space. Page three was the reproduction of a painting of Edward Gray, Jr. It was a ghetto scene. The copy stated, "It isn't a pretty picture. It tells a stark story and yet Edward Gray refused to paint it in drab colors. It is part of any city but it is specifically a part of Cleveland." Page four is blank.

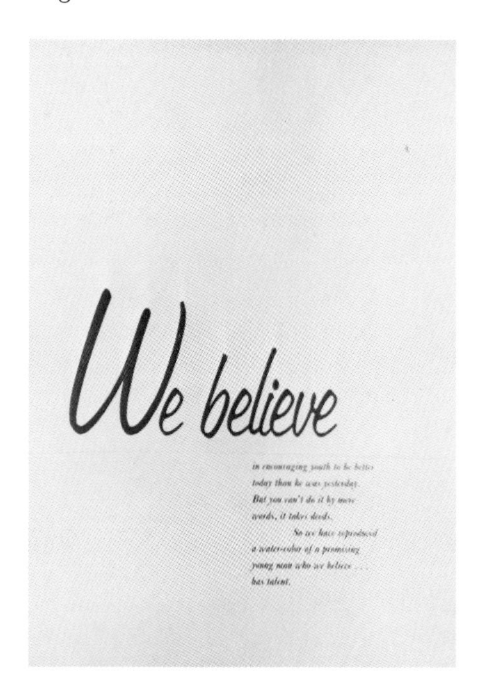

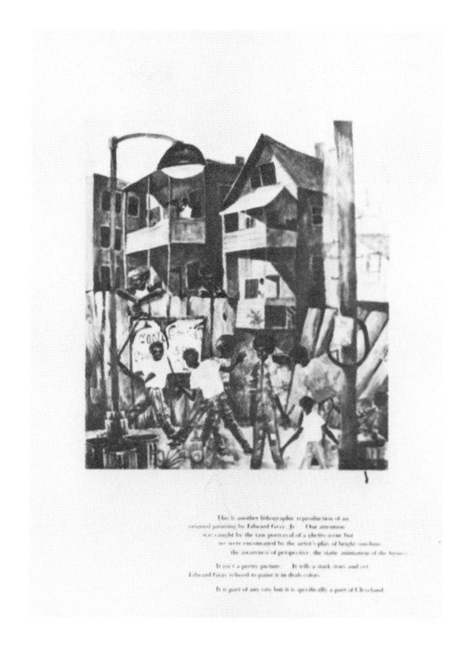

The second folder stated on page one, "We believe . . . in encouraging youth to be better today than he was yesterday. But you can't do it by mere words, it takes deeds. So we have reproduced a water-color of a promising young man who we believe has talent."

On page two is a cut-out halftone of the artist, age 17. They show his name and address. There is also the Great Lakes name, address and phone number. On page three is the reproduction of Edward Gray, Jr.'s water color. It is an excellent rendition of three or four broken down houses.

We hope and imagine that this series has continued, for Great Lakes has always advertised. We believe one more thing could have been added to these folders—a small sheet or card telling about the many services they offer, and a request to be of service. In other words, we would have included a little hard sell.

Great Lakes Press

Challenge

"Challenge" is the name of the 44-page, 10" x 14" book produced by Great Lakes Press, Rochester, N.Y. It is bound on the 10" side and covered with a heavy white Kromekote cover. The beauty of the sheet is preserved, as there are only four words and a small trademark printed in four colors on the sheet. The words in black are "Great Lakes Press" and "Challenge," which is 5 picas high. So often, a beautiful sheet of paper with an excellent finish is completely covered with ink. This is not the case here. The white space almost indicates what is to come—a high quality, dignified example of printing at its best.

Pages one and two inside are varnished and printed in solid black with the same size word, "Challenge," that appeared on the cover except that it is in reverse. On page two, set in 12-point Folio Medium, is the word "Challenge 1." On page three, there are four paragraphs of type describing the challenge to the creative artist to create a mood or tell a story, to excite or move the viewer as no one has before. The next ten pages are taken with photographs by outstanding photographers. Some pages show the small transparency used and then opposite will be a full bleed page of the same beautiful picture. There is a short description of the photographer's work with each photograph. The photographs have outstanding composition and interest. The printing is also outstanding.

On page 14, we find "Challenge 2," and on page 15, it is described as a challenge to the advertiser or seller. His graphic communications must be effective. The key, of course, to compelling communications lies in the visual presentation. And the key to a striking visual presentation lies in choosing the artists who create it and the printers who reproduce it. The next 21 pages are taken with reproductions taken from sales materials of companies served by Great Lakes Press. The companies are large, impressive ones. It proves the company that the printer keeps. Again, the printing is clean, crisp, colorful.

On page 38, we come to "Challenge 3." On page 39, it is described as the challenge to the printer. The challenge to bring together the creative artist's ideas with the seller's objectives on the printed page . . . reproducing the artist's work perfectly and communicating the seller's message dramatically. The remaining pages are used with copy and photographs describing the various departments of the plant and the employees' abilities to produce quality work. They offer "The desire to serve, the ability to create, the capacity to produce." The last page describes the facilities and equipment in their plant.

From cover to cover this is a beautiful sales tool. It is a very expensive book but the company is trying to sell some very large and demanding clients. The book thoroughly convinces the reader that he will get nothing but quality printing from Great Lakes Press.

With the type of competition that is in the printing industry in and around Rochester, New York, a book of this nature is logical. Rochester area printers have been known for their craftsmanship. Anything less than what Great Lakes produced would not sell their company in their area. Because of the cost, we would not recommend such an expensive piece where competition does not make it necessary.

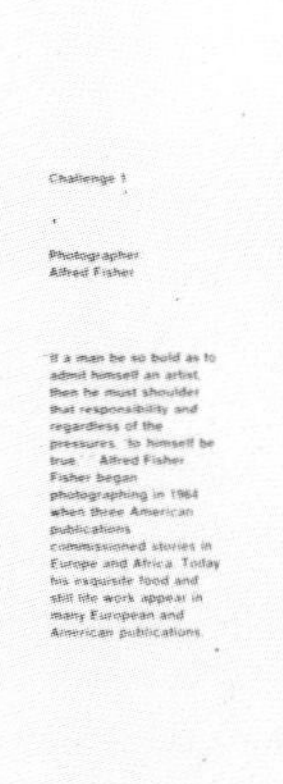
Challenge 1

Photographer
Alfred Fisher

"If a man be so bold as to admit himself an artist, then he must shoulder that responsibility and regardless of the pressures, 'to himself be true.'" Alfred Fisher. Fisher began photographing in 1964 when three American publications commissioned stories in Europe and Africa. Today his exquisite food and still life work appear in many European and American publications.

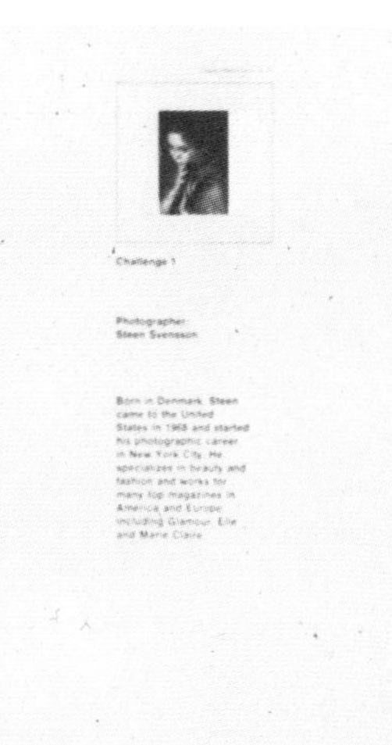
Challenge 1

Photographer

John Green Press

Miniature Forms

In the chapter headed "Direct Mail Hints," we mention a few "Idea Starters." One of them is to reduce the size—make it a miniature of the usual piece of advertising. The John Green Press of Rockford, Illinois, has done a wonderful job of miniaturizing their own printing. You really should see the five pieces that won a P.I.A. first award. We are sure we cannot do justice to them here.

The John Green Press specializes in unit sets of form printing. They have 31 employees, four of whom are salesmen. They have been in business since 1930, and their annual sales are around $900,000. They firmly believe in advertising, and these five pieces were just part of a continuing program. They had an outsider help them with copy and layout. Norman Jones, vice president, tells us they have had excellent results from their advertising. They increased their prospects by 6% with this particular campaign. They could trace about a 4% increase in sales. Customers were referring to the mailings even in their orders.

Four of the pieces are 3¾" x 9", four-page folders with the fold on the 3¾" side. The stock is Kromecote. One folder is headed on page one, "Right On The Button." The "O" in the word button is a button. There are ten different sizes and styles of buttons scattered and reproduced on a solid black background. Page one is printed in two colors, yellow and black. A screened red is used on page four.

On page two is this copy:

"The right paper
The right carbon
The right numbering
The right perforating
Right ON THE BUTTON
Your Business forms get individual
attention at John Green Press.
Mail the enclosed card today for
information and samples."

Page three contains the kicker—two of what we presume are 8½" x 11" forms reduced to 2¼" x 3". We put a magnifying glass on the type and rules and they are beautiful. No rules broken and no filled type. The one unit consists of four sheets and three carbons. The other unit consists of three sheets and two carbons. They are excellent jobs of miniaturizing and so effectively used. These two forms are tipped on to the white sheet.

On four panels, on page four, are listed the many items that are printed by John Green Press, Inc. There also appears their trademark and signature.

Another folder uses a giant "T" on the cover, and the words preceding it are, "Suits you to a—." Page two contains this copy set in 9-pt. type: "Our service will suit you to a 'T'—whether it's a ten-part continuous form, line-hole punched, a carbon inter-leaved form, forms printed on NCR (No Carbon Required) paper, complete machine accounting set ups, or just plain forms.

"Our high speed specialized equipment will fill your needs to a 'T.'

"Won't you drop the enclosed card in the mail today?

"No obligation, of course."

Page three contains two other tipped-on miniaturized forms. We cannot determine what was their actual size. One is an adjustment memo and is a single sheet. The other is a purchase order set of five various colored sheets and four carbon sheets. The purchase order is printed in two colors.

Page four again lists the various forms that John Green Press can produce. The signature and trademarks are on this page.

The third folder's page one is practically covered with various numbers printed on a solid black background. Three colors of ink have been used. The headline is, "We've Got Your Number."

Page two contains some short copy. The last paragraph reminds the reader that "Regardless of the Bank you do business with, John Green Press has your Account number."

Tipped on to page three is a small payroll check form with an attachment to show deductions. The complete form measures 1" x 5". The other check form unit measures 2¾" x 2¾", and consists of three sheets. Both checks are printed with a background that makes them look like safety paper stock. The forms are so well printed. These are also perforated.

The fourth page is a duplicate of the first folder we described.

The fourth folder shows five various-sized medicine bottles. On each label is printed a word so that the headline reads, "Just What The Doctor Ordered."

Inside, on page two, there is short copy describing the virtues of NCR paper for accounting forms and payroll setups. The small forms tipped in on page three are miniature accounting and payroll forms. Page four is identical to page four of the second folder we described.

The fifth piece is an 11" x 17" sheet folded twice to an 8½" x 5½" folder. It is printed on heavy offset stock in four colors. The first fold shows a stylized hand picking up an egg with the words, "Why Not" imprinted. There is a light green wallpaper design in the background.

Page one of the folder shows a stylized basket with eggs imprinted with John Green Press products such as, "Invoices—Sales Slips—Bills of Lading—Checks." The headline is, "Why not put all of your eggs in one basket?" The following copy is: "You can save time and money, speed up purchasing, assure prompt handling of orders and eliminate confusion by concentrating your form printing with John Green Press."

Pages three and four are taken with an overall tan tint with crossed pieces or lines of green hay or grass. On this background are six complete white eggs with four eggs bleeding off the sheet. Three of the eggs contain copy about Speed-A-Copy, Speed-A-Part and Speed-A-Tronic Magnetic Checks. Then on three of the eggs are tipped three miniature forms illustrating the three types of work. The forms are printed in two colors and are accurate in every detail. One form even has a tag with a brass eyelet within the unit which is made up of five sheets and three carbon sheets.

The last page of the folder shows an egg carton with this copy: "For Grade AAA, extra large improvements in your paper-work let a J-G-P forms expert survey your requirements—no obligations, of course." Then there is a listing again of the three "Speed" forms and the company name, address and telephone number.

These folders are outstanding because they illustrate the product so differently. Most samples of forms are pretty dreary, but here are forms that are cute. You just have to show them to someone else. Our hats are off to John Green Press for a different and interesting approach.

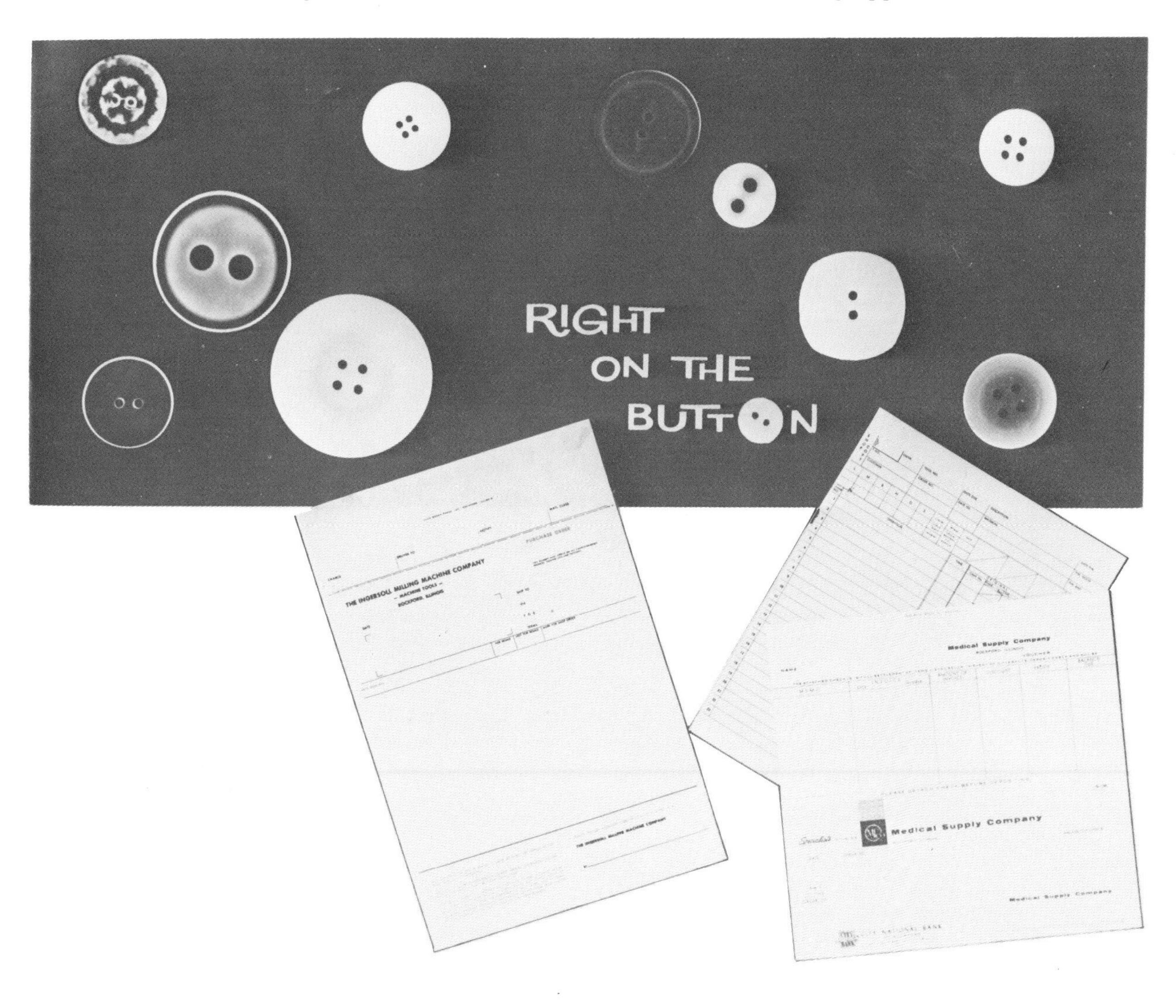

Greensboro Printing Co.

Christmas Cards

Christmas cards can become wonderful advertising pieces. If they are well designed and different, people will look forward to receiving them. As one who has designed his own Christmas card for 49 years, I have a soft spot in my heart for this form of remembrance and advertising.

Mrs. Margaret F. Earle, owner-manager of Greensboro Printing Co., Greensboro, N.C., can also tell you of the value of Christmas cards. She says: "Christmas cards, which were virtually our only form of advertising, have been a significant factor in the growth of the company from the 'little hole in the wall' which we purchased in 1949, to the 16,000-square-foot building which we built and occupied in 1972."

Before we tell you about the Greensboro or Earle family Christmas cards, let us tell you about the company. Greensboro Printing was founded in 1909 and purchased in 1949 by the late E.P. (Buck) Earle and C.H. Fowler, also deceased, husband and father respectively, of Mrs. Margaret Earle, the present general manager. Mrs. Earle assumed management of the company upon the death of her husband in 1952.

There are now 32 employees, many veterans of from ten to 22 years of service.

The Christmas cards started as personal cards back in 1936, when Mrs. Earle was a bride. The first card was simply a 4" x 6" french fold printed in two colors on tan stock. A Christmas tree was made out of type rules and a few stars scattered about. A red deckle was made by painting the one edge by hand! The message read, "Buck and Margaret Earle wish you a Merry Christmas and hope that the days to follow will be filled with love, laughter and content."

Following is just a sketchy account, without full details of these warm and friendly cards: In 1937, there was a printed photo of the happy couple beside their first Christmas tree, which was all of two feet high. In 1938, silhouettes cut from a linoleum block were seen through a die-cut cover.

In 1939, a wood-grained cover stock, overprinted with gold, red and black to resemble a book, was used. The message was embellished with terms used in the printing and publishing business.

In 1940, and twice afterwards, the cards became birth announcements rather than Christmas cards. These were not ordinary announcements but used the creativity and latent ability that every printer seems to have.

And this is where we wish we were ordained to preach. What a sermon we could give to printers about using their talents. There are very few printers who do not have the ability to create, adapt, steal—call it what you may—wonderful ideas to enhance a sales message. They have all the tools but they don't seem to use them for their own good.

In 1941, the baby Peggy's name was added to the Christmas card. A good touch. In 1942, the war economy and ration books were being used so the card resembled a ration book. The Earles' coupons were good for Health, Love, Peace, Wealth, Friendship, Laughter, Joy, Contentment, etc.

In 1943, the Christmas card featured the familiar service flag showing the address of Mr. Earle, who was in the Navy. 1944 and 1945 were skipped because of the Navy duty. In early 1946, a small booklet titled, "A Year Of Life" was published. The cover resembled a *Life* magazine cover and the arrival of the third child was announced. Included was a story of the family for the preceding two years. It announced that Mr. Earle was production manager of Riser Printing Co. in Greensboro. A Christmas card was produced that year, as well as in 1947. In 1948, there was no customary greeting, because Mr. Earle suffered a serious prolonged illness.

In 1949, they used an annual report format which brought everyone up to date on everything from the family pets, to the children, to the printing suppliers, competitors and creditors. This card was the first that went to customers as well as personal friends.

In 1950, it was "Earle's Home Journal," in which they told of the remodeling of their home. There was also an ad for Greensboro Printing Co. which told about such services as "Ideas Thunk Up, Money Changed, Errands Run, Paper Cut, Holes Punched, Contributions Made, Cold Drinks, Also Plain and Fancy Printing Done."

In 1951, the design was simple but the narrative told a homey story of maid trouble and how they found Lois the answer to all their problems or almost all.

In 1952, Mr. Earle died very suddenly and unexpectedly and no Christmas card was sent that year. In 1953, the first page of the card was illustrated with musical notes containing three pictures of the children and one of Mrs. Earle. Inside was a friendly note which referred to the children and that Greensboro Printing was still part of Mrs. Earle's interest.

In 1954, there was a card inspired by the song, "This Old House." In 1955, a clever crossword puzzle was used. In 1956, it was a letter to Santa Claus in the form of a booklet. Each child asked for something and Mrs. Earle wanted a book titled "How to Run a Printing Company in Eight Hours a Day."

The 1957 card was in the form of a resolution. The first line read, "Whereas: The Earle's Christmas card is usually the last one you receive, thanks to Mama's never getting around to printing her own until the paying customers are taken care of; and . . ." There were many more lines about the family and, of course, the season's greetings. This was signed by the Earles of Greensboro: Peggy, Preston, Mary and Margaret and witnessed by all the folk at Greensboro Printing Co.

In 1958 and thereafter, the card was referred to as an Earl-e Edition. Occasionally, it was impossible to have them mailed on time, so the expression "Another late Earle-e Edition" was used. However, a fairly dependable mailing schedule was kept until 1966 when Mrs. Earle became ill. An explanation was given in the 1967 card and the cards continued.

The 1969
EDITION
EARLIE
Are you sure this is going to bring me inner peace?
BOOK TITLES:
"21-Day Shape Up"
"Calories Don't Count"
"Psychocybernetics"
"Today's Horoscope"
"Managing Your Business"
"Work Smarter . . . Not Harder"
"Roberts Rules of Order"
"Jokes for Every Occasion"

The copy was always interesting, homey and obviously written by a proud mother who is also a businesswoman. Poems were used. No two cards were ever alike. There was a card in the form of a diary with pictures. A card like a scrapbook used clippings from newspapers to delineate the activities of the Earles in 1960. In 1961, a small 5¾" x 9" file folder was used with single sheets inside listing the many activities of each one of the family, as well as the Greensboro Printing Co. In 1962, the background was a monthly calendar with explanations of the Earle activities overprinted on each page. In 1963, it was a coloring book and very well done. In 1964, a take-off on Charles Schulz's book, *Happiness Is a Warm Puppy.*

In 1965, photographs were all placed within a television set shown on ten pages of a 20-page booklet. In 1967, a 24-page booklet was used and it was titled, "The Earle's Mother Goose." This was printed in four solid colors with interesting cartoons and poetry. In 1968, it was a four-color process cover headed "The Ballad of '68." Inside were six pages of "music" about the Earles.

Perhaps the most elaborate card was in 1969. It measured 4¼" x 5¼". Printed in four solid colors, die cut, scored and folded seven times, by hand, we are sure. The artwork was purposely made to look homemade but it wasn't! Some speedball pen hand lettering was used. And there were pictures of the Earles and those at the plant. A very effective piece, and it won my choice as the best of the years.

A card of 1970 was mailed in the summer of 1971. It was an elaborate jig-saw puzzle printed in four-color process with excellent pictures of the family, grandchildren and Mrs. Earle.

This is lengthy because we are trying to illustrate the consistency and to give you ideas for your own Christmas card. There are so many ways it could be handled. For some, the personal family ties which were used by Mrs. Earle and the Greensboro Printing Co. would not work. For Mrs. Earle, who must be a warm, friendly individual, it was a natural approach and a very effective one. She believes in advertising. Greensboro has won two or three P.I.A. awards and has received quite a bit of recognition for its advertising. For other companies who want an image of strict formality, there are various other ways to do it.

Our main point is that greetings at Christmas time, the first of the year, or at any time special to you, if unique, pay off. People look forward to receiving them. It is good advertising that works.

New Building

Most printers, even if they never advertised before, do so when they build a new building or move to a new location. Greensboro Printing Company has been advertising for years, but in 1972, when they built a 16,000-square-foot building, they went all out. They used five bright, intricate folders to announce the "happening."

The first folder was on a 12¼" x 19½" plus bleed sheet of good quality 80-lb. cover, printed five colors one side, three colors on the reverse side.

It was french folded to 8⅜" x 10" with pages one and two measuring 3¾" x 10". It was die cut and scored and hand folded. A modern cartoon figure of a construction man with a shovel in hand was printed on pages two and three. The arms of the man and the shovel popped out when the folder was opened. The first page headline was, "An earth moving event has taken place." The colors were bright and fluorescent. Everything was in register. The illustration and type were modern and the die-cutting was well done and very effective.

The second piece, mailed a few months later, was another die-cut piece. It was printed on a 19½" x 21½" sheet of cover stock. It was french folded to make an 8¼" x 9¾" six-pager with pages one and two measuring 3¾" x 9¾". There were four fluorescent colors printed on one side and two on the other side. To illustrate that every production detail seemed to be thought out for these pieces, we noticed that black ½" bleed borders were printed on the reverse side of three of the pieces, so that if the hand folding of the heavy cover stock didn't quite square up, it wouldn't be noticed as the black border would match the black on the front side.

The message of the second folder was "Watch us grow." The illustrations were photographs of the construction site taken at interesting angles to make them attractive. The copy emphasized the address of the new location. The intricate die cut was a pop-up of the Greensboro Printing Co. trademark. Again, the illustration, type and lay-out were modern and of high quality.

The third folder was from the same size sheet as the second folder with five colors printed on one side and three on the reverse side. It was also a six-pager and hand folded because of the die-cut. It had another interesting pop-up of a butterfly. Every detail was considered to make the folder attractive. There was no white paper showing where it shouldn't. Register was excellent. Illustrations were modern. Its theme was, "This is brand new," and it referred to the new camera, press and bindery equipment they were installing.

The fourth and final piece was the most elaborate of the four folders. It was printed on a 17½" x 28" plus bleed 80-lb. cover sheet. There were five fluorescent colors printed on one side and two on the reverse side. It was french folded to an 8⅜" x 9¼" six-pager with pop-outs coming from everywhere. On the bottom of page three an extra 4¾" x 8¼" shelf folded down and out popped a miniature building, and coming out of the roof was a 3¼" x 4½" white folded invitation to the open house on June 14, 1973, at the new building. The folder was beautifully executed. These four folders are a real compliment to the printing craft. The work, the engineering and the craftsmanship that went into these folders were great.

Mrs. Margaret Earle says, "The response has really been fantastic, if our business growth is any sort of indication. The grand opening folder may still be seen set up in offices around town. Whether the mailings are solely responsible or not, many doors previously closed to us have begun to open!"

We are certain that the advertising alone did not increase their business. They are doing many things right at Greensboro. We are certain that the advertising brought the wonderful crowd to their grand opening. We are also certain that these four folders illustrated to many buyers of printing that Greensboro Printing can do quality work.

If you are contemplating an open house and are located far away from Greensboro, write to Mrs. Earle. She is such a cooperative person, she may have an extra copy of these folders that she could send to you to see. She may even let you borrow and share in the expense of the dies! There's no reason under the sun why these folders couldn't be adapted to another printer's open house provided, of course, he isn't in the Greensboro market.

Greensboro Printing also has a facilities brochure. It measures 9¾" x 14", and consists of 32 pages plus a fly leaf. It is beautifully printed in one color—black. The cover is white Kromecote and they have let it shine.

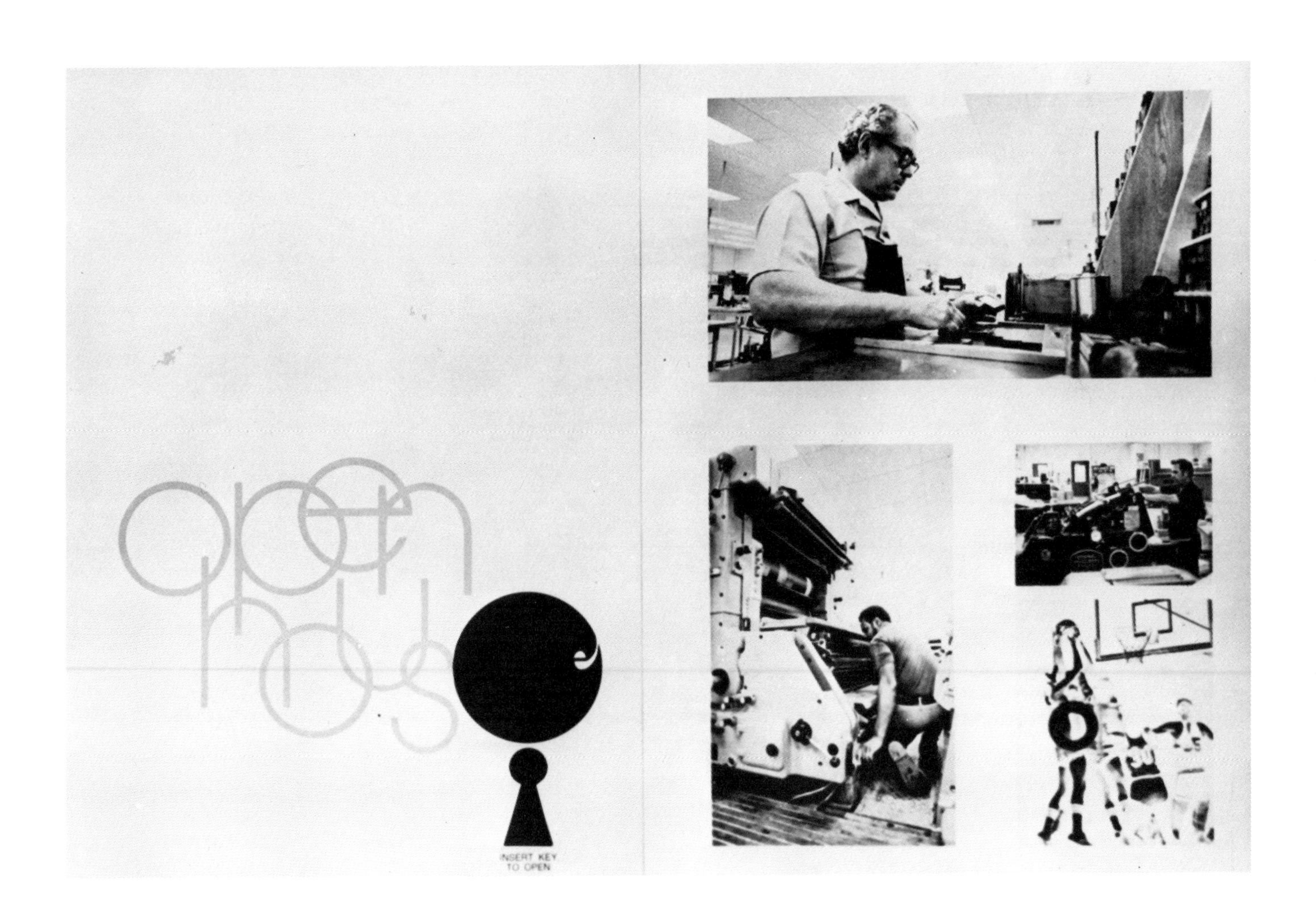

There are two lines of type, one on the front and one on the back cover. The line shows the company name in all lower case about 2½ picas high. Before you open the brochure you get a feel of class with that stark white glossy cover with just the company name at the bottom of the page. The address is on page two—nothing more. Then there is a parchment fly leaf with a picture of the front of the building showing through on which is printed:

"This is a printing office.

"Crossroads of civilization . . . Refuge of all the arts against the ravages of time . . . Armoury of fearless truth against whispering rumor . . . Incessant trumpet of trade.

"From this place words may fly abroad . . . Not to perish on waves of sound . . . Not to vary with the writer's hand . . . But fixed in time . . . Having been verified in proof.

"Friend you stand on sacred ground . . .

"this is a printing office."

On page three there is no copy except the 31-pica by 39½-pica halftone of the front of the building.

The copy throughout the book, from the introduction on page four to the acknowledgements on page 30, is well written and interesting. The layout uses broad expanses of white space. The photographs have sometimes been enlarged to cover the entire page. They are well printed with good black areas and no fuzzy dots in the lighter areas. It is an excellent brochure to leave with any prospect or to give to a visitor of the plant. It will convince anyone that they know how to print at Greensboro.

Printing is done by both letterpress and offset in our plant, with the latter accounting by far for the largest percentage of the total.

Letterpress, by which ink is applied directly to the metal type and transferred from it to the paper, performs many functions that cannot be accomplished by offset, such as numbering, perforating and die cutting. Furthermore, a job can often be produced quicker and cheaper by eliminating the camera and platemaking stages.

However, the versatility and speed of the offset process have accounted for its growth in recent years. Our printing presses are sheet fed, and vary in size from one which will take a sheet as small as 4" x 6" to a sheet size of 23" x 31". One of our newest presses, in the latter size is a Miehle 2-Color on which two colors of ink can be printed with each pass of the sheet through the press. On single color presses, each color of ink is applied in a separate run. Both require extreme precision which is aided by humidity control — one of the features of our new plant.

printing

Hennage Creative Printers

Anniversary Year

How do you describe the advertising and promotion of Hennage Creative Printers, Washington, D.C.? The company has won 13 Bennys from Printing Industries of America. It won a Direct Mail Advertising Association "Spectacular" award, a Marketing Executives' Club of New York award and hundreds of other awards.

Joseph H. Hennage is president of the company. He believes in good public relations, publicity and advertising, and he works to obtain it for his company. He believes that if you build a better mousetrap and tell everyone that you do, the world will beat a path to your door. Quality and service must not only be there—they must be heralded.

Joe insists that his company's advertising has been a big factor in the company's climb from almost nothing to a company having $3,500,000 in sales, with 60 employees working one shift and designing 60% of the printing produced. The company has grown at an average rate of 20% a year over the previous year.

We will try to describe three or four things that Hennage Creative Printers has done. Let's start with their 25th Anniversary year in December, 1970. They had 46 employees at the time. They had won a first award for an individual piece, a second award for their campaign and an award of achievement for an individual piece in the 1970 P.I.A. Awards. They publicized these awards in an eight-page fold-out folder.

One side of the 11" x 34" sheet was laminated. On the cover was a large photograph of the bronze medallion on the award plaque. This was on a black lacquered background and was very effective. Hennage has a wax life-like and life-size figure of Benjamin Franklin that they use in some of their advertising and which reposes in a replica of an old time print shop in their lobby. This figure was used to hold the awards and a full-page photograph was used on an inside fold. On a preceding page were a few words supposedly written by Franklin.

The four-page inside fold-out contained full-size photographs of the plaques and small reproductions of the prize-winning piece along with six editions of "Excelsior News" which was part of the advertising campaign. There was also a tipped-on, small four-color reproduction of an English coaching scene which they featured in "Excelsior News." There was copy describing the pieces and these words of appreciation: "To you, our clients and friends, we also want to express our thanks for many opportunities to serve you, and to assure you that Hennage Creative Printers will always have creative imagination, quality, and complete marketing service at your disposal."

The back page listed "Our Past Advertising Awards." There were 17 of them, a picture of the Hennage building, their signature and a line which read, "Celebrating 25 years of Creative Service."

This folder was sent with a four-paragraph note from Joseph H. Hennage, telling why it was printed and offering large coaching prints for framing to any who had not received them.

House Organs

House organs are excellent forms of advertising if you have enough interesting news to send to your prospects and customers. If your president is an active person in many ways, or if your employees are active in community works, a house organ makes a good medium for letting your public know about these activities. Since Mr. Hennage has his fingers in so many pies and seems always to rise quickly to the top of anything he gets into, the house organ is a natural for his company. We will go into some detail about Hennage's house organ so you will get an idea of the type of material they use.

"Excelsior News" is "published for the pleasure and information of our clients and friends by Hennage Creative Printers, Inc." At one time it was tabloid size but it was changed to an 8½" x 11" size of about eight pages and cover. Sometimes covers are die cut or unusually printed, such as using black ink on black stock. Various colored stock is often used on the inside. Type and layout are neat and easily read. One typical issue contains a speech by the president of Pennsylvania State University with an endorsement of what has been said by Joseph H. Hennage. Then there is a two-page article by Howard L. Sherman of *Financial World* magazine, entitled, "1969 Annual Reports Follow Own Bent." Included with this article are "Guidelines for a Modern Annual Report."

AN UNDERRATED GENERATION

by
ERIC A. WALKER
President,
Pennsylvania State University

From an address delivered to a recent graduating class.

Dear Friends:

This is a remarkable speech. It is wise. It acknowledges the accomplishments of my generation—and very probably yours—which many of today's young people have forgotten or have chosen to ignore. It is critical of violence and negativism without being violent or negative. I support it wholeheartedly and I wish I had made it. It is reprinted here for your encouragement and any missionary use you might wish to make of it.

Joseph H. Hennage

Ladies and gentlemen of the graduating class and those who got advanced degrees. Let me extend to each of you my personal congratulations and those of the entire University on the degree you have earned today.

This ceremony marks the completion of an important phase of your life. It is an occasion in which all who know you can share in your sense of pride and accomplishment. But no one has more pride in your accomplishment than the older generation. But I am not going to tell that older generation how bright you are. Nor am I going to say we have made a mess of things and you — the younger ones — are the hope of mankind. I would like to reverse that process. For if you of the graduating class will look over into the bleachers to your left or right, I will reintroduce you to representatives of some of the most remarkable people ever to walk the earth. People you might want to thank on this graduation day. These are people you already know — your parents and grandparents. And, if you will bear with me for five minutes, I think you will agree that a remarkable people they are indeed. Let me tell you about them.

Not long ago an educator from Northwestern University by the name of Bergen Evans, a radio performer known to your parents, got together some facts about these two generations — your parents and grandparents. I'd like to share some of these facts with you.

These — your parents and grandparents — are the people who within just the last five decades — have by their work increased your life expectancy by approximately 50 percent — who while cutting the working day by a third, have more than doubled per capita output.

These are the people who have given you a healthier world than they found. And because of this you no longer have to fear epidemics of flu, typhus, diphtheria, smallpox, scarlet fever, measles or mumps that they knew in their youth. And the dreaded polio is no longer a medical factor, while TB is almost unheard of.

Let me remind you that these remarkable people lived through history's greatest depression. Many of these people know what it is to be poor, what it is to be hungry and cold. And because of this, they determined that it would not happen to you, that you would have a better life, you would have food to eat, milk to drink, vitamins to nourish you, a warm home, better schools and greater opportunities to succeed than they had.

Because they gave you the best, you are the tallest, healthiest, brightest, and probably best looking generation to inhabit the land.

And because they were materialistic, you will work fewer hours, learn more, have more leisure time, travel to more distant places, and have more of a chance to follow your life's ambition.

These are also the people who fought man's grisliest war. They are the people who defeated the tyranny of Hitler, and who when it was all over, had the compassion to spend billions of dollars to help their former enemies rebuild their homelands. And these are the people who had the sense to begin the United Nations.

It was representatives of these two generations, who through the highest court of the land, fought racial discrimination at every turn to begin a new era in civil rights.

They built thousands of high schools, trained and hired tens of thousands of better teachers, and at the same time made higher education a very real possibility for millions of youngsters — where once it was only the dream of a wealthy few.

And they made a start — although a late one — in healing the scars of the earth and in fighting pollution and the destruction of our natural environment. They set into motion new laws giving conservation new meaning, and setting aside land for you and your children to enjoy for generations to come.

They also hold the dubious record for paying taxes — although you will probably exceed them in this.

While they have done all these things, they have had some failures. They have not yet found an alternative for war, nor for racial hatred. Perhaps you, the members of this graduating class, will perfect the social mechanisms by which all men may follow their ambitions without the threat of force — so that the earth will no longer need police to enforce the laws, nor armies to prevent some men from trespassing against others. But they — those generations — made more progress by the sweat of their brows than in any previous era, and don't you forget it. And, if your generations can make as much progress in as many areas as these two generations have, you should be able to solve a good many of the world's remaining ills.

It is my hope, and I know the hope of these two generations, that you find the answers to many of these problems that plague mankind.

But it won't be easy. And you won't do it by negative thoughts, nor by tearing down or belittling. You may and can do it by hard work, humility, hope, and faith in mankind. Try it.

Goodby and good luck to all of you.

1969 annual report

Hennage Clients Win Financial World Awards For Annual Reports

We are very proud to note that two of our clients' annual reports, which we designed and printed, have won *Financial World's* coveted Merit Award for excellence. As a service to readers, we also reprint *Financial World's* excellent article from its June 20 issue on trends and desirable features of annual reports. For those who may wish to do some thoughtful, advance planning now for their 1970 annual reports, we would be happy to make samples available from our own extensive library, and to provide assistance in planning and design.

FINANCIAL WORLD

Low Multiples—Higher Earnings
Interest Rate Paradox
Bank Security-Growth Field
Rebound for Toy Makers?

Bankers Security

9.2%

33.4%

$1.46

On another page are five photographs and on the opposite page are five articles describing the actions in the photographs. The subjects are: (1) Messrs. Hennage and Borum of P.I.A., distributing books from the P.I.A. Graphic Arts Awards competition to children at Children's Hospital. (2) Mr. Hennage accepting the P.I.A. award for "Excelsior News." (3) Second generation employee awarded master craftsman status. (4) Hennage client receiving award. (5) 60" cutter installed at Hennage.

On the last inside page is a picture of the new P.I.A. home which was of interest to Joseph Hennage when he was board chairman of P.I.A. The other picture on this page shows Mr. Hennage acting as a judge in the contest to select a design for savings bond envelopes from more than 20 entries contributed by the National Association of Greeting Card Publishers.

Anniversary Luncheon

Of course, Hennage Creative Printers made the most of its 25th anniversary. An anniversary luncheon invitation, measuring 8¾" x 11½", was sent to a list of Hennage clients and leaders of the business community. The Newport Blue, 100-pound Beau Brilliant cover was stamped in silver: "Twenty Fifth Anniversary." The words were hand lettered and leaves entwined around them. The four pages inside were 8½" x 11", 65-pound Granada Purple Beau Brilliant cover. All the pages inside were printed with a dark blue ink. Hennage Creative Printers was hand lettered in a cursive style on the first page. Pages two and three were used for the invitation and time table. The invitation is printed in reverse type on a dark blue background which is formed by a stylized printer's ink roller in a life size hand. We like the copy. It reads, "On the happy occasion of Hennage Creative Printers' Twenty-fifth year. Joseph H. Hennage cordially invites you to join a congenial group of friends who have shared in the company's growth at a Silver Anniversary Reception and Luncheon on . . . etc."

There also appears a time table which shows that the reception begins at noon. At "12:45 Promptly" luncheon was to be served and there would be a brief program commemorating the occasion. At 2:00 P.M., adjournment was scheduled "in deference to our guests' business commitments."

On the fourth page, inside, was this note of appreciation: "We are deeply and profoundly grateful for the support of our good clients and friends in the many communities that make up the Nation's Capital City—Associations, Business, Finance, Government, and others. In turn, we have supported as best we could the industry and the city of which we have been a part for twenty-five years. It is our pleasure to bring together good friends from all of these parts of our company's life for a pleasant and memorable occasion which will recognize the part they have played in our growth and success. Joseph H. Hennage."

Enclosed with the invitation was a formal reply card and stamped reply envelope.

TWENTY FIFTH
ANNIVERSARY

25th Anniversary Book

At the luncheon, each guest received a cloth bound 112-page book recording how the company was built. The book was dedicated to June S. Hennage, the president's wife and company historian who, over the years, kept and catalogued the photographs, clippings, records and advertising pieces that made up the raw material for the book. June was the first office employee and secretary for the company before she and Mr. Hennage were married. She has been bookkeeper, controller and the first vice president.

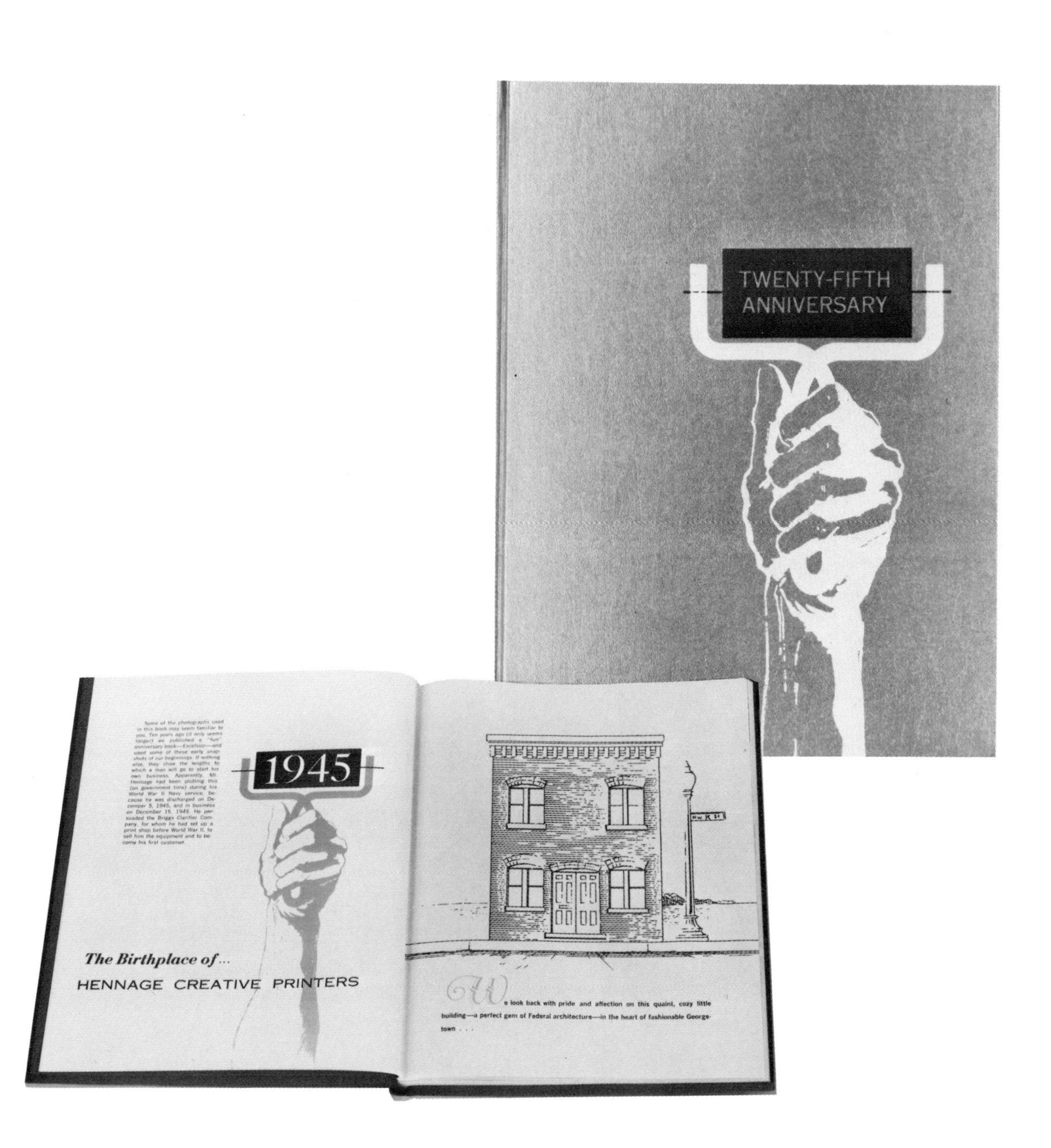

The book is very interesting. It tells of Joe Hennage, who was discharged from the World War II Navy on December 5, 1945, and in the printing business on December 15, 1945. He was a Multilith operator before he went into the Navy. The Navy used his printing skills and knowledge. When he came out of the Navy his old employer, having been heavily war production oriented, was seeing lean days ahead and asked Joe to liquidate the print shop. He bought it himself. His old employer was the first customer and some of the old invoices are shown in the book.

There are photographs of the first building, the terribly dirty interior and a list of the inventory which wasn't much. There are photographs of old and new equipment as it was added. We can see one of the first employees at work who was hired during the second year. He is now the foreman in charge of finishing operations. Luke Green was their first foreman. He is now vice president and plant superintendent. Their first creative staff person was William G. Hanlon. He is now vice president and art director. All through the book are photographs of these people at work.

Each of the twenty-five years are reviewed with pictures, advertising pieces and well written copy. As present employees were hired they are mentioned in the book. The many awards are pictured as well as the many civic duties and honors that involved Mr. Hennage. We cannot go into further detail but it is the most elaborate and interesting printer's anniversary book that we have seen.

Employee's Open House

Hennage also had a party and open house for their employees. Each employee and client was given an impressive Benjamin Franklin bust placed in permanent lucite as a token of appreciation and a constant reminder of Hennage Creative Printers' application of Franklin's principles of craftsmanship and imagination.

The silver anniversary issue of "Excelsior News" covered the employees' party with photographs and also illustrated some unusual treatments in the use of papers, halftones and the potentials in die cutting for special effects.

Spectacular Direct Mail

The direct mail campaign that won the Direct Mail Advertising Association "Spectacular" Award was just that—spectacular, especially for a printer. It consisted of 11 heavy, double-faced corrugated mailing boxes measuring 9½" x 13½" x 1½". We will quickly run through what each box contained:

Box 1. A heavy plastic envelope with a Cryptograph unit inside. This unit was prepared by the Institute for the Popularization of Science. It contained a slide rule, code-maker, graph paper and a package of Ferrous Sulfate to make invisible ink and a 12-page booklet describing various experiments. There was a Hennage card enclosed that explained in detail that Cryptograph and creative printing both have the same purpose . . . to communicate. Also enclosed was a sheet and reply card soliciting Association printing, a Hennage eight-page folder describing how they produced *Consumer Finance News* and a copy of that magazine.

GROWTH?
THINK BIG
Direct Mail
A LOOK
Award
we're buzzin'...
BE OUR GUEST...
REPRINT FROM
Proposal

Box 2. A heavy plastic envelope containing a Specialized Papers Unit. The unit contained 11 samples of paper and an eight-page folder describing the samples. There was also a card explaining what Hennage Creative Printers could do with paper. Also enclosed was a sheet describing moods with paper and a reply card asking to be placed on the Hennage mailing list. There were two eight-page booklets printed for a Tiber Island development—each one illustrating the different uses of paper.

Box 3. Contained a smaller corrugated box containing a Probability Unit—another science experiment. The Hennage card stated, "The Probability is about 4 to 1 that full-service creative printing, designed to meet a specific need will get you better results than the 'let's get out a mailing approach' to your problem."

There was also a sheet with a reply card telling of a Mail Order Portfolio that was available for the asking. Also, an eight-page folder telling how Hennage had worked with the General Federation of Women's Clubs to develop a Community Improvement Program.

Box 4. Contained a Static Electricity Unit and a card explaining that static electricity was no friend of Hennage's. There was also a sheet with a reply card telling of Hennage's creative convention portfolio that they would be glad to deliver. Enclosed were three pieces that had been printed for different conventions. One piece was a large folded poster.

Box 5. Contained a smaller corrugated box of Ancient Gems. There was a Hennage card, with copy, tied in with the gems. Also enclosed was a Cesso Polychrome Art book printed by Hennage; a smaller booklet about World Trade Fairs and a booklet printed in four colors extolling the virtues of Hennage creativity. Of course, there was a reply card to request being placed on the mailing list.

Box 6. Contained another science unit called Crystallization and a Hennage card stating that it is one of the things they do best. "You simply tell us what you want to accomplish, we'll crystallize your ideas . . . etc." There was an elaborate fold-out ten-page folder telling about designing and printing an award-winning annual report. Also, two well printed annual reports were enclosed, along with a sheet and reply card telling of Hennage's Annual Report portfolio that could be delivered to a prospect.

Box 7. Contained an Optical Illusion science packet and the usual Hennage card with copy tied into optical illusions and printings. There was an eight-page folder describing how Hennage worked together with an association to publish an official organ of Quota International Incorporated. There was a fact booklet of Financial General Corporation and a Corn Industries Research Foundation booklet, a National Association of Securities Dealers' booklet as well as a booklet of the Association of the United States Army—also a reply card.

Box 8. Contained a Papermaking kit with instructions and a card from Hennage. There were six enclosures in this box: 1. A direct mail piece of Hennage's. 2. An eight-page folder entitled, "The Story of a Successful Association Membership Promotion." 3. An envelope and letterhead of an insurance company. 4. A letterhead of P.I.A. 5. An American Corn Millers' Federation letterhead. 6. A sheet telling of the availability of a Hennage Letterhead portfolio.

Box 9. Contained a Simple Machines unit, and the Hennage card referred to simple machines not being found in printing plants. There was an 8½" x 11" french fold piece showing a pink high top hat on page one and the question, "Old Hat?" on page two. Then a large full color picture of the employees grouped around a press holding 17 awards that Hennage had received for its printing or advertising. Well written copy told of their accomplishments. Also enclosed was a 48-page booklet designed and printed for the National Machine Tool Builders' Association. The reply card enclosed was for requesting to be placed on the Hennage mailing list.

Box 10. Held a Mathematical Paper Folding Unit and a Hennage card about folding and trimming printing. A fashion gift catalog was enclosed that surely demonstrated how Hennage could use paper, die cutting and folding to produce an outstanding selling tool. The reply card sheet referred to design with a purpose. The box also contained a 16-page and cover brochure entitled, "To Acquaint You With Us." The cover was heavy and die cut. The brochure was an excellent piece of printers' self-advertising.

Box 11. Contained another small box which held a Pinhole Photography Unit. The Hennage card referred to photography and reproducing photos for printing. Two different exhibition 12-page booklets were enclosed in this box, and also the usual reply card.

We have gone into much detail about this campaign because it was a very unusual and expensive one for a printer. It was done in great style and, like so many things Joe Hennage undertakes, every detail was well covered. They did their homework on this campaign.

Mail Campaign

Hennage, as this book is being written, has another campaign going. We have seen six pieces. They are 4" x 8½", cast coated cards mailed in various colored envelopes. Here is a quick run-through.

The envelope states, "1974 year of the tiger at Hennage." The inside card has an embroidered caricature of a tiger pasted on the card. It can be lifted off to wear. Below the tiger, the copy states, "You'll find us ready to pounce . . . on any printing project you have." There's a small picture of the Hennage building, the company signature, address and phone number. On the reverse side is a picture of the new Hennage strip-lister for easier mail list maintenance. The eight-point copy explains the machine in detail.

Another envelope states, "Here is the heart we put in every printed piece we do for you. Happy Valentine Day." The inside card is addressed to "Lovers of fine printing—our Customers . . ." Then the envelope message is repeated. There is a caricature of Cupid and a pasted on red embroidered heart with the suggestion that you lift it off and wear it. The same picture of the building, signature, address and phone number appear on each card on the front side. The reverse side again shows a larger picture of the

A
NEW
LOGO*
FOR OUR
FIVE
COLOR PRESS
TRY
IT
YOU'LL LIKE
IT
NA8-8282
Here's
Something
Green
for Luck
To Wear
On
St. Patrick's
Day...
... but luck is one
thing you won't need
when you do your
printing with us.
* Lift off and wear it.
NA8-8282
HENNAGE CREATIVE PRINTERS
814 H ST., N.W., WASHINGTON, D.C. 20006
QUICKER
THAN
THE BUNNY
HOW OUR COLOR
PRESS
DID ROLL
TO PUT
YOU
AT THE TOP
OF OUR
SPECIAL
TOTEM POLE
Happy
Easter
NA8-8282
1974 Chinese year of
the tiger at Hennage
Lift off and wear it.
You'll find us ready to
pounce . . . on any
printing project you have
NA8-8282
HENNAGE CREATIVE PRINTERS
814 H ST., N.W., WASHINGTON, D.C. 20006
BUSY
BUSY
BUSY
*
BUT
NOT TOO
BUSY
TO
WORK
FOR YOU
* Lift off and wear it.
NA8-8282
HENNAGE CREATIVE PRINTERS
814 H ST., N.W., WASHINGTON, D.C. 20001
Lovers of fine printing-
our Customers . .
here is the heart we put
in every printed piece
we do for you.
Happy Valentine Day
*Lift off and wear it.
NA8-8282
HENNAGE CREATIVE PRINTERS
814 H ST., N.W., WASHINGTON, D.C. 20006

building, "Located Downtown To Be Near You" and then there is a headline, "The Complete Graphic Arts Center," with copy going into detail.

"Busy—Busy—Busy—" is on another envelope. Inside is a card with the same words and an embroidered bee pasted on with the words below it, "But Not Too Busy To Work For You." All of the cards have been printed in two colors. On the reverse side is a large picture of the Hennage building with copy describing "The Annual Report Center . . ."

On a green envelope appear the words, "Here's Something Green For Luck." On the card inside, the copy is repeated with these added words: "To Wear On St. Patrick's Day . . ." and then an embroidered four-leaf clover which can be lifted off and worn. The copy continues . . . "but luck is one thing you won't need when you do your printing with us." On the reverse side is a photograph of the 12 Bennys that Hennage has won. The headline states: "Washington's Award Winningest Printer . . .", and short copy follows.

A cartoon of a totem pole of bunnies is on the envelope enclosing another card. Inside, a pink embroidered bunny is pasted on the card, and this copy: "Quicker Than The Bunny* How Our Color Press Did Roll To Put You At The Top Of Our Special Totem Pole—Happy Easter." On the reverse side is a picture of the five-color perfector offset press and its master console. The headline reads, "Automation, It's Here . . . Five-Color Perfecto Offset Press." Copy describes the printing quality of the press.

The last envelope we have states, "Try It You'll Like It." On the inside card the copy is, "A new logo for our five-color press." An embroidered logo in five colors on a white background is pasted on the card. Then "Try It You'll Like It" is found below. The reverse side of the card is similar to the last card described above.

Preparing Pieces For Contests

One more thing we have to write about Hennage Creative Printers which may help other printers: Joe Hennage knows how to advertise and publicize his company and himself. And, say what you will, a company reflects the image of the top man. If he can and will publicize himself, he will benefit the company. You see this man's name and picture in almost every printing magazine, but more important, he is seen and known around his own city, Washington.

Personally, we don't like to see his company win another P.I.A. award. We believe that his continual winning must keep printers in that category from entering their pieces. Joe is the vice president of P.I.A. Public Relations, and that committee handles all the details of the two P.I.A. contests. We know that some people think the contests are rigged in favor of Joe. We can guarantee that they are not. I have been a judge three or four times. I play a little game when there is a Hennage campaign or piece being considered as a winner. There are always three judges. I purposely keep my decision till last so that in no way will I influence the other two judges. They almost always pick the Hennage piece if it is one of the top three high scorers. Only then do I give them my opinion, which invariably agrees with theirs. Of course, all of the Hennage entries don't win but they have had one or more winners consistently.

Every Hennage entry is prepared according to the rules. The pieces are carefully mounted. The purpose is spelled out in simple language. Highlights of each piece or campaign are mentioned. Results are definitely stated. The judges don't have to wonder what happened. They are told. If every entry were as well prepared the judges' work would be easy. Many possible prize winners have been passed over because the judges aren't told the purpose, or else the results or continuity has not been spelled out. Each campaign is rated from 0 to 10 on the idea, copy, design and physical appearance, quality of reproduction, plan and continuity, results or effectiveness. If the judges don't know how the pieces were used or what the results were, they can only score those subjects zero. A few zeros will quickly reduce the score of a well conceived campaign.

William C. Hanlon signed the entry form for the 1974 Hennage Creative Printers' campaign entry, so we will assume that he should get the credit for preparing the entry and explaining the details. They now have 56 employees at Hennage. Their campaign entry was contained in a 24-page plastic bound, heavy cover book.

The cover displayed the company name and a design from one of their booklets. Prest-type was used on the cover. Each piece of their advertising was firmly glued down and type set reversed copy used to explain the piece. Six times in the book, this statement was made: "Sales were up 15.7% as the result of this campaign."

The purpose of their campaign was simple: "To demonstrate to our customers and prospective customers our continued interest in them. We believe that 'example is better than precept' and that our self-advertising material is proof-positive that we are indeed creative printers."

Throughout the book such statements as these were used: "We have never before received as many compliments from customers as this booklet has elicited. Even more important, saleswise, it is opening doors that heretofore have been closed to our sales staff. We are selling more and more jobs to newly developed customers and we know that this booklet is bringing them to our door."

Beside a Hennage booklet about annual reports was this statement, "We designed and printed some 30 annual reports this year. Once again we proved that taking the time to plan and develop a different kind of self-advertising piece pays big dividends."

Hennage Creative Printers believes in showing samples of work they have done for other people. They attach a short note explaining the job. This is always an excellent form of advertising, especially if the piece was printed for a large company or organization. It shows the kind of quality customer you have.

Hennage also makes excellent use of the past awards they have received. They "merchandise" them at every opportunity. Each year they have a special luncheon to celebrate the winning of various awards. It is another form of their advertising. Along with full-color photographs of the occasion we found these words in the book: "Luncheon to honor those customers whose material printed by us won national recognition. This year's luncheon brought us $200,000 of repeat business." Mr. Hanlon left no doubt about the success of this promotion.

Somewhere in the book was this statement: "If you are going to do something, do it right or not at all." In preparing their PIA entries, Hennage Creative Printers has always practiced what they preach. Year after year their entries are well prepared and informative. Their entries recall the ones prepared by Herbick and Held of Pittsburgh when they were winning awards year after year. The H&H campaign books were always presented in such detail that nothing was left to the imagination.

Joe Hennage and his Hennage Creative Printers do their homework when it comes to advertising and publicity. Their efforts have paid off, so why not go out and do likewise?

Hennegan Company

Award Inserts

If you don't tell people you print, how will they know it? Likewise, if you win awards for your printing, who will know it if you don't tell them? So, when you go to the trouble and expense to submit your printing or advertising to these various award programs and win an award, then for goodness sakes, tell the world. Or, at least, tell prospects and customers.

The Hennegan Company, Cincinnati, Ohio, believes in merchandising its awards. In 1970, they won six. In 1971, there were seven. In 1972, there were 12. We have samples of three magazine inserts, customer mailings and salesmen's handouts. Each piece is printed on white Kromecote. Four colors have been used. They are all 8½" x 11" and well printed. The Hennegan trademark includes the words, "Showmanship In Printing." The three pieces illustrate exactly what they mean.

The 1970 awards insert consists of two pages. Page one is headlined, "Winner of Six 1970 P.I.A. Awards." There is a large trademark in the center of the page and the company name is at the bottom. On the reverse side of the sheet are illustrated the six pieces with short identifying copy below each reproduction. The copy at the bottom of the page is short but sells. Here it is:

"So we won six awards. Did we have to put together an ad about them?

"Well, excuse our lack of modesty, but we are proud and gratified about them for two reasons. First, the awards come from our peers—The Printing Industry of America. Second (and the reason for this ad): The work illustrates a unique combination of talent and facilities rarely found in a single plant.

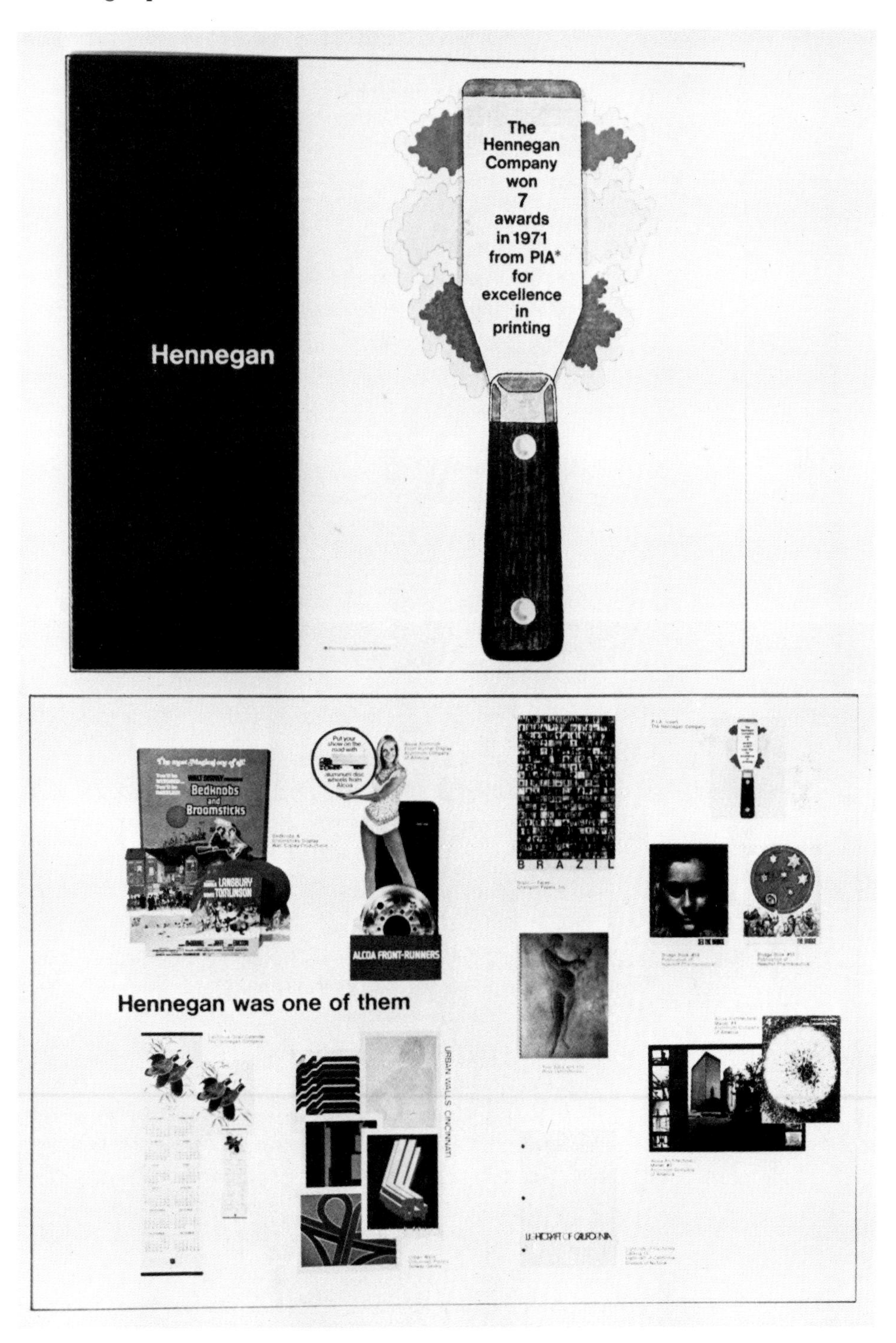

"The winners include art prints, displays, company publications and promotion brochures . . . Each has something special to relate—a portrayal of our maxim, 'Showmanship in Printing.'

"And, next time you want your printing to have a little more showmanship, try Hennegan. We're holding a place for you in next year's ad."

The Hennegan signature and trademark also appeared at the bottom of this page.

The second insert was also a single sheet. The first page showed a drawing of an ink knife. Underneath the blade are three stylized blobs of different colors of ink. On the blade these words are overprinted: "The Hennegan Company won 7 awards in 1971 from P.I.A. for excellence in printing."

On the reverse side of this sheet they have shown the seven prize-winning pieces which consisted of a nearly life-size, animated display, an art print, a brochure for architects, a cardboard castle and corporate publications. The copy was again excellent and asked for an order.

The third magazine insert was four pages with pages three and four being 7" x 11". The first page was divided by a solid black panel to the left and a white panel to the right. The word "Hennegan" is all that appears on the black background. The white panel contains six paragraphs of 10-pt. type. The Hennegan trademark is centered in the panel and printed in three colors. The copy refers to the 12 awards and the diversity of the work.

Inside, on pages two and three, they reproduced the pieces that won the awards. One piece was the insert described above. Another piece was the Hennegan 1972 calendar.

On page four, they have grouped all the framed certificates of awards and captioned the display, "Only six printers in the entire country won 12 or more P.I.A. awards in 1972."

Bill Charles, the Hennegan sales manager, says that they received many congratulatory notes about the inserts. He is sure they helped to sustain the company's image of quality printing. They make six to eight mailings a year and strongly believe in advertising.

Calendar

The Hennegan calendar has been published for many years. It is printed in two sizes and is often accompanied with a print of the artwork for framing. For the past few years they have used the paintings of a nature or wild animal artist, John Ruthven.

The large calendar is 12" x 46". The painting is 14" high and 11" wide. The balance of the calendar sheet is used for two rows of monthly calendars. They use good, readable type. A small space at the bottom is used for an attractive signature and trademark. The calendar is stapled to wooden hangers, top and bottom.

They also reproduce this same calendar in a 5" x 18" size, tinned top and bottom. The calendars are attractive and the executives at Hennegan believe strongly in their value as reminder advertising.

1973
1 JANUARY
FEBRUARY 2
3 MARCH
APRIL 4
5 MAY
JUNE 6
7 JULY
AUGUST 8
9 SEPTEMBER
OCTOBER 10
11 NOVEMBER
DECEMBER 12
The Hennegan Company
Lithographers
Color Printers

Herbick & Held Printing Company

One Grand Effort

We could fill many a page of this book with descriptions of the advertising of Herbick & Held Printing Co., Pittsburgh, Pa. However, we will describe only one of their efforts although they have won many, many P.I.A. printer's self-advertising awards. We will go away back in history for this one.

It was one grand effort that had lightning-like effect on the printing buyers of Pittsburgh. It was in the year of 1953. Bert Held, now deceased, was the president of Herbick & Held Printing Co. H&H, over the years, had done a large amount of "Shopping News" printing. The "Shopping News" was a large run on cheap paper, always a rush job, and not too fancy. It was distributed free by young boys, house to house.

Mr. Held had pulled H&H up by its boot straps in 1952 and 1953, and it was doing quality work—some annual reports and quite a large amount of advertising brochures and color printing. Although they had quit printing the "Shopping News," all the advertisers and buyers of printing thought of them as just "Shopping News" printers, not too high on quality.

Bert Held decided to change all that and he wanted to do it in one fell swoop. He called in Ketchum, MacLeod and Grove, a small agency in that day, and told them his problem. We have never heard the cost of the solution, but it had to be great and it was good.

Engraved invitations to a noon reception and luncheon were sent to the business leaders in the city and some in the state. They were sent to all the advertising fraternity and buyers of printing, and what a crowd they had! The mayor of Pittsburgh, the governor of the state, the presidents of U.S. Steel, Gulf Oil, Aluminum Corporation, Heinz, Mellon Bank—you name them—and we will wager they were there.

H&H took over the grand ballroom and Urban Room on the top floor of the William Penn Hotel and put on a reception like Pittsburgh had never seen before. There were bars everywhere. Every employee of H&H was acting as host, and what hosts they were! Every executive who amounted to anything in the industrial life of Pittsburgh was there. Flash bulbs were popping, and excitement was in the air. It was a most lavish, unusual affair. The decorations alone were something to behold. There were small musical groups spotted around the rooms. There were large tables of hors d'oeuvres, the luncheon was sumptuous, and everything was on a grand scale. Herbick & Held was acting like big time. They just had to be something special to put on such a show. Their image changed overnight. Bert Held's goal was accomplished in a few hours. They followed up this effort with many other fine pieces of advertising, but the grand reception really did the job.

That was 1953. How about today? If you have the money and the planning, it will still work.

I always felt that the Printers' Self-Advertising Awards instigated that party and started Herbick & Held to advertise. The first Printers' Awards banquet was held in St. Louis in October, 1952. Some time after that, Mr. Held called me on the phone at Miller Printing Machinery Co. I was their director of marketing. Miller sponsored the awards, handled the details and furnished the cash prizes and Bennys. He suggested that I go to see his new office and take one of the Benjamin Franklin statuettes with me.

I went to the H&H plant and they had just about finished a new office for Bert. He was proud of it. He told me he needed some graphic arts pictures or something for decoration. He thought the Benjamin Franklin statuette would look good on an end table he had. He asked me what it cost. I told him and he told me to leave it.

I swallowed hard, for Bert Held was a good customer of Miller's. I told him I couldn't leave it. I hadn't discussed such a situation with Dick Tullis, president of Miller, but I felt that I was right. I told Bert that he could get one only by winning first prize in our Self-Advertising Awards contest. At the time I knew there weren't any statuettes of Franklin available anywhere except in one man's collection in Philadelphia. I had searched high and low for something we could copy and finally found one cast in bronze in Philadelphia. The original awards were lost wax bronze copies of that one in Philadelphia. Bert didn't like my answer. In an exasperated tone, he told me to take the statuette and he would get one somehow.

I went back to my office and within five minutes Mr. Tullis asked me what I had said to Mr. Held. Bert had phoned him. I explained the situation and Dick thought that was a bit rough but he also wanted the statuettes to mean something. There were only three of them in prize-winners' hands at the time. He called Bert and told him he would have to win one.

Three or four months after that, Herbick & Held had its big party. They entered an elaborate entry in the 1953 contest with on-the-scene photographs, newspaper and magazine clippings, letters from those who attended, and samples of follow-up advertising. The H&H entry won first prize in the second year's contest and Bert Held got his Benny. They won Bennys in '53, '56, '57, '61, '63 and '67.

Heritage Press

Institutional

Some printers use advertising as some industrial companies do—purely for its institutional or image building values. Heritage Press, Dallas, Texas, does just that. In the 1970 P.I.A. Awards, Heritage took the first award for campaigns of printers with 20 to 49 employees. Heritage said that although its campaign was purely institutional, they showed significant increases in volume after it was mailed. They even acquired one new account in a new market that came as a direct result of the program.

Heritage caters specifically to advertising people. It is not only fine printing oriented but also advertising oriented. As such, they have always been an advocate of printers' self-advertising.

The campaign that won the award consisted of ten elaborate four-page pieces. Each piece featured illustrated selections from great works of literature. Along with the first mailing, they sent a sturdy Kromecote-covered slip case in which the entire series could be accumulated.

The folders measured 10¾"x14" when scored and folded. Pages one and four were plain finish, solid-colored cover stocks. Pages two and three, inside, were cast coated sheets pasted to the cover stock.

On page one of each of the ten folders was pasted a 2½"x2¾" label. This label was in the center of the sheet. At the top of the label was printed, "Heritage In Print" in 16-pt. type. The balance of the label was taken with a large reverse figure (1 to 10) on a two-color background. On page four, in the top left-hand corner, appeared the company name, address and telephone number. There was no selling copy nor indication that Heritage Press sold printing.

Page two was used to give a short biographic sketch of a famous writer and then an excerpt of his work. The series covered Dylan Thomas, Cervantes, Mark Twain, Herman Melville, John Milton, Chaucer, Virgil, Jonathan Swift, Shakespeare and William Faulkner. Page three was used to reproduce paintings and drawings illustrating the subject matter. All the illustrations were modern impressionistic forms of art.

The executives at Heritage Press felt that the mailings developed a stronger attitude toward the company among its existing clients . . . made them feel more confident that they were dealing with the right printer.

Holden Industries

Corporate Facilities Brochure

"Our selling force needed an all-new corporate facilities brochure reflecting the many changes, the growth and expansion of the company, for use in their daily selling efforts," said James Morrison, Director of Advertising and Public Relations of Holden Industries, Minneapolis, Minn. They now have 48 salesmen, so we can readily see why they would need such a brochure. It will provide each salesman with the same story. They won't be able to forget to mention any of their services because they are all mentioned in the brochure.

Holden grew from a two-employee company with sales of $26,000 to sales of $19 million and 700 employees under the direction of Harold L. Holden. The 28-page and cover booklet was handled in house and it is a fine job. They have a slogan—"complete graphic arts service"—and the booklet proves it.

Holden Industries consists of seven Minneapolis companies and a corporate headquarters: Holden Printing Co., creative and commercial printing; Jensen Printing Co., web fed printing; Holden Business Forms Co., snap-a-part and data processing forms; Proma Co., promotions, mailing, assembling; Fastype, Inc., magnetic tape composition; Graphic Arts Computer Service, specialized computer applications and Washington Square Corp., real estate.

The Holden book is 9"x11". The cover stock is a heavy-weight, light gray linen-like finish. It is printed in four solid colors and black. The cover is hot, blind embossed with the words, "Holden Industries." There are six small photographs of graphic arts equipment. The brochure was enclosed in gray envelope which was printed in two solid colors and black. The envelope stock matched the cover in color and finish.

There are five full-page halftone or line reproductions of printing equipment inside. These reproductions also illustrate various photographic techniques. There are pictures of men and women at work in the various plants. All of the 45 black-and-white photographs are interesting and well printed. There is not one gray or washed out reproduction.

There is a large amount of copy in the book but it is interesting reading. The Holden philosophy appears twice in the book and it is a good one, so we will reprint it here: "To remember always that our company's existence depends on our ability to serve our customers. To insure growth for the company and opportunities for all employees. To let the Golden Rule guide us in our association with customers, suppliers and co-workers. To perpetuate the free enterprise system. To support our industry, church and community." No long, involved words there. It is quite plain what they mean. When a corporation refers to the Golden Rule, church and community, a person is inclined to believe that they will get a square deal from such an organization. We believe that is a fine philosophy and we think they have a fine brochure.

Since the company's inception in 1940, Holden has always believed in advertising its services. They say their biggest problem is finding "open time" in lithoprep and in the pressroom (between commercial jobs) to get their own promotional material produced. Mr. Morrison says, "Not entirely an unpleasant situation." We will agree but it can be unpleasant if you don't do any advertising. As we have said at least three times in this book—you have to put your own advertising in the production schedule like a customer's job or you won't get it done.

Howarth & Smith Limited

50th Anniversary Brochure

Howarth & Smith Limited, Toronto, Canada, was founded in 1921, by Bruce G. Howarth and Charlie Smith. It is a type house but they do so many other things involving type that they prefer to be known as graphic arts craftsmen. Their 32-page and cover booklet observing their 50th anniversary is an interesting one. Both their history and their present operation are covered in an unusual manner.

The cover is printed in four colors and varnished. Superimposed over a head and shoulders picture of Mr. Howarth is a photograph of some of the keys, push buttons and flashing lights of a computer. An excellent illustration of the old and the new. Bruce Howarth retired in June, 1971, at a young 76. There is four-color process printing on every other page of the 9½" x 12" brochure. It is bound on the 9½" side. The photographs cover almost every operation and many of the offices in the new 40,000-square-foot plant.

They employ 140 people and five are salesmen. Their sales are approximately $2.5 million. After publishing this booklet, sales showed a 17% increase after some low growth years. Of course, the new building and new equipment contributed something to that growth. However, the good comments from customers and prospects indicated that the booklet was a good communication tool.

The interesting copy treatment was one that could be used by other printers. The main text, telling about present operations and plans for the future, was set in 18-point Baskerville. Along the side of each page was a column approximately 12 picas wide set in 9-point Vega Medium.

These columns contained Mr. Howarth's story, in his own words, recounting some of the incidents and highlights of his career. It was a warm, personal and very interesting history of the company. It was an excellent way to tell Mr. Howarth's story and not get it confused with the modern everyday happenings in the new plant. It provided entertainment along with good hard sell copy. We would recommend such treatment in other anniversary brochures.

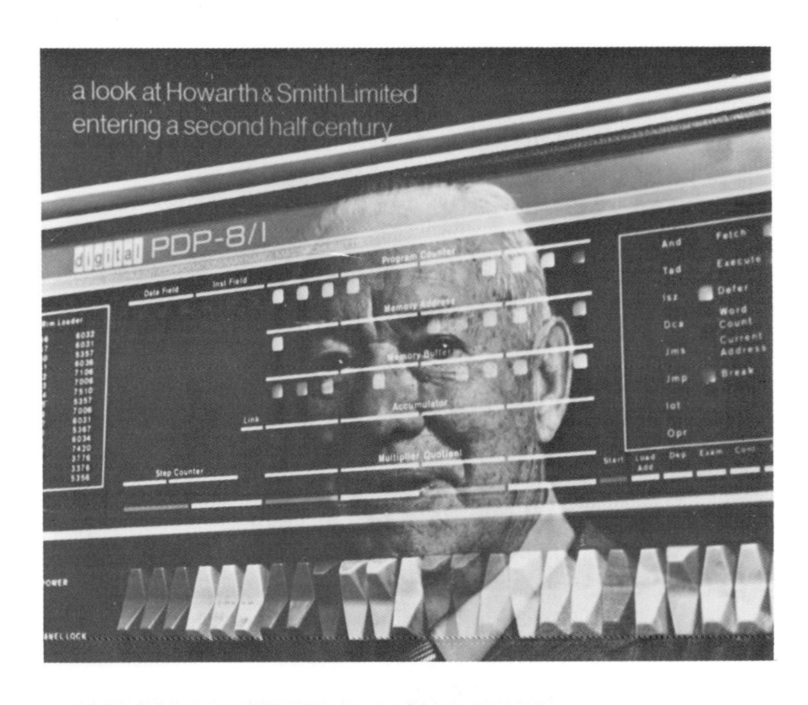

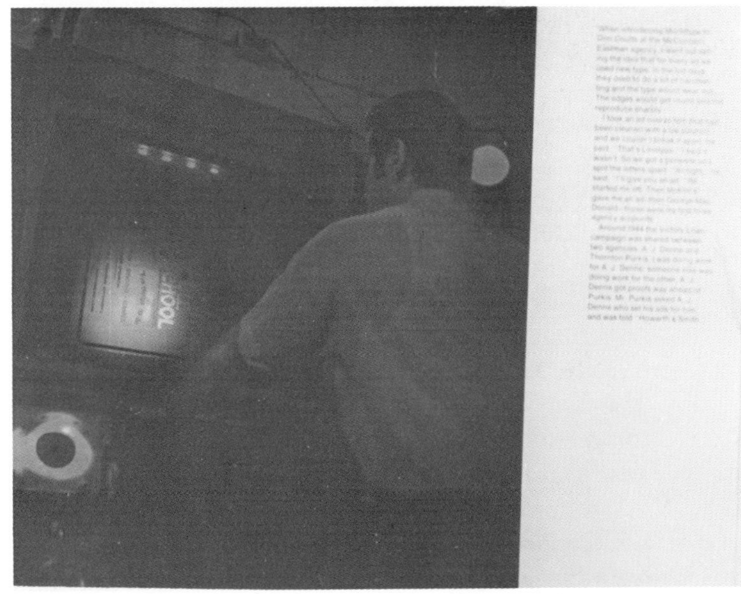

Judd & Detweiler, Inc.

A Survey

As we have said, there are many ways to advertise and here is a unique one. Judd & Detweiler, Inc., Washington, D.C., specializes in publication printing. They have published a small booklet, 4½" x 6", entitled, "As Others See Us." It is bound on the 4½" side and contains 16 pages and cover. The laid cover is a rust color. The inside pages are ivory and the type is quite readable. The copy and concept are what is important in this booklet.

On the first page they discuss change, and then their most important asset—their reputation. The last sentence states, "Therefore, with the ever accelerating tangle of change, management wanted to know if others saw us as we saw ourselves."

Copy on the next two pages tells about the hiring of Strategic Futures, Inc., a New York research organization, to conduct a series of personal interviews to discover if (1) J & D were in step with what printing buyers want today. (2) What kind of relationships do their sales and production people have with customers and prospects? (3) What are the strengths and weaknesses that others see at J & D and are they keeping pace with competitors?

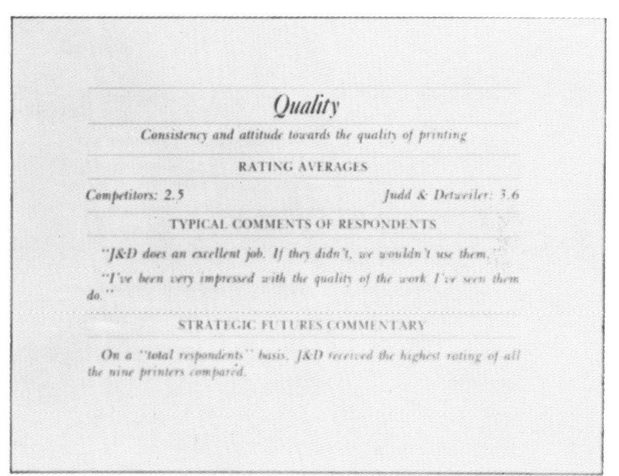

Quality

Consistency and attitude towards the quality of printing

RATING AVERAGES

Competitors: 2.5 *Judd & Detweiler: 3.6*

TYPICAL COMMENTS OF RESPONDENTS

"J&D does an excellent job. If they didn't, we wouldn't use them."

"I've been very impressed with the quality of the work I've seen them do."

STRATEGIC FUTURES COMMENTARY

On a "total respondents" basis, J&D received the highest rating of all the nine printers compared.

The respondents to this survey were asked to establish a relative ranking of twelve factors involved in the selection of a printer and the continued assignment of work to him. Within each factor, J & D was rated quantitatively against nine competitors on a scale of 1.0 (poor), 2.0 (fair or average), 3.0 (good) and 4.0 (excellent).

The next 12 pages were used to report the findings. Each page had the same layout of information. The subjects were separated with fine line rules. The heading was explained in one line below. Then came

Rating Averages of Competitors and J & D. The one or two "Typical Comments Of Respondents" were shown. Then a "Strategic Futures Commentary."

The 12 subjects were:

Quality—Consistency and attitude towards the quality of printing.
Delivery Speed—Speed with which the delivery is made.
Delivery Dependability—Overall dependability of the delivery.
Personnel—Relationships and dealings with the in-house personnel.
Expertise—Expertise and leadership in technological progress.
Orientation—Orientation of the printer to his customer.
Price—Price structure relative to the competitive market.
Location—Efficiency and convenience of plant location.
Growth—Stability and potential of future growth.
Management—Caliber and attitude of the top management.
Sales—Caliber and attitude of the sales representation.
Aggressiveness—Aggressiveness shown by the printer.

Judd & Detweiler reported the good with the bad and thereby made the report quite believable. Of the nine competitors, they received the highest rating in Quality, Delivery Speed, Delivery Dependability, Orientation and Personnel. Their rating on Price was not good but only one printer was rated excellent; four rated good and four fair. J & D published these quotes: "J & D is higher than the others I'm familiar with." "J & D is premium-priced, although less significantly than they were in the past . . ." It takes courage to print statements like that but it proves to readers that this is an honest report. The comments were interesting and entirely a different advertising approach.

The last inside page was a summary and a statement that achieving top ranking in five factors was no accident. They thanked their customers for their good will and cooperation. They suggested to prospects that if they wanted some of these benefits, a call to the nearest office would bring a prompt response.

We imagine this survey was very helpful to J & D. It showed that there were a few spots where they could improve. We thought it was an excellent and bold form of advertising that surely would pay off.

John H. Harland Company

Annual Report

"It is appropriate that a unique annual report be used to tell about a unique company." That is a sentence in the John H. Harland Company Annual Report for 1972. It was a most unique annual report. It appeared to be a gold record with one side cut flat 3" in order to wire stitch the 20 heavy enamel pages on the inside. Over the gold stock cover was pasted a clear plastic record which could be peeled off and played. The bright red label indicated it was a Harland record. The title was, "Another Record Year (plus selections from our 50 Golden years)." Around part of the label's circumference was a line reading, "John H. Harland Company Annual Report For 1972." The inside cover copy suggested that the record be played in order to hear about the eventful years from 1923 to 1972.

The record was well done by someone with a professional announcer's voice. The background music was nostalgic. There were excerpts from President Roosevelt's speeches, radio announcements of the Pearl Harbor attack and the armistice. The announcer told of the meager beginning of the company with one second-hand litho press in 1923, the depression years when Harland was commissioned by the Atlanta Clearing House Banks to print three million one-dollar certificates to be used as script in case of a run on the banks. The script was never used but this helped

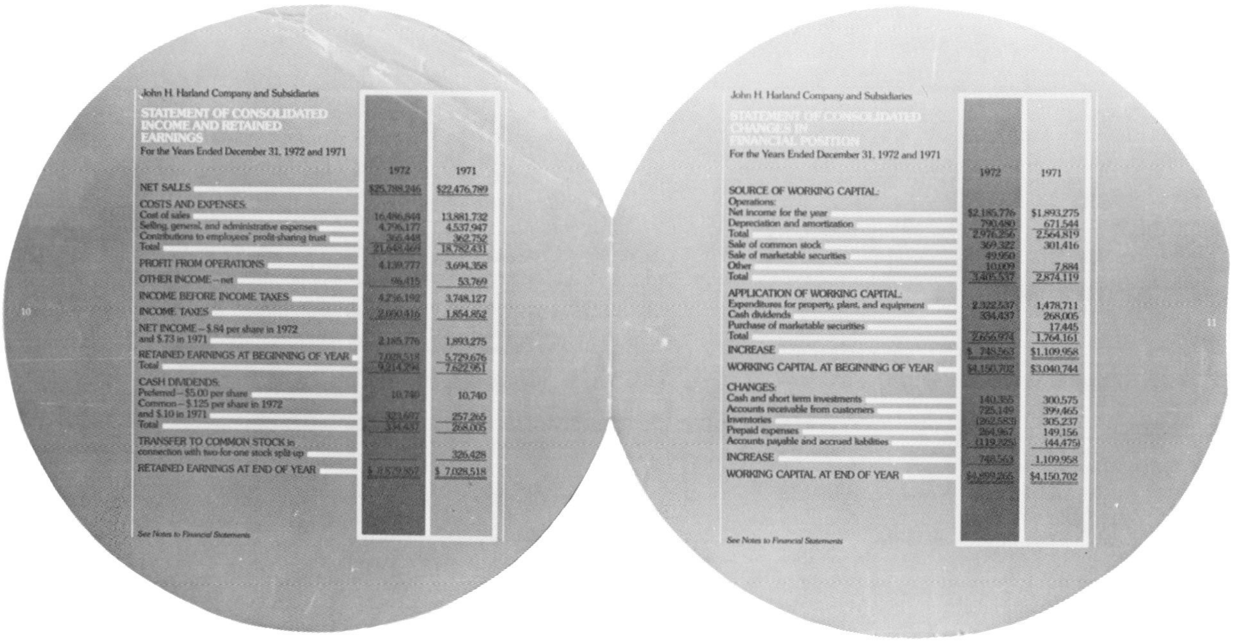

John H. Harland Company and Subsidiaries

STATEMENT OF CONSOLIDATED INCOME AND RETAINED EARNINGS

For the Years Ended December 31, 1972 and 1971

	1972	1971
NET SALES	$25,788,246	$22,476,789
COSTS AND EXPENSES:		
Cost of sales	16,486,844	13,881,732
Selling, general, and administrative expenses	4,796,177	4,537,947
Contributions to employees' profit-sharing trust	365,448	362,752
Total	21,648,469	18,782,431
PROFIT FROM OPERATIONS	4,139,777	3,694,358
OTHER INCOME—net	96,415	53,769
INCOME BEFORE INCOME TAXES	4,236,192	3,748,127
INCOME TAXES	2,050,416	1,854,852
NET INCOME—$.84 per share in 1972 and $.73 in 1971	2,185,776	1,893,275
RETAINED EARNINGS AT BEGINNING OF YEAR	7,028,518	5,729,676
Total	9,214,294	7,622,951
CASH DIVIDENDS:		
Preferred—$5.00 per share	10,740	10,740
Common—$.125 per share in 1972 and $.10 in 1971	323,697	257,265
Total	334,437	268,005
TRANSFER TO COMMON STOCK in connection with two-for-one stock split-up		326,428
RETAINED EARNINGS AT END OF YEAR	$ 8,879,857	$ 7,028,518

See Notes to Financial Statements

John H. Harland Company and Subsidiaries

STATEMENT OF CONSOLIDATED CHANGES IN FINANCIAL POSITION

For the Years Ended December 31, 1972 and 1971

	1972	1971
SOURCE OF WORKING CAPITAL:		
Operations:		
Net income for the year	$2,185,776	$1,893,275
Depreciation and amortization	790,480	671,544
Total	2,976,256	2,564,819
Sale of common stock	369,322	301,416
Sale of marketable securities	49,950	
Other	10,009	7,884
Total	3,405,537	2,874,119
APPLICATION OF WORKING CAPITAL:		
Expenditures for property, plant, and equipment	2,322,537	1,478,711
Cash dividends	334,437	268,005
Purchase of marketable securities		17,445
Total	2,656,974	1,764,161
INCREASE	$ 748,563	$1,109,958
WORKING CAPITAL AT BEGINNING OF YEAR	$4,150,702	$3,040,744
CHANGES:		
Cash and short term investments	140,355	300,575
Accounts receivable from customers	725,149	399,465
Inventories	(262,583)	305,237
Prepaid expenses	264,967	149,156
Accounts payable and accrued liabilities	(119,325)	(44,475)
INCREASE	748,563	1,109,958
WORKING CAPITAL AT END OF YEAR	$4,899,265	$4,150,702

See Notes to Financial Statements

Harland's profit picture (They made only 32 cents profit in 1932) and was the beginning of a close and continuing relationship of service to banks. Harland helped with the introduction of MICR printing in the fifties. They now have a network of 18 company-owned plants producing bank checks, forms and other business stationery.

The unusual report was designed and all creative work was handled by Harland employees. However, it was printed by Huggins, McArthur, Longino & Porter, Inc., because the job would have interfered with Harland's own production for its regular customers. That is one way to get your advertising done. If you aren't able to put it into your own production then let another printer print it and get it out.

There are four pages taken with old nostalgic prints: one of Rudolph Valentino; another a political sign, "Keep Cool-idge"; a reproduction of a 1923 gold piece and a "Drink Moxie 100%" sign. There is also a page with a full-color picture of Mr. William Robinson, president, and John H. Harland, chairman of the board. The other pages are used for the financial report, the Harland Growth Philosophy and pictures of the business and personal check line with the scenic backgrounds.

Besides Harland's own advertising, they provide some advertising services to their bank customers. The report was received extremely well by the financial community and just about everyone else who saw it, reports William Mills, Jr., the director of marketing. It won two or three awards for design and was placed in many annual report libraries for reference.

Knickerbocker Press, Inc.

36-Month Campaign

Knickerbocker Press, Inc., Grand Rapids, Michigan, mailed one piece of four-color printing each month to its 450 prospects and customers. We have 36 of the sheets in a plastic bound book that would make an excellent selling tool for their two salesmen. Knickerbocker has 16 employees and their annual sales are around $750,000.

The single 100-lb. offset enamel sheets were 8½" x 11". Each sheet was laid out to look like a magazine advertisement. The copy and illustration were a complete message on each sheet, yet there was a built-in continuity in general tone and selling message. Each sheet was mailed flat in a catalog envelope. They placed a sheet of spider-web parchment over the sheet which added to its value. The copy, layout and design were done in-house.

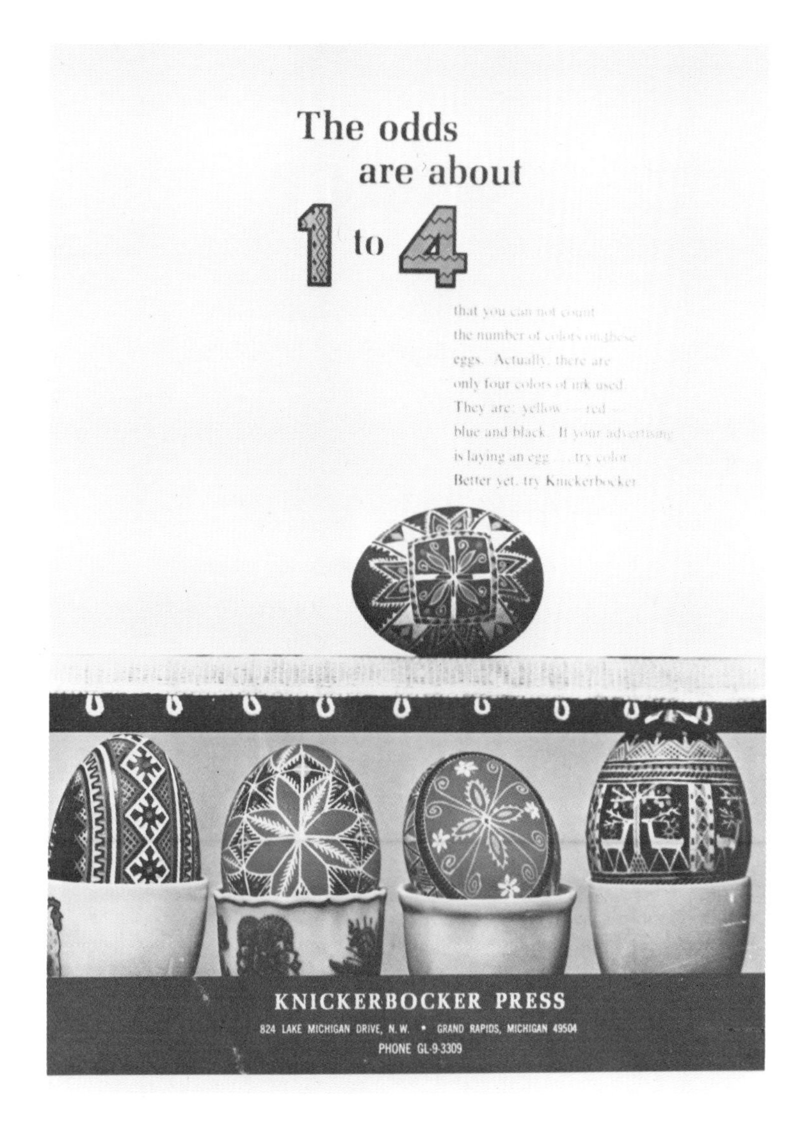

The excellent photographic subjects ran from children's toys, to old southern mansions, to a glass of beer, to winter scenes, to jewelry, to butterflies. The sheet with the beautiful butterfly contained this short copy and a large amount of white space: "So You Don't Sell Butterflies." "We doubt if you even want to buy butterflies. Most people don't. But just about everyone appreciates good color printing and is aware of what it can do for a product. The attention-getting power of color was not invented by man . . . it was Nature's idea. Our job is simply to make the most of it."

A large head of a white cat lapping up some milk from a white saucer is one of the illustrations and here's the copy: "Closer than a cat's whisker . . . That's the kind of close register it takes to print fine detail in full color. That's what we do . . . best."

We won't go on describing the 36 sheets but we want to give you a rough idea of the subject matter and short copy which make these sheets so interesting. They surely sell Knickerbocker's ability to print industrial and consumer advertising.

This will be the last one. They show four highly decorated Easter eggs in egg cups and a cut-out halftone of one. The copy and headline reads, "The odds are about 1 to 4 that you can not count the number of colors on these eggs. Actually, there are only four colors of ink used. They are: yellow—red—blue and black. If your advertising is laying an egg . . . try color. Better yet, try Knickerbocker."

Let us pharaphrase that last thought: If your printing business is laying an egg . . . try advertising like Knickerbocker has.

Kohler & Sons

Christmas Greeting

Kohler & Sons, St. Louis, Mo., won an award of achievement in the 1974 P.I.A. Printers' Self-Advertising contest for a very elaborate ten-page Christmas greeting that we can't possibly describe. You would have to see it to believe it. It is a 5¾" x 8½" book that had to be planned and laid out by a graduate engineer. No ordinary printing craftsman devised this one. It is a die-cut, scored, folded marvel. They give credit to Maris Cirulis for concept and creative directors.

It is "The Story of the Christmas Rose," an adaptation from traditional Scandinavian folklore by Michael Powers. The illustrations were drawn by Jeannette Muller, Patricia Watkins and Leslie Wolf. No credit was given to the person who made the keys for the printing and binding. He or she had to be a genius.

There are four "scenes" in the book. The "scenes" could be likened to stage scenery. Each scene might remind one of looking through a peep hole in an old world Easter egg and seeing the scene in three or four depths. The story is set in 8-point type. The measure is very wide—45 picas. It runs at the bottom of each "scene" and is 9 picas deep.

The "scenes" are printed on three sheets of heavy lithograph stock. All sheets are 8½" wide and they range in length from 34" to 36" to 40". The 34" sheet makes the outside plane of each "scene" and it is scored and accordion-folded eight times. The 36" sheet has been folded 7 times, as has the 40" sheet. The three sheets have been printed in four process colors one side. Two of the sheets have been intricately die cut. The longest sheet acts as a back drop.

All of these sheets are pasted at the 8½" edge to a light gray cover. The cover shows the title and a large rose sprinkled with white snowflakes. It is printed in four colors.

This Christmas greeting is the most elaborate we have seen. If Kohler & Sons can produce such a masterpiece, they have surely proved that they can handle just about any type of printing that man can devise. It is a very costly piece and had to be a labor of love.

Lasky Company

A Large Company's Campaigns

If you aren't convinced that advertising pays off, we wish you could have an opportunity to talk to Sherwood A. Barnhard, president of Lasky Company, of Millburn, New Jersey. You would come away with no more doubt in your mind that good advertising works. The tone of his voice, the enthusiasm he has for Lasky advertising would immediately convince you. He says their advertising is most successful. They have a large budget for advertising because they have found that advertising helps to produce business. Mr. Barnhard tells us that they plan and have their artwork ready at least six months ahead of the actual campaign. That alone indicates that Lasky advertising is important. It isn't knocked out at the last minute. It is planned and scheduled. Of course, all anyone has to do is look at one of the campaigns and he will see quickly that it is a professional job. They win many awards for their advertising but the most important thing is what Mr. Barnhard says, "It is effective; it pays off in new business from new and old customers."

The Lasky Company employs approximately 250 persons. They have been in business for 54 years. They have a totally self-contained creative department to handle their own advertising as well as layout and design work for customers. They have their own four-color process separation department and 15 other fully staffed departments. They offer offset and letterpress printing. They have a typesetting department as well as camera, platemaking and a bindery. Their advertising mailings are sent to approximately 14,000 names which are on Addressograph plates. The pieces are mailed first class to the customer list and third class to prospects. They believe that the direct mail campaigns have a public relations value in terms of creating recognition of the Lasky name and help to pave the way for their sales force in making new business contacts.

The Senses Of Color

The first series of seven mailings that we discovered was called "The Senses of Color." They won a Silver Mailbox from the Direct Mail/Marketing Association, Inc., as well as many other awards. We noticed a copyright date of 1972.

The first piece was contained in a magenta envelope, 6¾" x 13⅛". The other pieces were mailed in 9½" x 12½" envelopes—each one using a bright, almost fluorescent color. No colors were repeated. The envelope corner cards showed the headline of the mailing piece and the return address but not the company name. The first piece was 9" x 9", 100-lb. offset enameled sheet, printed in four colors, liquid laminated and folded once into a triangle. This piece announced: "A Provocative New Series Will Be Coming Your Way Soon." The subject, "The Senses Of Color," was graphically illustrated with type and blocks of color. There were at least ten colors shown. The Lasky trademark is always printed in four colors. The copy was short, complimented the reader, explained what was coming and pointed to a benefit: "Created for people like you, who recognize the value of fine printing, the Senses of Color series will show how the imaginative use of color through lithography can stimulate, can spark, can amplify your printed promotional pieces to greater achievement."

The Taste Of Color

The second mailing was a 12" x 18" sheet folded twice to a 9" x 12" piece with the two narrow pages, 4½" x 12", opening as two doors to the focal point of the piece—an Indian fire eater. The full-color photograph showed the head and shoulders of the man with a belching yellow-red flame coming from his mouth. All of this on a bright blue background. The two folded doors or narrow pages were printed in a beautiful solid black with the headline in white block type, "The Taste Of Color." The five letters of the word "Color" were printed in five different colors.

The business reply cards, fastened by a sticker to each of the six folders, were all printed in four process colors. Each of the folders was liquid laminated, which greatly helped to intensify the brilliant colors that were used. As usual, the lamination also gave the jet blacks an added touch.

We do not have space to reprint the fine copy from each folder but we will give you a taste by using the copy from the second mailing. This appeared on the inside of one of the double-door folds. The return card was attached to the inside of the other door. Notice the use of the words and how they sell. Each piece made use of that line asking for the order, "May we have the pleasure of your Company?"

"The Taste Of Color. Puts spice in your printed message. Color can be so radiant and red-hot that it seems to dance down your throat. Color can pulsate so passionately, it envelops and engulfs you. Color can flame and flare, flicker and burn with intensity. Color can kindle the imagination. Color can spark the difference between dullness and drama.

"Everyone in the world hungers for color and more color in everything they do and see. Color is the spice that creates a hunger, a sharpened appetite, a keen and exciting delight. For what? For anything and everything you have to sell and tell.

"Color your printing and product with Lasky and you're on your way to the kind of sales that can only be called: colorful. With Lasky two-, three- and four-color printing, your promotional material is fired up to new impact, new impetus.

"Fantastically accurate color reproduction—the kind we at Lasky are known for—comes from superior standards. Our fifty-two years of knowledge and experience with the use of the right color, the right stock, the right color separations, the right press (all under one vast, brand-new roof), make our color printing a fine art, not just a skilled craft.

"Let your printed promotion experience the quality taste of color through Lasky. May we have the pleasure of your Company?"

The copy on each folder has the same sparkle and sell. On the reverse side of each folder there is always a listing of the 16 departments of Lasky. Many printers neglect to tell their customers and prospects about the many services they offer. These mailing pieces leave no question. Also, on each piece there was a short colophon describing how the piece was created, printed and finished, including stock specifications, size and make of press, as well as the impressions per hour.

The Sound Of Color

The third mailing was entitled, "The Sound Of Color," and featured the arm and hand of a man with a hammer smashing a multi-colored glass container on an anvil. It was a fine action, full-color photograph.

The Scent Of Color

The fourth mailing was, "The Scent Of Color." The folder was the same size as the others but the two front "doors" were a bright magenta and were die cut with a pleasant curve or scroll and opened from top to bottom rather than right and left. They opened to a large four process color photograph of a skunk sniffing some roses with a bouquet of flowers in the background. The copy was excellent and referred to color as the stimulator of senses, sensations, scents.

The Look Of Color

"The Look Of Color" was the fifth mailing and, again, the two folds were made but this time the "doors" were of uneven widths. The "doors" were printed in the bright blue and the headline was the largest of the series. As in each folder, the word "color" was printed in many colors. The photograph was of an Indian with a beautiful feathered headdress and a painted face wearing a modern tie and holding two ties in his hand as though he were selling them. The photography is excellent in every piece. We thought we caught an error in this photo, as the Indian had a shaven but black beard and a good bit of hair on his chest. We researched the subject and found that some Indians had hair on their faces as well as their chests. So, we couldn't even fault them on the photograph.

The Touch Of Color

A photograph of a young lady's head, taken, we presume, with the use of black light, gives an unusual effect in the sixth mailing entitled, "The Touch Of Color." The eye shadow, finger nails and lips have had a fluorescent color applied and they glow in the darkness. There is no doubt that this piece illustrates the creativity and ability of Lasky's people to design and create unusual eye-catching pieces.

The Depth Of Color

The seventh folder uses dark greens and blues on the cover as a background for the headline, "The Depth Of Color." The letter "O" in the word "Color" has been die cut so we can see through to page three where there is a goldfish looking out at us. When we open the folder we see a close-up of a table setting on page three and the goldfish is swimming inside a crystal goblet.

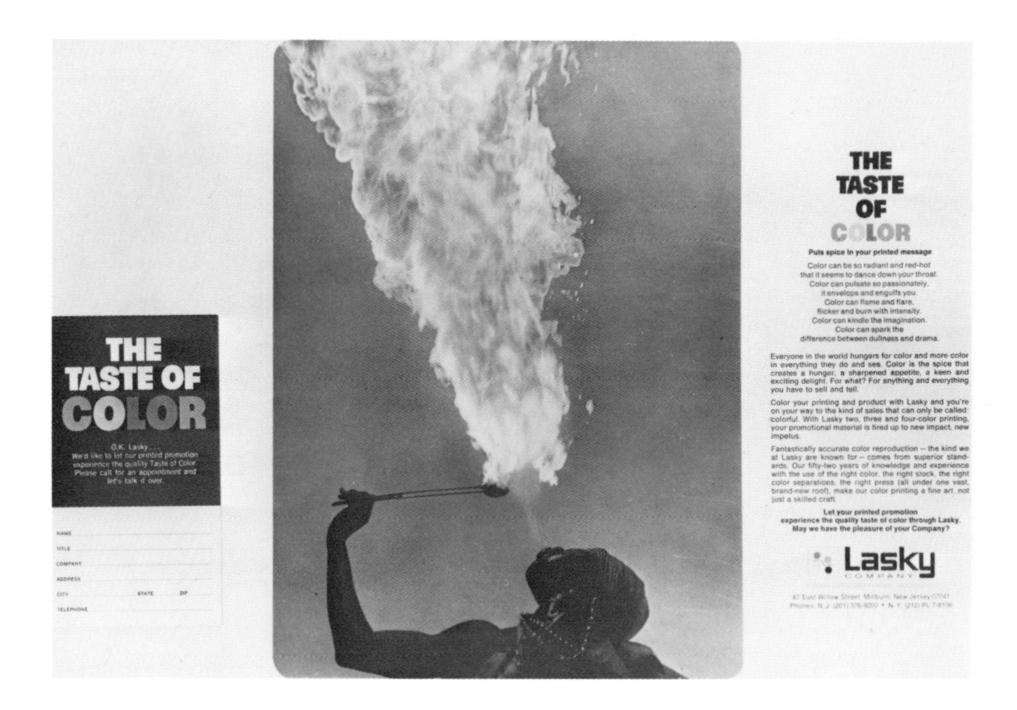
THE TASTE OF COLOR
O.K. Lasky . . .
We'd like to let our printed promotion
experience the quality Taste of Color.
Please call for an appointment and
let's talk it over.
NAME
TITLE
COMPANY
ADDRESS
CITY
STATE
ZIP
TELEPHONE
THE TASTE OF COLOR
Puts spice in your printed message
Color can be so radiant and red-hot
that it seems to dance down your throat.
Color can pulsate so passionately,
it envelops and engulfs you.
Color can flame and flare,
flicker and burn with intensity.
Color can kindle the imagination.
Color can spark the
difference between dullness and drama.
Everyone in the world hungers for color and more color in everything they do and see. Color is the spice that creates a hunger, a sharpened appetite, a keen and exciting delight. For what? For anything and everything you have to sell and tell.
Color your printing and product with Lasky and you're on your way to the kind of sales that can only be called: colorful. With Lasky two, three and four-color printing, your promotional material is fired up to new impact, new impetus.
Fantastically accurate color reproduction – the kind we at Lasky are known for – comes from superior standards. Our fifty-two years of knowledge and experience with the use of the right color, the right stock, the right color separations, the right press (all under one vast, brand-new roof), make our color printing a fine art, not just a skilled craft.
Let your printed promotion
experience the quality taste of color through Lasky.
May we have the pleasure of your Company?
Lasky
COMPANY

THE
SOUND OF COLOR
AMPLIFIES YOUR PRINTED MESSAGE
Color can crash its way to the senses, breaking the sound barrier with new images, new imagery.
Color can cut through silent resistance with its own special magic and mastery.
Color can sing out, loud and clear. Color can roar and resound and reverberate. Or
Color can purr. Color can whisper. Color can be the softest sound around.
A crystalline bell tone. A delicate tinkle. A soothing symphony of serene shadings.

THE SCENT OF COLOR
MAKES IT REAL

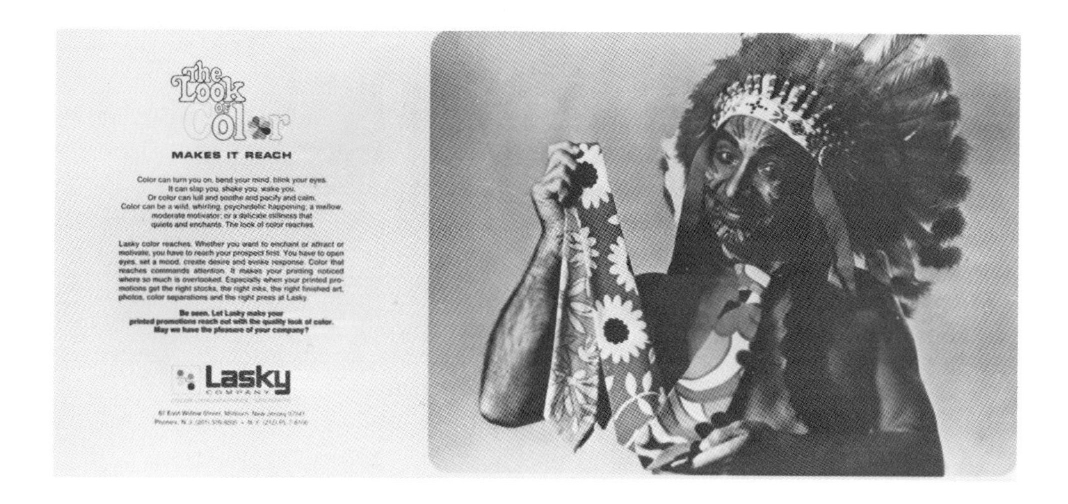

Strawberries

From that series of seven pieces they went to a series of four mailings in 1973. Lasky's theme was centered around strawberries.

The first mailing was a single sheet, 9" x 9", and announced "have we got Strawberries for you! Watch for them. They're coming soon. While you're busy watching . . . we'll be happy to take care of your printing needs. Call us. Then sit back and enjoy your strawberries." Notice—they ask for an order even in this announcement piece. This piece was mailed in a 9½" x 9½" white envelope. The other three pieces were mailed in 9" x 9" white envelopes and the pieces measured 8½" x 8¼". The corner cards on the envelopes were printed with red ink and showed the subject of the piece but not the Lasky name, although the address was used. The first piece was printed in four process colors. The background was black and the colors really jumped at you. The piece was liquid laminated.

The second piece was headed, "there are strawberry cones and there are strawberry cones." It was printed on one side of an 8½" x 24" heavy sheet in four process colors and folded twice. The 14-inch illustration was an ice cream type cone filled with beautiful large strawberries. The copy was short and stated, "This is ours. Homemade from start to finish right in our own plant. If you'd like, we can make one for you. We start by making our own luscious color separations. Then we add some zesty 4-color presswork and sprinkle it with real old-fashioned customer service. And you've got a strawberry cone that's good enough to eat. If that sounds good to you, call us. We deliver." A four-color process 4" x 5" business reply card was enclosed.

The third piece was headed, "have you ever seen a . . . Strawberry Submarine." Inside was a photograph of a 12-inch strawberry submarine sandwich and it really looked good enough to eat, although it included lettuce and Swiss cheese. Again, short copy was used to indicate that they could do the whole "mouth watering quality" job right in their plant. Another four-color process business reply card was enclosed. Each reply card in this series had the same design but colors were changed.

The fourth piece headline on the first page of the fold was, "who ordered the Strawberries and Spaghetti." The inside two pages showed a beautiful dish of spaghetti topped with what looked like about fifty strawberries. The copy was practically the same as on the other folders. It mentioned that the entire job was handled in their plant and "if you want a feast of color flavor, call us." The illustrations and subjects were so different that these pieces had to be mentioned. They obtained attention, the first requisite of any ad campaign, through the unusual headlines and photographic subjects.

Bed Sheet-Wire Sculpture

Let me quickly review the 1973-74 series. I have seen five pieces. I don't know if there were more. As in each one of these series, the first piece announced what was coming and asked the recipients to keep their eyes on the mail. The illustrations of this series were based on sculptures made of bedsheets, wire, color and a lot of props. Carol Anthony, of Boston, created the "unusual people" sculptures. They were surely unusual, yet they had a hidden character that anyone could immediately recognize as someone they had known or seen on the streets of New York. Again, Lasky found a group of illustrations that would immediately attract attention.

One illustration was Mary, a little girl on a bike who likes to visit the Lasky plant. Another was a pressman's mother. Then there were a pressman and a color-separator operator sitting in front of a hot dog diner eating their sandwiches made by "a wife who cares." Giuseppe, a printing customer and also a fruit and vegetable vendor, was another subject. All of these people, "sculptured" from wire sheets, old clothes and hats, shoes, and using antique carts, stools, chairs, seemed to be free standing and so unusual, but so natural.

These folders were mailed in the same bright-colored envelopes that Lasky used in the first mailings. The envelopes were 10½" x 13½" and contained a cardboard stiffener. Always attached to the 10" x 13" four-page folders was a business reply card printed in four colors. Again, the folders were liquid laminated. The fourth page always listed and described Lasky's many services under one roof and the colophon.

The copy on page two of each folder was tied in with the illustration and Lasky service. There was always the invitation to come in or buy Lasky printing. The type, hand lettering and general design were excellent. Color was used with good taste and the complete series illustrated what Lasky could do in their plant. These pieces were printers' advertising at its best. They worked for Lasky and this type of advertising will work for you.

Litho-Art, Inc.

Small But Effective

Litho-Art, Inc., Madison Heights, Michigan, produced a 4½"-square eight-page booklet to tell about an award they won. It is lithographed on white stock with plenty of white showing to make an effective, high-quality folder. There are 132 words in the booklet which includes credit lines and company signature, address and phone numbers. It is an excellent example of restraint—yet it sells.

The first page shows an inch black square with the words, "Black is Beautiful." On page two, they have two one-inch black squares, one overprinting the corner of the other. The copy is "So is Black on Black." On page three, the copy reads, "But can it Win a National Award?" There is a 1⅝" x 2¼" black halftone, which was taken from the award winning piece, we presume. On page four is another black halftone and the words, "It can." Page five, the copy reads, "And has" and there is a small halftone of the Award. Page six describes the piece and on page seven there is a P.S., with this copy beside a 1¼" x 1½" four-color process photograph: "We also print old fashioned sheet fed four-color process work. Our clients like doing business with an Award Winning firm—you will, too! We invite your inquiry." The last page shows some credits and the company name and address.

This booklet is proof that advertising doesn't have to be pretentious or to shout to be effective.

Litho Colorplate Inc.

Calendar

10" x 17" is an unusual size for a calendar but it works out well for Litho Colorplate Inc., with offices and plants in Minneapolis and Dallas. They produce four-color process litho positives and plates. The company was founded in 1949 by Charles P. Wesner and the calendar that we have was dedicated to him. Scenes taken on his travels around the world were used on the monthly calendar sheets. The four-color photographs were 7" x 10". The balance of the sheet was used for the calendar which was printed in brown ink. The figures stood five picas high so they were quite visible. It was a useful calendar. The sheets were bound in plastic and there was a punched hole for hanging.

The first sheet had a die-cut 2¾"-diameter circle. The flowers on the January sheet showed through. The words, "Litho Colorplate—complete facilities for color reproduction," were on the cover sheet. The first and last sheets were of a little heavier stock than the monthly sheets which were at least 100-pound dull-coated enamel. The last sheet showed the various departments at Litho Colorplate and rough sketches were used to illustrate them.

Jack Cole, president, has been pleased with the returns from the calendar. It has been an annual advertising effort and he believes they acquire about a 10% increase in new customers each year because of their advertising. He feels they have to advertise to maintain their image and that advertising is a necessary part of their overall sales function.

Litho-Krome Company

Keepsake Reproductions

If you have been in the printing industry for any length of time you have no doubt seen the beautiful full-color lithographic reproductions of photographs and art that have been printed by Litho-Krome Company, Columbus, Georgia. J. Tom Morgan is the president and he has been active in printing associations for years.

The reproductions have mostly been printed on large 20¾" x 23¾", heavy quality stock. They are quite suitable for framing for offices or homes. Many have spent $50 or $60 for frames alone. They have been used as a continuing advertising program since 1950. That year, Harris-Seybold Company commissioned Mr. Morgan to print a reproduction that would help sell lithography. Tom produced the now famous "Wine and Cheese" prints.

Salesmen usually hand carry a print to the prospect. They are rarely sent to a prospect, but when they are, air express is used for shipment.

Litho-Krome has consistently produced these keepsakes and believe that they are excellent forms of advertising. They demonstrate how well Litho-Krome can print. The reproductions have won prizes wherever they have been entered. This is a case of finding an excellent advertising medium and staying with it over the years.

Los Angeles Lithograph Company

Presentation Folder

We have a Los Angeles Lithograph Company, Redondo Beach, California, file folder or printing sample holder that every printer should have. It gives a printer something to use when sending quotations or carrying samples. They make fine presentation folders.

This one was cut from a 12" x 27½" ivory, linen-finish cover stock. It was scored and folded twice. Page three, or the center page, had a 3" x 8¾" flap on the bottom which, when turned up, provided a pocket for various pieces of literature. The pocket was die cut so a calling card could be inserted. The three inside pages had light rules running horizontally across the pages. The first 16 were narrowly spaced and printed in black. Then 15 rules were spaced about ½ pica wide and they were printed in a process blue. Then came 15 rules spaced one pica wide, printed in magenta. The following 15 rules were spaced in various widths and were printed in a process yellow.

The cover was printed in four process colors. The company name was at the top of the sheet. On the lower part of the sheet were four 3¼" circles representing the four color rollers, and an embossed rule separated the two top circles from the bottom two. The circles were solid red, yellow, blue and black. Page five was folded in. In the top left hand corner were these words, "Another quality job from the West's most versatile web press plant—Los Angeles Lithograph." Its trademark was also shown. Page six was blank.

Selling Print

One of their prize-winning pieces was an eight-page 8½" x 11", booklet showing a shadow of a bird in flight over an unusual textured background. The headline was, "you can turn the page, he won't get away." Pages two and three show twenty 1⅞" squares printed in four colors of various nostalgic items such as an old fashioned radio, a gum ball machine, a Calumet baking powder can, an NRA insignia and things of that nature. The copy, set in 8-pt., mentioned that there's a funny thing about printing—it lasts. The details don't vanish when it's time for the station break. Neither do the ideas. Memories are kept alive in print. Printing is a trap. It plants a thought and then clips its wings for discussion.

The center page spread was a four-color reproduction of a montage of nostalgic things and people in the news. Pages six and seven used thirteen 2½" blocks of modern photographic prints, using fish eye lenses and other methods of distortion. The copy was headed "revolutions are starting in print." It then goes on to mention that the electric age of communications has electrified Los Angeles Lithograph Co. It takes 80,000 square feet to do it along with a specially trained staff to manage it. They have added new equipment such as a big web press and they state, "We're going to be now where most printers will be tomorrow."

Page 8 showed a small halftone of the bird in flight and some more copy reviewing what was printed inside. The company signature, address, telephone numbers and trademark also appeared on this page.

The company has 200 employees and 12 salesmen. Their annual sales are approximately $10 million. They have opened a new plant and they hope to continue to increase their business, which has been increasing since 1969. They began operations in 1950.

Mailographic Company, Inc.

Monthly Memos

Mailographic Company, Inc., New York, had a mailing list consisting of names of prospects and customers in the New York metropolitan area as well as in many states across the country. It was a large enough list to preclude its calling on each one in person or by telephone on a regular basis.

Research also showed that its customers were not always aware of its three major areas of service—creative, printing and mailing. Therefore, the purpose of its campaign was three-fold: (1) To "call" on its customers and prospects on a regular monthly basis, (2) To remind its customers of its three services, (3) To stress the friendly, personal approach they take in producing assignments.

They decided on a standard, coordinated format using contemporary artwork, friendly copy, a useful calendar, a personalized business reply card, an occasional insert card listing some of its latest assignments from customers, plus important dates to remember. They used commemorative stamps on the envelopes.

They also wanted to practice what they preach: that a direct mail campaign based on specific objectives, prepared in advance and mailed on a regular basis, is effective in bringing in qualified leads resulting in increased sales.

Victor Ancona, vice president-marketing, tells us that through an informal survey they found that: (a) inactive customers were nudged into action, (b) customers asked about other services, (c) mailings were turned over to others within the customers' organizations, thus enlarging the reach, (d) several prospects became customers.

The campaign consisted of 13 pieces, one for each month in the year and one extra. They were all mailed in white envelopes printed in three colors showing the Mailographic trademark, address, an illustration or line of copy from the piece and a line, "Address Correction Requested."

We will try to review a few of these mailings. Each mailing consisted of a four-page folder, 3½" x 8½", printed in at least three colors. The first page always had a neat calendar at the bottom of the page. Also, there was a small design to coincide with the month or the copy on page three. At the top of page one were the words, "Mailographic Monthly Memo," each word printed in a different color. There was a lot of good clean white space showing. Page two was always taken with an overall bleed design that was very attractive, and the design was appropriate for the month. Page three contained the nicely set copy in 12-pt. type. Page four was a solid color with the type in reverse. The trademark, company name, address and phone number were on page four, along with two lines stating, "Specialists in the Creation, Printing and Mailing of Direct Advertising and Sales Promotion Material—Since 1920."

In each envelope was also a very well designed business reply card, 3½" x 8½", printed in three colors. Each card was different. Then they added a new twist. Another 3½" x 8½" card was printed for each mailing with the page two design of the folder on one side, and on the other side, a list of the recent assignments produced by Mailographic. This further made the customer aware of the type of work being done by the company.

The January folder was about resolutions and the fact that, it being leap year, Mailographic looked upon it as an added 24 hours in which to serve its customers.

February was about Love. At Mailographic, they translated love into personalized service to its customers every day of the year.

March was about wind, kite flying and quickened spirits.

April covered rain and the tender shoots of green awakening. At Mailographic they were exhilarated by the planting of ideas, etc.

Flora was the subject for May's mailer. June was weddings. July was about vacations, and so they went. Each one very cleverly tied in to the Mailographic service. November handled Thanksgiving very well. Then there was the extra mailing entitled, "Encore." Mailographic had won a P.I.A. Award of Achievement for campaigns, so they told their clients and prospective clients. They thought if they could produce award-winning printed communications for themselves, they could see no reason why they couldn't do the same for their clients.

This was an excellent campaign, well planned, nicely printed and very effective.

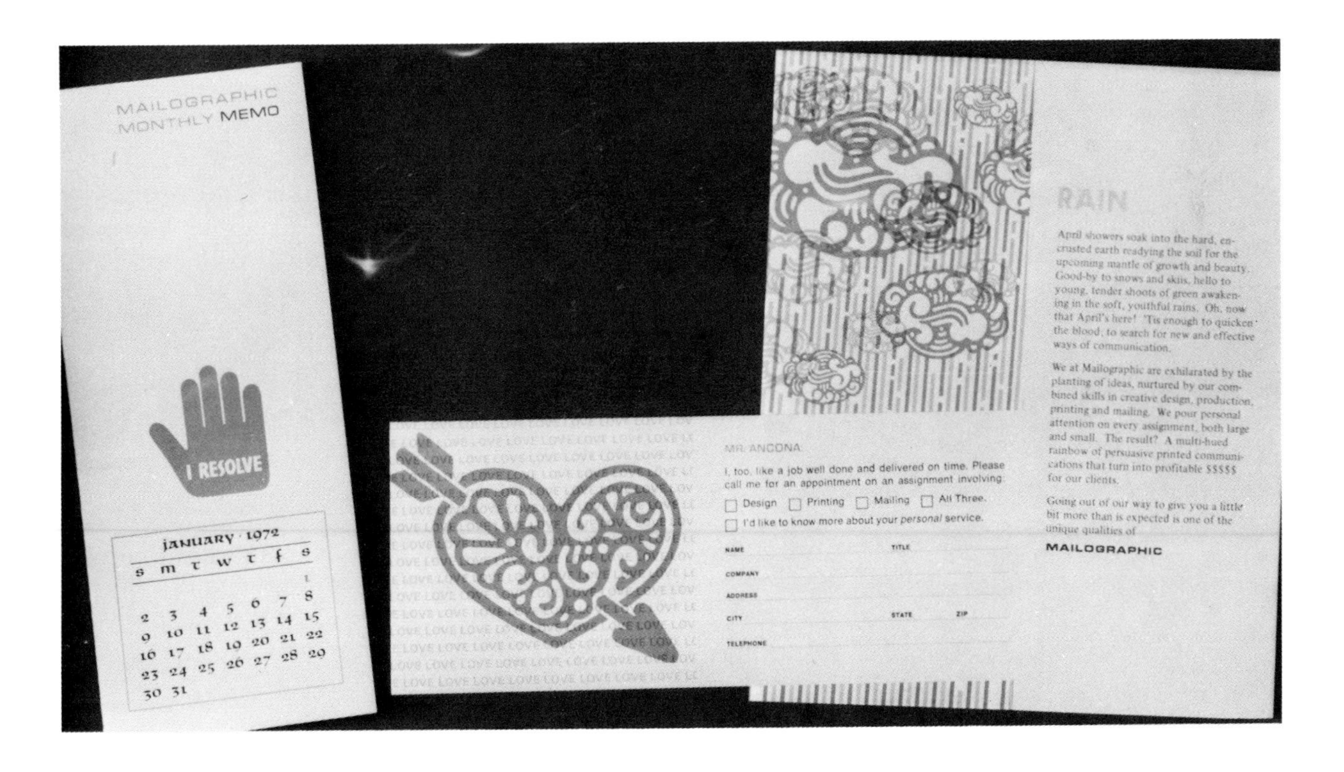

The Maple Press Company

The Printed Page

"The Printed Page" was a booklet published three times a year by The Maple Press Co., York, Pa. They also published a Christmas book keepsake. There was a series of 26 issues. Each issue was a distinct and separate idea on many different subjects. They were enclosed in specially printed envelopes for each issue. Thirty-six hundred were sent by first class mail to customers and prospects.

The booklet size was always 6" x 9". A few issues were bound on the 6" side but the majority was bound on the 9" side. We have four issues. One issue describes the furnace at Cornwall in Lebanon County, Pennsylvania, which was operated from 1742 to 1883. Another issue describes Fortress Louisbourg in Nova Scotia. The Time of Day is the subject of another issue and covers clocks and other means of telling time. The 25th issue was about John W. Keely, an inventive man who lived in Philadelphia in the late 19th century.

These booklets are mostly 16 pages and cover. They are well illustrated with photographs. The paper stocks are mostly text paper, although enamel has been used. The layout and typesetting are excellent; wide margins: short measures for easy reading and beautiful type faces.

The last page is employed to tell the Maple Press story. They specialize in book manufacture. They have produced over 10,000 book titles bearing the house imprints of the best known publishers in the country, including university presses. They have been in business for 75 years. They have 600 employees, and annual sales are approximately $30 million. They have 16 salesmen. Vice President, Howard King, believes these booklets were certainly a factor in cementing relationships with all of their accounts, particularly the large ones. Mr. King says, "I am a firm believer in self-advertising, year in and year out. It is necessary to continue to advertise whether you are busy or dull. Too many think of advertising only when they experience low periods."

The Master Eagle Family of Companies

Art Shows

The Master Eagle Family of Companies, New York, is an association of several organizations, each with separate and specialized capabilities with centralized management and centralized responsibilities. Engravings for letterpress are produced by Master Eagle Photoengraving; color separations for lithography by Craftsman Color Lithography; and metal and film typography by The Type Group. Mario Gambaccini is president.

They are all located in one building along with the Master Eagle Gallery. This group has been able to develop good publicity and recognition from its gallery. One of its exhibits that seems quite worthy of note is in conjunction with The School of Visual Arts, an institution of instruction in the fine, graphic, film and photographic arts.

They conduct one of these exhibits each year. It is a continuing example of industry and education cooperating to present the work of young American artists. One year's exhibition was titled, "The Bald Eagle: Survival or Extinction." It attracted extraordinary attention from the public and press.

The Master Eagle Family of Companies helps with the typesetting of the announcements to the students. They also print posters for the occasion. For the Eagle exhibit they were joined by The School of Visual Arts and, as an announcement, produced a poster featuring a large symbolic drawing of a bald eagle's head and an hour glass. The copy referred to the extinction and future state of the bald eagle being destroyed by pollution, pesticides, elimination of breeding areas and hunter.

The poster was well printed in four colors by Craftsman Color Lithographers. The art was by Joseph Ianelli of the School of Visual Arts.

Another poster produced by the same group measures 24" x 34", and features a giant stained glass portrait of a bald eagle with its 35-foot wings spread over the ceiling of the Master Eagle Gallery. It was designed and produced by the students of the School of Visual Arts.

This poster is a beautiful job of four-color process printing and is enhanced by being laminated. The stained glass reproduction is on a jet black background. The copy is in reversed type. The entire job is beautiful and quickly illustrates the abilities of the Master Eagle Family of Companies.

The posters are used not only to announce the exhibit but also to publicize the work that is being done by the company. Some are mailed, others are hand carried to customers. When visitors come to see the exhibit, of course, they are also exposed to the work of the company.

Another exhibition was entitled, "The Side Show." Each one of the 60 paintings and sculptures was selected from approximately 200 entries. They were based on the old outdoor amusement park "photo fun" stands where a customer's head, photographed in the oval cut-out of a painted scene, was pictured on the body of a mule rider, a strong man, a diapered baby and things of that type.

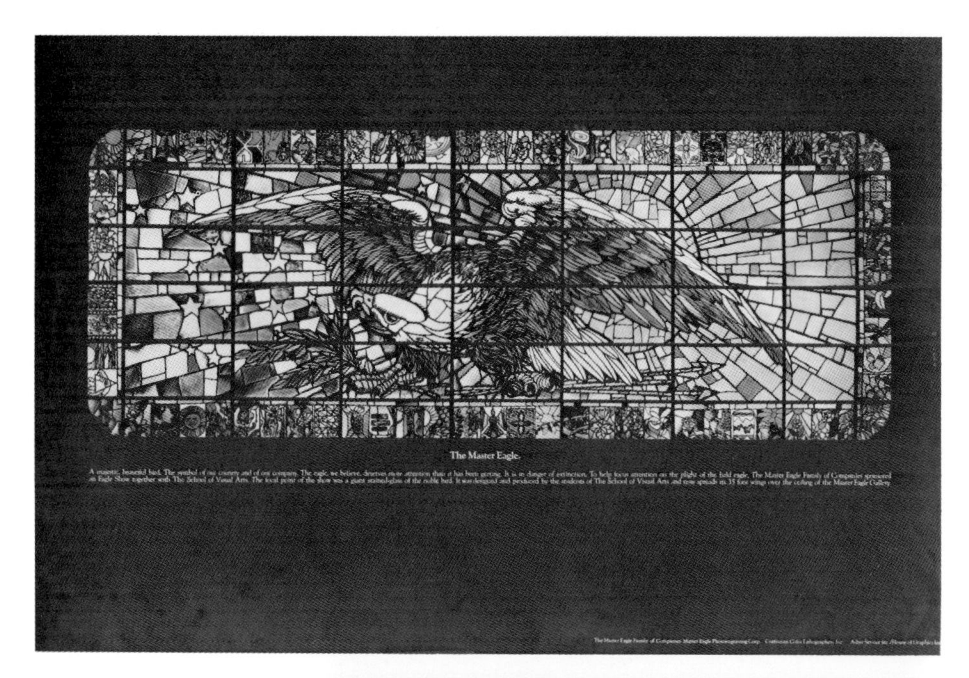
The Master Eagle.
A majestic, beautiful bird. The symbol of our country and of our company. The eagle, we believe, deserves more attention than it has been getting. It is in danger of extinction. To help focus attention on the plight of the bald eagle, The Master Eagle Family of Companies sponsored an Eagle Show together with The School of Visual Arts. The focal point of the show was a giant stained-glass of the noble bird. It was designed and produced by the students of The School of Visual Arts and now spreads its 35 foot wings over the ceiling of the Master Eagle Gallery.

Extinction: The future state of the Bald Eagle? Being destroyed by pollution, pesticides, elimination of breeding areas and hunters. The School of Visual Arts and The Master Eagle Family of Companies present, The Bald Eagle: Survival or Extinction? On exhibit at The Master Eagle Gallery, 40 West 25th Street, 6th Floor. March 26th through May 4th, 1973. From 10 a.m. to 4 p.m. Monday through Friday.

The artist instructors at the school supervise the show. The company selects the jury from working professionals in the graphic and illustration fields. The winning artists receive U.S. Savings Bonds and some of the work is printed for publicity purposes. There is a formal reception, by invitation only, at the Gallery to announce the winners to the trade press. For the "Side Show" exhibition, Mr. Gambaccini arranged for the Polaroid Company to photograph those who attended. The souvenir photograph was given to each one as a keepsake.

These exhibitions are an excellent way to assist youth. They also give the graphic arts people an opportunity to find promising talent. Above all, they are good will builders for Master Eagle.

Christmas Booklet

The Master Eagle Family of Companies does other forms of advertising. One form is a beautiful Christmas booklet. We have one that deserves reviewing. It is 5¼" x 7", case bound, with a soft, exotic, scattered-silk-floss white sheet used as a dust jacket over a light-weight laid text paper cover. The jacket is printed with a 2" feathery medallion in a screened blue and black. The type work in the entire book is beautiful. There is every evidence that a craftsman worked on the type. It is set ragged right and left—in other words, each line is centered. There are no hyphens, widows, broken type or jammed lines.

The eight water-color illustrations are on the right-hand pages. Each one is printed in four colors. The colors are soft and almost translucent. The drawings are very well done; the costumes are of yesteryear. The book

was designed and illustrated by Charles Attebery. The pages are of a light-weight text stock folded once. The other edges on the 7" side are folds.

The subject of the book is, "Christmas is Being." Here is the copy from the first page: "Earth's crammed with Heaven and every common bush is afire with God. But only he who sees takes off his shoes. –Elizabeth Barrett Browning."

"Christmas is the affirmation of love, hope, joy and brotherhood. Christmas is Being! Probably no greater revelation has ever been taught than the realization of the divinity within us. Every man is unique, alike only in his oneness with the whole of nature, created to unfold, to express himself, thinking, working, producing and being. In this booklet we have collected a few thoughts of some enlightened people who have expressed this enthusiasm for being and accepted their own innate oneness with nature. We hope you will find them meaningful and, perhaps, in some small way will make yours a merrier Christmas and a happier New Year."

Then follow eight pages of quotations with illustration opposite, of such creative people as Voltaire, Thackeray, Emerson, Twain, Jack London and others. The last page shows the company name and the companies that make up the family of companies. This is a very beautiful book that bespeaks of the craftsmanship available at these companies. It is a real keepsake.

McArdle Printing Company

A "Teaser" Campaign

The Washington, D.C. area is a competitive market for printers. You have to keep your name before the prospects or someone will do a better job of advertising and you will quickly be forgotten. Printing is the second largest commercial industry in Washington. McArdle Printing Company, Washington, had a twenty-fifth anniversary coming up so they decided that it would be an excellent time to put their name before the public. They called in some outside consultants who designed a "teaser" announcement campaign to mark the occasion. The pieces were created to reinforce good will, acquaint the public with McArdle's history, leave a reminder of the name and also be entertaining.

There were seven mailings of 1,300 pieces each. They were sent out at one-week intervals. Five of the 5½" x 8½" silver-foil, coated white cover stock 4-page folders were printed in two colors. The first folder had a small hanger to inform the reader that it was one of a series of fun and nostalgia and over the next several weeks more would come.

Since this was a "teaser" campaign, nowhere in the copy or on the envelopes was the company named. There was a small insignia of the same size on each folder with the words over the top, "Look back and remember." The folders covered Al Gionfriddo's catch in the sixth game of the 1947 world series and other sports incidents; Loretta Young's winning of an Oscar; the Tuesday night Bob Hope show and other leading radio shows in 1947; the "Open The Door, Richard" tune and other wacky lyrics of the day; the meatless Tuesdays and egg-and-poultry-less Thursdays.

On the cover of each folder was a large "1947," and copy asking a question about the event depicted on the inside with a photograph of the happening. The sixth mailing was a 16-page booklet, 4½" square, which was enclosed in a box. The cover was also silver-foil, coated white cover stock with a large "1947" thereon, and the words, "Look back and remember with McArdle Printing Company." Inside were pictures and copy about the first McArdle plant, the second plant they moved into, and then the third plant. The little cartoon figure of "Art Graphic" was introduced again. Over the years this cartoon figure has been used as McArdle's spokesman and we are sure it is recognized by many Washington printing buyers. On the last inside page was a note signed by Walter McArdle, president, thanking the customers for their friendship and confidence over the 25 years. He asked them to accept a replica of "Art Graphic" that was also enclosed in the box.

The final mailing to 800 names was an invitation to an anniversary luncheon and an RSVP card and envelope. The 98% response was very gratifying. Eighty percent accepted the invitation and from what we heard, it was quite a nice affair.

"Teaser Campaigns," if they are well conceived, often prove very successful. Creating a spokesman for the company, such as McArdle's "Art Graphic," is another good idea, provided it is continually used. It would have no value if it were used one month and then forgotten for the next six months. If something like "Art Graphic" is going to be used, it should be used on everything in order to establish its identity and to be of value.

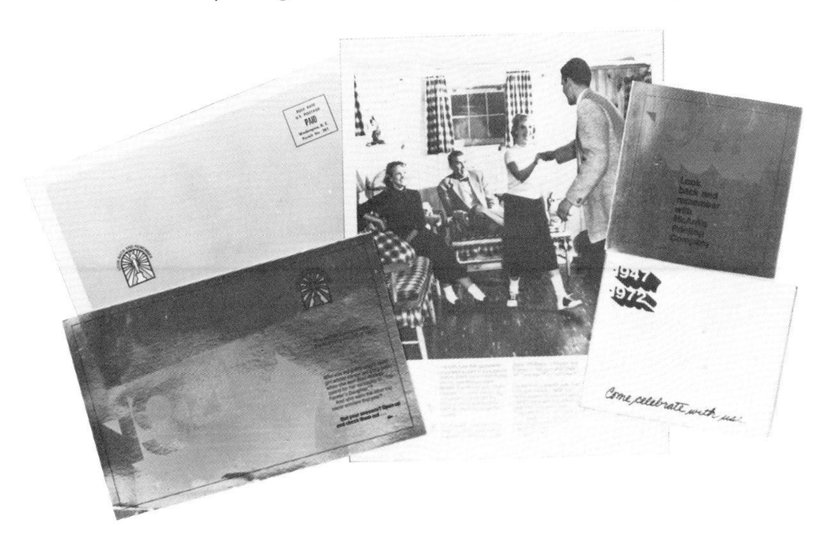

McCormick-Armstrong Company, Inc.

"Rumpus Room" Prints

When a piece of advertising has "lived" for at least 23 years, it has to be good. McCormick-Armstrong Co., Inc., Wichita, Kansas, has a series of four mailings that they still use, which won an honorable mention certificate in the first P.I.A. awards contest in 1952. E.W. Armstrong, better known as "Pete," is the president, and he tells us that though they quite vigorously pursued the responses, results in terms of sales and new customers were quite intangible. He adds, "Nonetheless, we're glad we did it!"

The drawings used on the covers of this series are all by Bill Nye, who now serves McCormick-Armstrong customers in a sales capacity. He is a top creative artist. The drawings are all reproduced in four-color process and they are cartoons of characters from bawdy ballads and earthy observations that pale in light of today's "literature."

The subjects are: "Casey At The Bat," "The Face On The Barroom Floor," "Casey Jones" and "Cremation of Sam McGee." Then there is a series of four more that they will send if you want to frame them for the rumpus room. They are: "The Shooting Of Dan McGrew," "Frankie and Johnnie," "The Death of Jesse James," and "The Passing of the Backhouse."

The folders are 8½" x 10¾". Pages two and three are printed with an overall solid color and screened here and there to enclose blocks of copy. There is a small head or head and shoulders black-and-white sketch of the character on the cover, reproduced on one of the inside pages. The type is easily read and the copy is friendly and excellent. In each folder they tell you what they can do and how well they can do it because of being all under one block-long roof. We will give you some of the highlights of this copy:

"Our illustrations aren't contemporary, either. When we first produced Casey At The Bat and the others, everybody wanted them. We gave them to customers and to people we'd like as customers. That was just the beginning. The first printing went fast. We printed some on order. Suffered mild tsk-tsks over some of the words, and shocked a few old ladies with some of the pictures.

"Addressing: by Elliott, Xerox, or full Cheshire mailer . . . and three shifts' worth (if necessary) of trained and experienced operators!"

This on the "Face on the Barroom Floor" folder: "As a disciplined artist, he was a flop. That bum wouldn't have lasted at McCormick-Armstrong. Nobody here can spare the time for temperament. Our graphic designers fit their art into restrictions: Time, Size, Budget. Every design during working hours is framed within a purpose set by the buyer of printing: it will sell, build an image, set an ultimatum, inform, persuade—sell. And it will look good doing it.

"We offer under-one-roof service—McCormick-Armstrong customers insist that our greatest value to a buyer of printing is that we'll take total responsibility for your whole job, right here in our plant. From first glimmer of idea through creation and production and into the mail—we can do it here.

"And don't overlook operations that no machine can do, but we can. Our fine permanent bindery staff knows how to hand-assemble special projects—spot glue, special fold, strip gum, insert anything from feathers to rocks, assemble samples, swatches, paint chips or even free-hanging mobiles for your point-of-purchase advertising."

There are many fine paragraphs of selling copy but those few will give you some ideas of how friendly copy can be written. It doesn't have to be stuffed shirt.

Metzger Printing and Publishing Company

Helping New Salesmen

Metzger Printing and Publishing Co. of Denver used advertising to help two new salesmen. One of the men was totally inexperienced in the printing industry, although he had made his mark as a salesman in another industry. The company executive wanted to get some new business for a new Multibinder they had purchased. They also wanted new customers. They had two new salesmen to do the task. So, in order to help the salesmen explain what the new equipment would do, they advertised.

We though Freddy Pannebaker was the only creative printing genius in Denver, but we discovered that there is at least one more. That high altitude must be good for creativity. John Metzger produced a 26-page book, "Creativity Through Unique Equipment," to help his salesmen to sell. He believes that this, their first piece of advertising, cut the time by two years for their two salesmen to build a profitable volume. He feels that this piece of advertising which, incidentally, won a P.I.A. award, along with his two new salesmen, produced a 30-percent sales increase.

Metzger Printing does quite a bit of advertising printing and it is trying to develop its market into financial printing. There are 37 employees. The largest presses are two 23" x 36" offset presses. There are about 14

presses, hot-metal typesetting equipment and a well equipped bindery department. Metzger's annual sales volume is well over a million dollars.

The 26-page book (there were two pages pasted in) measures 8½" x 11" and has 3½" high pockets on the inside and back covers. There are seven different paper stocks used. They are different colors, different weights and different textures. Each paper stock was identified so the salesmen wouldn't have to do any guessing.

Since the new equipment was a Multibinder, every opportunity was taken to illustrate what the machine could do. There was a short letter loosely inserted in the book. It was selling watermark letterheads. It was also telling customers that they could insert a letter anywhere in the book while the book was being bound, without stitching it in. Of course, their other bindery equipment was mentioned. There were pages in regard to calendars, typesetting, warehousing, embossing, efficient printing factors and a statement mentioning that the book could have been two or three times as large because Metzger Printing employees just couldn't stop submitting ideas for using their new unique equipment.

The book cost about $5,000 to produce. It undoubtedly was worth every penny of that because it helped two new salesmen to become quickly familiar with the plant's capabilities. With the book they could illustrate what their company could do. It was really an advertising piece that worked.

Modern Press

Introducing The Sales Team

"The Winning Line Up" was the headline on a narrow first page of an eight-page, 8½" x 11", folder produced by Modern Press, Saskatoon, Canada. This dark green cover was die cut so the shape of a small football appeared to the left of the headline. The white paper on page three, with the company trademark on it, showed through. On page three, there were also two wide rules set to resemble goal posts and an illustration of two football players, printed in four colors and showing as part of the cover, as the cover sheet was cut short. The small headline read, "Meet The Professionals . . The Modern Press Sales Team."

On pages four and five there was a spread showing photographs of just the faces of the five salesmen and one score keeper. Around the faces were drawn heavy lined cartoons of football players. The background was a printed green to match the cover stock. There were yard lines, in reverse, running across the pages to help with the football theme. The copy read, "Sign up with the PROFESSIONALS. You'll score on your next printing job if you call one of these experts. They'll tackle any job, large or small, and you're the winner." Beside each salesman's figure was a block of copy telling how long he had been in the business (their combined experience was over 100 years), and other pertinent data giving reasons why he could help the customer. The young lady who was the score keeper, and cartooned as a cheer leader, was the rookie.

On page six was pictured in cartoon fashion, with photographs as heads, "The Backfield," who were the estimators. Pages seven and eight were blank and we felt they were wasted as there was room for a listing of the company's services or, at least, its address. There was a telephone number at the bottom of page six, but no address.

This was an interesting and novel way to introduce a sales group.

Monthly Calendar

Modern Press also distributed a monthly calendar that was well printed on a cast coated, 6" x 16" heavy sheet and then scored three times so it could be easily folded into a tent and stapled. The monthly calendar was printed in three colors on one 4½" x 6" side. The numerals were large so they could be easily read. There also appeared a preceding and succeeding calendar and a panel of type showing the company name and phone numbers—no address.

On the other side of the angle was printed a beautiful four-color photograph of scenery in and around Canada. These photographs were exceptionally good and added to the retention value of the calendars.

On the base side of the triangle was a complete yearly calendar printed in three colors. These monthly mailings secured several new accounts, and the inquiries from persons on the mailing list when calendars were late in coming through the mail, signified interest. The calendars won an award in the P.I.A. contest.

Mono Lino Typesetting Company, Ltd.

Envelope Stiffener Advertising

What a waste of good advertising space is an envelope stiffener, unless it is one from Mono Lino Typesetting Co., Ltd., Toronto, Canada. They have utilized their proof envelope stiffeners for quite a few years. They have won awards for them. We have a series of eight, 11" x 14" cardboard stiffeners, with a separate quotation from Oscar Wilde on each piece. All of them are printed in two colors. One has a 5" x 6" piece of bright silver foil pasted on it as a mirror.

This mirror piece uses the quotation, "Other people are quite dreadful. The only possible society is oneself." The frame on the mirror is quite ornate and well drawn. It is printed in a dark red and black. The type is "Modern No. 20—Number one in a Series of Selections of 'Wilde' and Wonderful Faces from Mono Lino."

Each piece uses a humorous quotation and demonstrates another type style. There are small illustrations on every card. Every card is beautifully printed. Here are a few of the quotations:

"Imagination is a quality given to man to compensate him for what he is not, and a sense of humor was provided to console him for what he is."

"When we are happy we are always good, but when we are good we are not always happy."

"Fashion is a form of ugliness so intolerable that we have to alter it every six months."

"Women represent the triumph of matter over mind, just as men represent the triumph of mind over morals."

"None of us are perfect. I myself am peculiarly susceptible to draughts." The illustration is an old bald-headed man sitting in a chair contemplating a wig.

Derek Browning tells us that some recipients collected whole series of the stiffeners and pinned them up in their offices and at home. We imagine people would be delighted to get proofs from Mono Lino and get the extra dividend of the motto keepsakes.

The Morrison Company

Posters

Posters seem to be a popular form of advertising again. We see more of them being used every day. With the paper shortage and the postal increases, they become a very expensive advertising medium. However, it seems that colorful, well designed posters are taking the place of the old wall calendar in modern offices. Management will not permit calendars to be plastered on their decorator-designed office walls, but a good poster is often considered modern art and acceptable.

In the 1890's, in France, posters were extensively used as advertisements for cafés and theatrical performances. They were created by fine art men who dined and went to these entertainment spots. There is little doubt that some of them used poster art as a means of livelihood. Henri de Toulouse-Lautrec is today the most famous of these artists. His lithographs are considered fine art subjects rather than commercial art.

Commercial artists are creating similar works today. Their posters are colorful, use beautiful design and attract attention wherever they are seen. People want to place them on their walls. There is no doubt that they are excellent forms of advertising. Our personal objection is the cost. They need large expanses of paper of fairly heavy weight. In most cases they must be printed in many colors. They must be carried or mailed in a heavy tube. Postage rates are so high that delivery becomes quite expensive. In other words, you can mail two or three advertising folders or letters for the cost of one poster.

The Morrison Co., Philadelphia, has created a series of seven posters that are particularly outstanding and have received acclaim from many local sources as well as others around the world. The Philadelphia Convention Bureau has begged and borrowed copies for their use and has mailed them to many far-away places.

Morrison has 23 employees. Its posters were designed and, of course, printed internally, since the company wanted to illustrate its in-house capabilities. While it enjoys creative and sales promotion type of printing, it also does run-of-the-mill printing.

The four salesmen Morrison employs have been in business about nine years. The poster series was their self-advertising venture and they are pleased with the results. Jerry Pomerantz reports that the initial response was fantastic. They received special mention in the newspapers. As mentioned, the Chamber of Commerce and the Convention Bureau couldn't get their hands on enough of the posters. Prospects were high in their praise of the printing as well as the public spirited gesture. Their salesmen had something to talk about and explain. They were sure the posters demonstrated their creativity as well as their printing ability. A few new customers were created from leads generated by the posters. We believe Morrison missed a bet in not selling the posters to a bank. The sets could be used as premiums for new depositors.

There were 500 of each of the seven posters printed. All seven were mailed in a tube to customers, prospects and friends. Each poster measured 18" x 24", and was printed on a white 80-lb. Camberra stock.

The poster subjects were Philadelphia. One design was a posterized small section of the Philadelphia Orchestra with the words, "Philadelphia is Great Music." The lemon yellow background with the large orchestra illustration printed in black was striking. The word "Philadelphia" was in white type, a reverse plate of the yellow. As on all the posters, there was a small 8-pt. line, "One of a series created, designed and printed by the Morrison Co., Philadelphia, Pa."

Another poster featured "Philadelphia Parks," with 20 of them mentioned. The dominant illustration was part of a statue of William Penn, rendered in a black and gray wash drawing. The hand of the statue held a bouquet of vari-colored flowers. This was a four-color process job.

Another poster, with a blue background, stated, "Philadelphia Is History." The largest point of interest was a 13-star American flag. There was also a posterized view of Independence Hall. As all good posters should be, these designs were all simple, clean and bright with color. This one was printed in solid reds, blacks and two tones of blue.

"Philadelphia Is Fine Art" was the hand-lettered brush-stroke heading of another poster. It mentioned six schools and museums devoted to fine art. There was a 3¾" x 5" fine art reproduction, and one-half of the poster devoted to bright swatches of color and a museum facade reversed out of a large blue background. This poster was also printed in four colors.

Another in the series featured—on a solid glossy-black background—the words, "Philadelphia Is Faith," in brilliant white. Five similar spots or designs to represent stained glass were used very effectively. This poster was printed in four colors.

Green and black were used to print the "Philadelphia Is Urban Renewal!" poster. A drawing of a long row of obviously old, remodeled homes was the illustration across the lower part of the poster with the letters of the word "Philadelphia" broken up in a readable and interesting design, taking two-thirds of the poster space. These letters were reversed out of the solid green background.

Four drawings illustrating baseball, basketball, football and hockey dominated the "Philadelphia Is Sports" poster. (We thought this statement was boasting a bit when we first received these posters. However, Philadelphia now has the Stanley Cup Championship hockey team, so we will permit their bragging a bit.) This poster is also printed in four colors. All seven are excellent examples of poster art and would be a fine addition to anyone's collection.

PHILA
DEL
PHIA
is urban renewal!

Philadelphia
is Great Music

philadelphia is sports

Philadelphia
is Parks
fairmountawburybartramburholmecobbs creek
disstonfernhillfranklindrooseveltgorgas
huntingjuniatamorrispastorious
stentontaconyvernonwhitehall
wissahickon wissinoming
wister's woods

Motheral Printing Company

Texas Open House

It's a big state, and they always believe they have to do something big. As far as advertising is concerned, that isn't a bad idea. The three Motheral brothers who own Motheral Printing Company, Fort Worth, Texas, had finished an extensive remodeling job. They had some interior decorators help them with some of the offices and a conference room and they thought the place looked good. In fact, so good that they wanted to show their customers and prospects. They also decided to get a new 28" x 40" four-color litho press. So this was a fine time to promote their new capabilities.

They started planning and decided that in six months everything would be in fine working order. As they planned, more good ideas came forward. Creativity ran rampant and no one stopped it. So, they had an open house in real Texas style with 1,800 people present. That's a crowd of people for a printing plant. It is a good thing they didn't all come at one time.

Their six months' planning paid off because they were able to cover every detail in that time. For instance, parking. The borrowed a Coca-Cola Company lot across the street. They arranged to use a Baptist church lot five blocks away and had buses to transport the people. They had a good, detailed map with parking instructions. To take care of the crowd at the plant they erected a tent outside. They had six girls as hostesses, welcoming people and getting their name tags which were pre-printed and ready. There was no delay.

What brought so many people? The fanfare ahead of time. The Fort Worth Chamber of Commerce teamed up with the Motherals to make it a gala occasion. The reason for this cooperation was that the Motherals invited the Lord Mayor of Heidelberg, Reinhold Zundel, and the Managing Director of the Heidelberg plant, Dr. Wolfgang Zimmerman. They both accepted the invitation. They were the guests of honor and were feted for three days.

First, a 25" x 38" four-color poster was mailed to prospects and customers. The illustration was a bridge over the Neckar River in Heidelberg. There was also a photograph of the four-color press. The words "Wunderbar" in large decorative type appeared on one side, "Heidelberg" on the other side.

Then the invitations were mailed. These were also in four colors, showing on the cover a reproduction of the poster. The invitations were die cut, scored and perforated from a 6½" x 17¾" sheet of white litho stock. They measured 4⅝" x 6" when folded.

The fifth page folded in showed a wine bottle and glass with a border of grapes and leaves. The words, "You are invited" were on this page. On page two, the guests were asked to join in tasting the wines of Germany, see the Heidelberg press and meet the Mayor of Heidelberg. On page three was printed a nice drawing of homes in Heidelberg and the words, "An Evening in Heidelberg with the Motherals." On the bottom of this page was a 2" flap folded up and perforated. On one side was the printed word "Mr.", and then the man's name was filled in. On page four, there was a similar flap with the word, "Ms.", and the woman's name filled in. On the other side of the flap was a door prize ticket for a five-day trip to Heidelberg for two—all expenses paid. The fourth page also contained some short copy about the open house and the door prize.

There was an R.S.V.P. card enclosed. Since people don't always show their manners, Motheral prepared and sent out another card a few weeks later, and mentioned that they hadn't heard from them. For an event of this size they had to know how many were coming so that name tags, gifts and refreshments could be prepared. As it was, they expected 1,500 and 1,800 came.

The printing equipment was roped off, and large signs explained each piece. Motheral Printing employs about 100. They have both letterpress and offset equipment. The new four-color Heidelberg press was the only thing running as the crowd would make it impossible to operate other machines.

There were two bands playing German music, one in the plant and one in the tent. There were also tables in the tent and plant where German wines and cheeses and crackers were served. There were folders describing the four wines that were being served. The folders suggested that guests depart from the rear entrance where special favors awaited them as well as buses to the parking lots.

The Lord Mayor of Heidelberg was a fine fellow and circulated among the guests shaking hands and helping with the hospitality. Miss Fort Worth, the mayor of Fort Worth, the Texas Secretary of State, all the executives of the Fort Worth Chamber of Commerce and many Heidelberg representatives in the United States were present. It was an important, festive and gala occasion.

As the visitors left they were given a Motheral Company brochure, a 22" x 33" poster of a view in Heidelberg, a package of scratch pads, a key holder, and a folder stating, "It was great having you with us" and a small bottle of Heidelberg wine. Keepsakes of a very enjoyable visit.

After the event, two letters were sent. One was to those who attended, thanking them for attending, telling them who won the trip to Heidelberg and suggesting that they do not make that their last visit to the plant. The other letter went to those who were invited but couldn't attend. They were told that the welcome mat was still out and they were sorry they missed the fun evening. Very good follow-through.

There were private parties before and after the open house—many arranged by the Fort Worth Chamber of Commerce. The Heidelberg News published a six-page insert, printed in four colors, telling about the event and the visit to the Heidelberg plant by the door prize winners and the Carl Motherals. The main point is that Motheral Printing Company received an enormous amount of publicity and gained a large number of new friends and prospects. Their planning paid off.

Mueller-Krus Corporation

Single Sheets

Mueller-Krus Corporation, Milwaukee, Wisconsin, who has an offset and engraving service, used single-sheet, 8½" x 11" pieces to advertise its services. One sheet won a P.I.A. award. It was a good drawing of an ostrich's head and long neck. The face had a silly grin on it. There was a small leather collar on the ostrich's neck with the Mueller-Krus trademark hanging from it. That was the only illustration on the white sheet. It stood eight inches high and was an eye catcher. The only copy was a long headline which read, "Head-n'-Shoulders above . . . for the 'New Look' in color separating, offset-n'-engraving . . . Mueller-Krus Corporation."

There was a trademark and signature with address and phone number at the bottom of the sheet.

Another sheet, printed in four colors on two sides that had eye-catching illustrations, was one using a wood carving. The carving was exceptionally well done. On one side there was the question reversed out of a stone background, "troubles with reproduction problems?" This side of the carving showed a Farmer with a dog and a cow on a tether. The caricatures were amusing. At the rear of the cow was a veterinarian with his one hand on the cow's hind quarters. The other hand was behind his back. There was also the usual doctor's bag.

On the reverse side of the sheet we found the other side of the wood carving—a cutout halftone on the white sheet. Only then do you see that the vet has a syringe in the hand that was not showing in the other view. The headline read, "Mueller-Krus has your answer in hand." Then followed some short copy about their "every patient measure" and service. The company trademark and signature were at the bottom of the sheet.

Burt Jahn tells us they have 55 employees, including eight salesmen. These sheets have been part of a continuing self-advertising effort. They could trace about $50,000 worth of sales and many new prospects from their advertising. They had excellent customer reaction as it was a terrific image builder. They plan to continue their advertising.

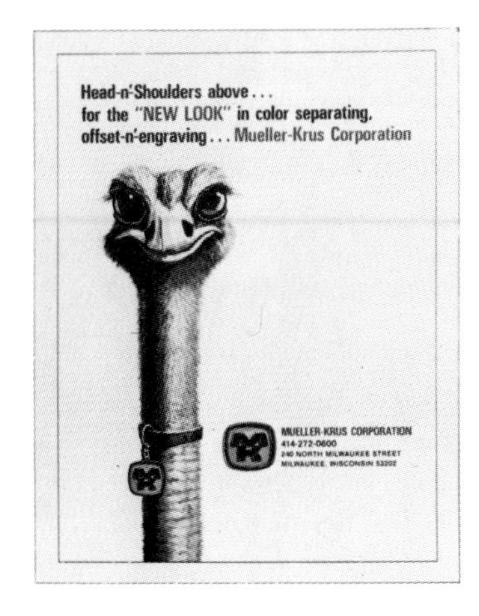

Oshiver Studio Press, Inc.

Mottoes

"Sending out this motto gives us a chance to show off a bit of our craftsmanship, and to remind our friends that we give as much thought and care to all the printed pieces we produce. We help to plan and design them, clothe them in our usual fine typography, and print them uncommonly well—as we have done for over 40 years." That is part of the message that is sent with some of the mottoes used by Oshiver Studio Press, Inc., Philadelphia, to publicize its work.

These mottoes are printed on a heavy stock. They measure 9" x 12" or 8½" x 11". If the company name and address are not on the sheet there is a hanger attached which explains why the motto was printed and then the company name and address appear.

The mottoes include, "Youth Is Not A Time Of Life. It Is A State Of Mind," which has been reprinted two or three times. It is printed on ivory stock in black, orange and gold. The decorative initial is very beautiful and the type has been set by a craftsman. Stephen Grellet's statement, "I shall pass thru this world but once . . ." is another piece. It is printed on white stock in black, a light blue and gold.

Eleven Important Commandments Of Good Business is another keepsake they have produced. It is printed on ivory stock in black and blue using an initial letter, C, to give the piece a decorative effect. The initial is repeated in 11 paragraphs. People enjoy receiving these fine examples of printing and they don't throw them away. They make good image-building advertising.

YOUTH IS NOT A TIME OF LIFE
IT IS A STATE OF MIND

IT is not a matter of ripe cheeks, red lips and supple knees, it is a temper of the will, a quality of the imagination, a vigor of the emotions; it is a freshness of the deep springs of life. Youth means a temperamental predominance of courage over timidity, of the appetite of adventure over love of ease. This often exists in a man of fifty more than in a boy of twenty.

NOBODY grows old by merely living a number of years; people grow old only by deserting their ideals. * * * Years wrinkle the skin, but to give up enthusiasm wrinkles the soul. Worry, doubt, self-distrust, fear and despair—these are the long, long years that bow the head and turn the growing spirit back to dust.

WHETHER seventy or sixteen, there is in every being's heart the love of wonder, the sweet amazement at the stars and starlike things and thoughts, the undaunted challenge of events, the unfailing childlike appetite for what next, and the joy and the game of life.

YOU are as young as your faith, as old as your fear; as young as your hope, as old as your despair. In the central place of your heart there is a wireless station; so long as it receives messages of beauty, hope, cheer, courage, grandeur and power from the earth, from men and from the Infinite, so long are you young. * * * When the wires are all down and all the central place of your heart is covered with the snows of pessimism and the ice of cynicism, then are you grown old indeed and may God have mercy on your soul.

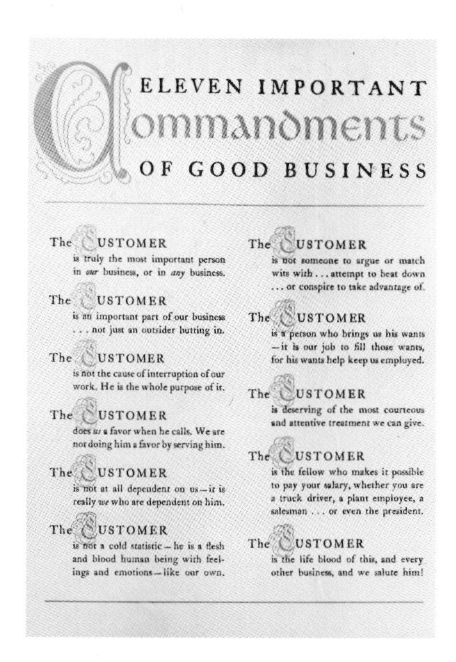

ELEVEN IMPORTANT Commandments OF GOOD BUSINESS

The CUSTOMER is truly the most important person in *our* business, or in *any* business.

The CUSTOMER is an important part of our business . . . not just an outsider butting in.

The CUSTOMER is not the cause of interruption of our work. He is the whole purpose of it.

The CUSTOMER does *us* a favor when he calls. We are not doing him a favor by serving him.

The CUSTOMER is not at all dependent on us—it is really *we* who are dependent on him.

The CUSTOMER is not a cold statistic—he is a flesh and blood human being with feelings and emotions—like our own.

The CUSTOMER is not someone to argue or match wits with . . . attempt to beat down . . . or conspire to take advantage of.

The CUSTOMER is a person who brings us his wants—it is our job to fill those wants, for his wants help keep us employed.

The CUSTOMER is deserving of the most courteous and attentive treatment we can give.

The CUSTOMER is the fellow who makes it possible to pay your salary, whether you are a truck driver, a plant employee, a salesman . . . or even the president.

The CUSTOMER is the life blood of this, and every other business, and we salute him!

Package Products Company, Inc.

Newsletter

Package Products Co., Inc., Charlotte, N.C., produces very interesting annual reports but we want to tell you about their newsletter. Package Products specializes in roll and die cut labels, tags, folding cartons and printed flexible packaging. It is not a small concern. They have 450 employees and annual sales of approximately $16 million dollars. They have 31 salesmen.

Their newsletter is called "Wrap-up." It is a continuing promotional effort, designed primarily to tell of their creativity and innovative problem-solving ability in the field of printed packaging materials. They mail about 5,500. Each issue is a separate communication primarily built on successful case histories of innovative problem-solving packages.

This is not an inexpensive typewritten newsletter. It is 8½" x 11", four pages, always printed in two colors, sometimes up to four. A few of the issues we have are: cover hosiery packaging, chemical packaging, men's underwear packaging, a label promotion for bananas, a new wrap for candy, pantyhose boxes, bakery goods wrapping, new roll label stock, perfume packaging, razor blade packaging and film packaging.

In some issues they show pictures of salesmen. The copy explains where they are located and what their qualifications are. We feel certain the salesmen approve of this publicity.

There are plenty of illustrations or photographs of the subject being discussed. The copy is well written and type is all very readable. Duotones are used as well as good black halftones. There are no fuzzy pictures that you often see in a newsletter or house organ. Everything is first class.

Mr. Sam Ryburn, vice president, tells us that "Wrap-Up has created, year after year, a high number of inquiries and favorable communications, many of which lead to new business from old customers or to new accounts. We feel it is one of our most valuable forms of self-advertising. It offers the opportunity to call to our customers' attention our creativity and quality. We have a continuing program of self-advertising through the years and feel that it is increasingly effective and important to us."

Although Package Products is a large company using an expensive form of a newsletter, we feel that a small printing firm could adapt the newsletter principle to its advertising programs. It need not be so elaborate but still it could give case histories of printing jobs going through the plant, introduce the people in the plant and keep the customers and prospects aware of what is being accomplished. It is an excellent form of advertising, but don't start it if you aren't going to keep it going in a regular pattern. It should be mailed at least every quarter. Every month would be much better.

Frederic M. Pennebaker, Lithographer

One-Man Shop Advertising

Some small printers believe that they haven't a chance to gain recognition by winning one of the many awards that are available today. We would like to remind them of the P.I.A. Printers' Self-Advertising Awards. In that contest they don't have to compete with the large companies. There is a category for printers with 19 or fewer employees. That brings us to the first-prize winner in that category in the first awards contest away back in 1952. At that time he won a solid bronze Benjamin Franklin statuette and a check for $1,000. He was the owner, estimator, pressman, binder and janitor of his company.

If you ever go to Denver, take time to visit Frederic M. Pannebaker, Lithographer. His is a one-man operation and he has his walls just about covered with awards. His 1952 prize winning effort was a 4½" x 6" deckle edge, french fold, four pages, on a textured ivory stock, printed in four process colors in perfect register, on a Multilith!

Freddy could have written the copy himself but he says he obtained outside help on that as well as the layout. The artwork featured various bugs which were drawn by Ray Chatfield, a gentleman of 11 years of age. The first page showed the bugs with a large one fashioned from a walnut shell and which was embossed. There was also an old fashioned flatiron. The copy read, "Let freddy iron out your printing bugs." On page two were the address and phone number in black, overprinting a large yellow flat-iron and various red bugs going from page two to page three. Page three copy, printed in black, read, "In the charming never-never land of advertising, comes from time to time a desire for the perfect or near perfect. But then, alas, the best laid plans gang aft agley, and bugs crawl out of the woodwork to gnaw away at mice and men.

"For perfect (or near perfect) printing, we at Freddy's fairly drool at the opportunity to iron out your bugs. Our bug ironing service is staffed by diploma-holding bug-ironers from way back. Please feel free to consult us at any time. You'll really be delighted with our work."

On the left of page four, there was a column of nine small flatirons. Each iron was a different color and identified as gold ochre, or carmine red, or moss green or real black black. To the right was a large green bug fashioned from a walnut shell with the artist's name overprinted. It was an excellent advertising piece. Fred mailed about 1,000 by first-class mail in a matching envelope. The cost was between 75 and 90 cents each.

We recently asked Fred about this piece and he said, "The winners (he had three of them: 1952, '56, '57) helped continue building prestige, and have to this day been remembered by some. They made possible firming the conviction of the worth of a product from Pannebaker, which has helped bring profitable, good-looking things to do. And there was, of course, the usual amount of vanity involved . . . it was all coming from a very small press."

In Denver, we are sure his advertising has been a good image builder, for Freddy does some beautiful work for the ski resorts, and he gets his price.

Moving Notice

Freddy Pannebaker's moving notice was great. The envelope corner card was a wash drawing of a man stepping on the running board to get out of an old Model T Ford. Below were the words, "Denver Chapter of Periodic Peregrinators, 1411 Fox Street, Denver, Colorado." If you don't know what a peregrinator is, don't feel badly. We can't even pronounce it. The dictionary says it is one who walks or travels over—traverse.

The 5½" x 8½" four-page folder inside was printed on a white litho sheet. The first page background was a line photograph of the Denver mint printed in brown ink. Overprinted was a blue halftone of Freddy (Incidentally, he now calls himself Frederic M.) in a miner's hat and with his finger to his lips as if it were a big secret. The copy reads, "litho luminary goes underground near the mint." On page two is this copy, which is fun to read: " 'The press is just a cover. If I can stay out of the News I'll strike a Mint,' leers the laughing lithographer. With these words, Freddy Pannebaker, nationally recognized printing expert, explains his recent move to 1411 Fox St. (between 14th and W. Colfax). 'Parking is no problem now,' smirked the self-satisfied egocentric of ink. 'Just drive your team down the alley in back of the shop and park right in the lot. The main thing is this . . .,' said the hero of the DAC badminton courts, ' . . . I'm near the mint, let me watch your printing dollars for you.' In his

new quarters, Freddy will continue his superb production of printed pieces, among the large variety of which includes: Letterheads and Envelopes, Pie Labels, Invoices and Statements, Direct Mail Pieces, Pie Lables, Financial Statements, Sales Letters and Pie Labels."

On page two, on a yellow background, is a map to indicate where the new building is located. There is also a square halftone of an old buggy with a caption, "effortless parking in the back lot." On page four is a large cutout halftone printed in brown ink of an old wall telephone with the bell handle that had to be turned to ring a number. Across the halftone in two black panels are the words, "same old phone, KE4-2747." There is also "Freddy Pannebaker, Denver, Colorado."

Extra Dividend

When you purchase any printing from Frederic M. Pannebaker, Lithographer, today, you get a dividend. In the package of printing and with your invoice you will receive some 2" x 3½" varied colored cards on which are printed some silly sayings. Nowhere is it indicated that they are printed by Pannebaker but most people remember. Here are just a few excerpts from his collection:

"My work is very secret. We make the front end of horses and ship to Washington for final assembly."

"I know women aren't perfect but they're the only opposite sex we have."

"There's one trouble with Russian Roulette—not enough Russians are playing it."

"I'm a bargain hunter and can't resist anything that's half off. That's how I got my husband."

And on and on and on. This is just another form of reminder advertising for Frederic.

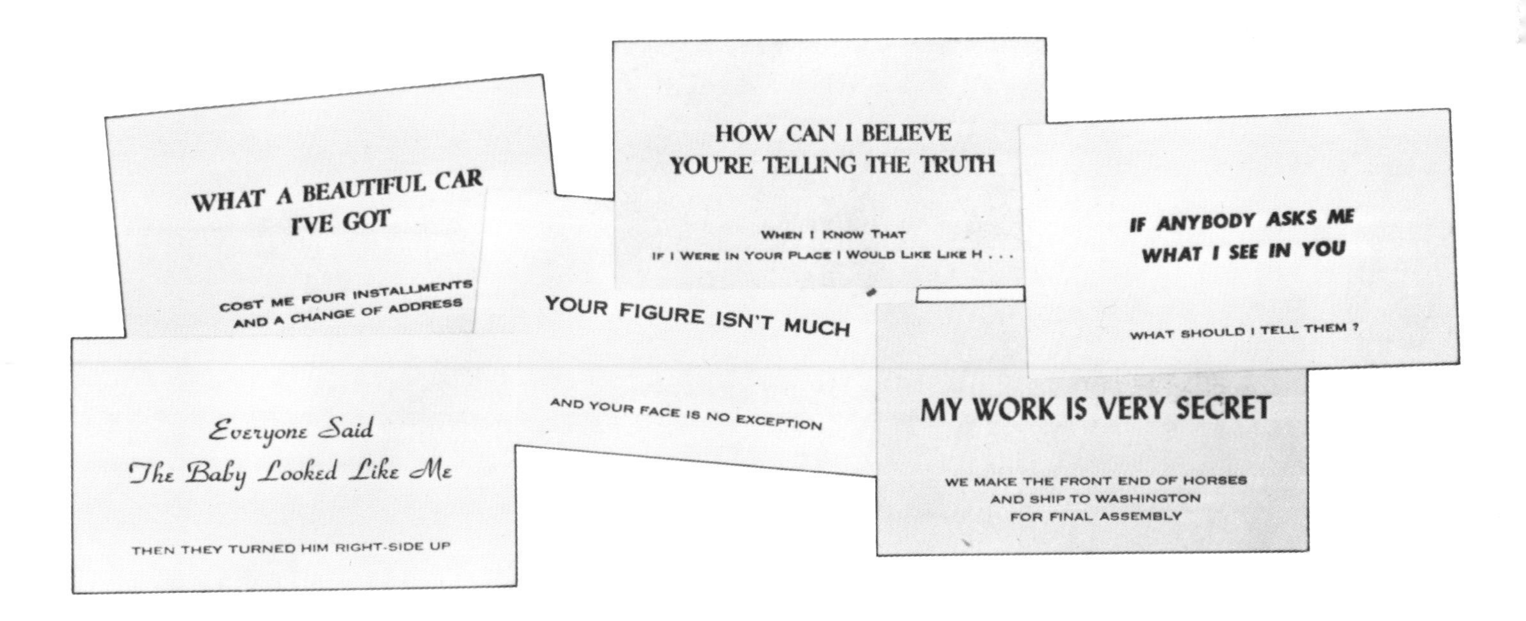

Printing-Advertising-Plus, Inc.

Sardine Can

P.A.P. Inc. (Printing-Advertising-Plus, Inc.), Monrovia, California, won an award for its moving notice that looked like a sardine can when it was folded.

It was mailed in an envelope showing a cutout halftone of a sardine can key for opening the can, and these words: "A new key with an old twist."

The folder inside, printed on a white stock with aluminum foil on one side, was approximately 4" x 5⅜", folded. It was die cut from an 8" x 15" sheet and scored and folded three times. The first page showed the can being partly opened, with the key extending beyond the fold about ¾". This was printed on the foil side. Page two, as it was turned up, showed a blue cutout halftone of the key with these words, "Thanks For A Good Turn." Below page two, and printed on the foil, was the can fully opened with seven persons packed in the can. When the other two folds are opened, there is a picture of the seven employees standing around, some on a press, and stretching their arms and legs. The copy reads, " . . . We're stretching out in our brand new building . . . come see." The address and phone number appear at the bottom of the sheet with a three-color trademark.

This is just one other clever way to advertise a move. They say they received numerous phone calls about the mailing piece and received some good newspaper publicity.

Phipps Press Inc.

Calendars

The Phipps Press Inc., Freeport, New York, produced a very interesting calendar in 1974. I believe it was designed for a wall calendar because it had a hole punched in the backing for hanging. It also could have been used as a calendar pad for the desk as there was a small space after each date where notes could be written.

The calendar was delivered in a 6⅛" x 11" envelope or pouch. It was hand made from tan cover stock. A large drawing, with a wood cut effect, of the head and shoulders of Franklin, was reproduced on the flap of the pouch. It was printed in brown ink and bled three sides.

The calendar was mounted on heavy board 6" x 10⅞". One side of the board was brown and showed the company name and address. The reverse side was white. The calendar pad was 6" x 9" and was mounted ½" from the top of the board. That left a 1⅜" space at the bottom of the board so the company name was always visible.

The tan front sheet contained some well written copy describing, in three paragraphs, Franklin's history. There were two paragraphs about Phipps Press. The last one stated, "If you agree that printing should not be based on price alone and that printing is a growing personal, cooperative relationship between the customer and the printer, we may be just the printer you're looking for. Telephone us now and let's talk. As Benjamin Franklin said, 'never leave that 'til tomorrow which you can do today.' " The company name, address and a fair sized reproduction of the Franklin head artwork also appeared on this page.

The 52 pages of this calendar were very interesting. 5¾" x 6" of each sheet was taken for the illustration and quotation of Benjamin Franklin. Each of 25 pages was carefully planned. Illustrations were repeated. Different type faces were used and each quotation was cleverly illustrated. A tan and a brown ink were used to print each page. One page contained the dates for one week. The date and the day were listed on the left hand side of each page with fine rules separating each day. This took 3¼" x 6" of the page at the bottom.

Let me try to describe a few of the 52 quotations and illustrations which made this calendar so interesting:

Set in approximately 40-point type were the words, " 'Glass, China, & Reputation Are Easily Cracked & Never Well Mended.' Benjamin Franklin." Then these words were cracked as if they had been printed on a piece of glass and the glass shattered.

Running through this quotation was an old fashioned sugar spoon with a fly in the bowl: " 'A spoonful of honey will catch more flies than a gallon of vinegar' Benjamin Franklin."

An old-fashioned ribbon watch fob was illustrated and the clip that held the watch was broken. No watch was shown. The quotation was, "Lost Time Is Never Found Again."

Creative credit for the calendar goes to Richard Commer of Dick Commer's Ad Factory, Melville, N.Y. The graphic design was by Mo Lebowitz, Bellmore, N.Y., who made great use of old catalog engravings.

The calendar won a P.I.A. award, a Beckett Paper Company award and a Long Island Ad Club Golden Boli (Best of Long Island). President Matthew D. Bernius believes a calendar is a good silent salesman. It keeps the company name in front of potential customers for a whole year. The result was the addition of a number of new accounts for The Phipps Press, Inc.

The 1975 calendar was of two sizes: one, 8½" x 11", wire-o-bound on the 11" side; another, 17" x 22", wire-o-bound on the 22" side. The pages were printed varied colored stocks in varied colored inks. The cover showed a drawing of Franklin's head and shoulders and there were two paragraphs: one described Franklin and the other described the Phipps Press philosophy.

There is a December, 1974, sheet, which is often a good idea, as it gets the calendar in use before the other calendars come around. The numerals are large. Various holidays are shown, and on every sheet there are at least two, sometimes three, quotations of Franklin's, with thumbnail cartoons. These have been injected into the calendar by omitting numbers, so one has to assume the dates of one or two days in some weeks. The quotations are mostly humorous and the cartoons are amusing.

Both the small and large sizes are identical in layout, design and copy. We suppose that if a person doesn't have the space to hang the large calendar, he could find space for the small one. By hook or crook, Phipps Press gets its calendars hung.

PMA Industries

Killing Rumors

Direct mail advertising works in so many ways it is sometimes unbelievable. Anthony Morelli is president of PMA Industries, Farmingdale, N.Y. He had some trouble with a few employees "who spent more time creating extra coffee breaks than churning out clients' orders." So, he had to dismiss them. Before it was all over he had to let approximately 30 go. He employs 23 in the printing department, 52 in the mailing department and 10 in data processing. Rumors started flying, he lost customers and almost went bankrupt. Then he mailed a letter to 3,500 customers and prospects. He increased his business, solved his financial problems and is now doing very well—thanks to a bold, frank, direct mail letter.

PMA Industries, Inc., has a sales volume of approximately $1,700,000. They organized in 1958. They have two 25" x 38" perfectors and a couple of multiliths. They have a complete direct marketing communications service. They print both offset and by computer, make mailings, maintain computer mailing lists and even have an order fulfillment department. Here's the computer letter that Mr. Morelli used:

"Some people have a lot of nerve, Mr. Brown.

"But, I'm still here to tell about it.

"Mr. John Brown

"Brown and White

"111 Blue Street

"Red Hill, Pa. 18076

"Good Morning, Again:

"Guess what happens when you fire a loafer?

"He picks up the phone and calls everyone.

"He gripes and groans and complains that he was super-terrific. Tells the world that he was the most important person in your company. That you're really in trouble. That your business is going down the drain-pipe and you're about ready to throw in the towel.

"Certain competitors hear about it. They jump on what they think is a dead carcass. Like vultures, they swarm after your accounts. They spread false rumors. They undercut prices. They offer to pick-up a client's job and 'rescue it' when there is no rescuing to be done. They talk about padlocked doors and missed deadlines.

"Quickly, like a wind-driven fire, the rumors spread. Then comes disaster. People start believing the rumors. Few of them check the stories they hear. They hear so many stories that they don't know what to believe.

"Well, Tony's here to tell you the truth.

"I fired some clock-watchers who spent more time creating extra coffee breaks than churning out clients' orders. Yes, I fired some dissidents and some dumb bunnies. They do more to louse up your reputation than you might believe. So I got rid of them.

"However, the rumors spread, and only a few competitors and a handful of clients stood by us. And we did get into trouble.

"Put yourself in my shoes, Mr. Brown. What would you do in this situation?

"I came out fighting.

"Fighting for the loyal, efficient employees who put in a day's work for a day's pay. Fighting to protect my reputation, and my business.

"I reorganized the staff. Hired new supervisors. Eliminated the gossipers. Did everything I could to remake an entire company.

"I called every client and pledged my personal attention to every job. I set new standards of performance for every man and woman on my staff.

"And guess what happened?

"Certain competitors fed us their overflow work. We love them and thank them.

"Certain accounts stood by us and gave us as much work as they could. We love them even more.

"And, some clients who left us suddenly came back. They realized that Tony wasn't going to dry-up and blow away. I'm not that kind of person. I know my business and I am bringing it back, a little bit each day.

"But, I'm no florid salesman.

"I'm a knowledgeable, hard working, reliable person who loves this business. I can quote prices and recommend methods to cut your costs. But, I'm not a joking Don Juan or an ever-present pest.

"And because I'm not a whirlwind salesman, I'm using the medium I know best—direct mail—to solicit business from you, at a time when I truly need it most. Please look around your desk, Mr. Brown, and see if there's a job (even a small one) that I can quote on. Printing, addressing, inserting, computer work, or mailing services.

"I won't give up this fight. I need your help NOW. Won't you please call me, TODAY.

"Gratefully,
"Anthony Morelli
"President"

A business reply card was enclosed listing PMA's many services and a box to check off what the customer needed. There was even space headed, "I'm a need-it-yesterday person. Here are some specs. Please quote quickly."

Mr. Morelli received 84 cards and phone calls. He is convinced this bold approach worked for him in his situation. Sometimes people like to have it laid on the line.

Pollack Printing Corporation

New Press

Press announcements are not unusual, so there are many varieties. Pollack Printing Corporation, Buffalo, N.Y., won a prize for theirs, so we will describe it. They have 90 employees and sales are approximately $2 million. They have seven salesmen.

They took a 42¾" x 62¾" heavy white enamel sheet and folded it six times to a 10¾" x 15¾" mailing piece which they placed in a gray kraft 12½" x 16" envelope. "It's A Boy!" was emblazoned on the envelope in red and blue letters. The company name, address and phone numbers were used on the corner card.

As you open the mailer the word "It's" jumps at you in 6½" high red block letters, with two decorative borders top and bottom. As the mailer is unfolded, you can read these big block letters printed in solid red, blue and green, and saying, "It's A Boy (we think) A Restless Steel-Hearted Terror." With half the sheet open, there are six multi-colored balloons with black strings. The specifications of the press are printed in large black type on these balloons. Such statements are used as "6,000 times an hour he wets his 43" x 63" paper sheets! He snacks on 24 lbs. of ink an hour (any two colors seem to satisfy his appetite)". Weight at birth, length,

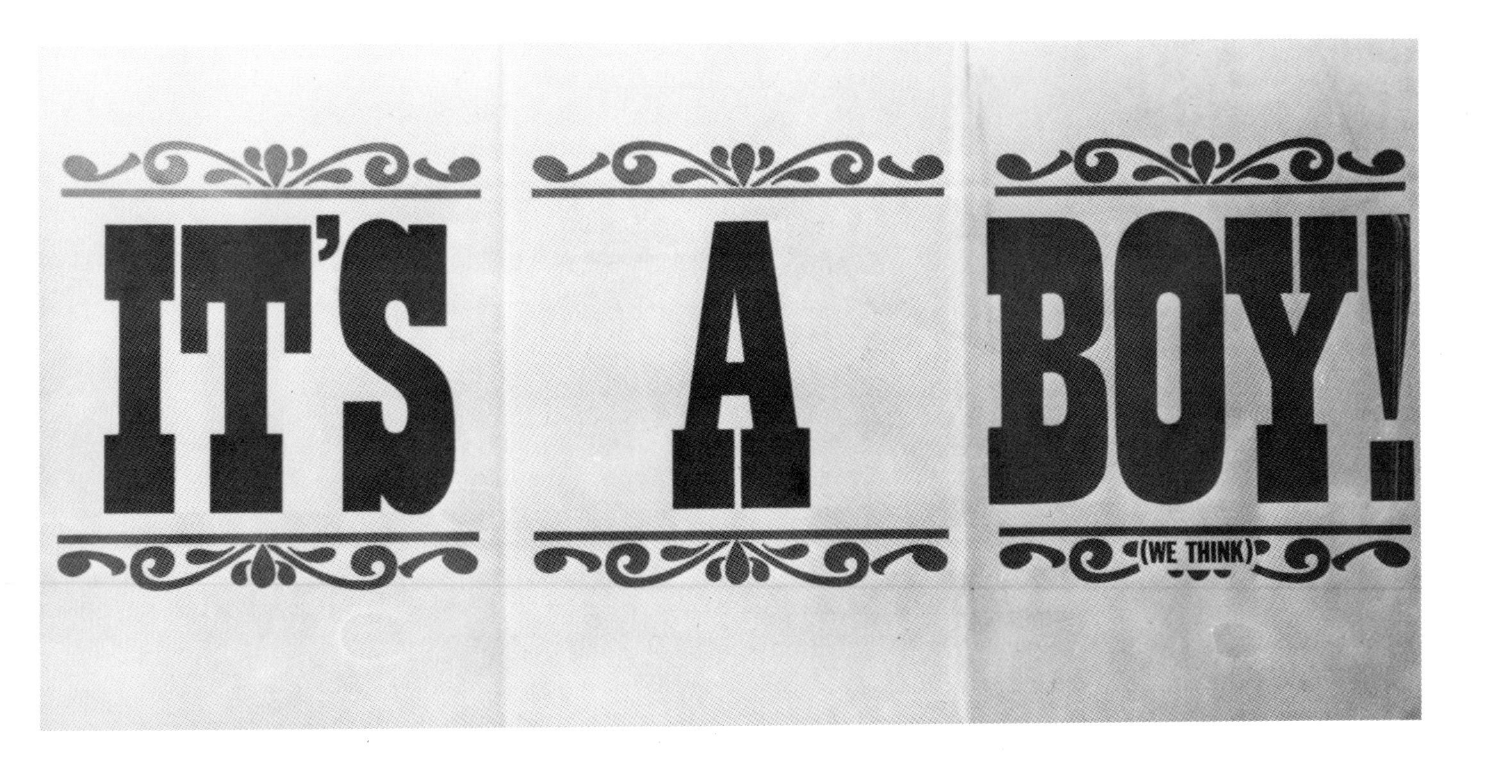

width and height are given. "60 gallons of oil circulate through his mechanical, arterial systems to keep his rugged precision-built body in perfect running condition! He's one Helluva big boy with a performance capacity to match!"

Open to the reverse side of the entire sheet, there is a combination duotone and line drawing of the press in a pink bassinet with a large card stating, "This important announcement was produced by our 'Baby' on maximum size sheets 43" x 63", (2 color offset lithograph press)." There's another spot of copy showing the name, home, proud parents and a note, "Please don't send gifts . . . Our 'baby' thrives on *Printing* . . . Feed him everything you've got!"

Mr. William Pollack, president, said, "It was difficult to ascertain results since there were other self-advertising pieces appearing at the same time. They received innumerable verbal and written comments from customers and prospects regarding the clever presentation of this special announcement." He also stated, "Since our business is built on advertising customer products and promoting their corporate images . . . self-advertising is a natural for us and from time-to-time, we do 'toot our own horn,' in an effort to prove our creative ability and production capabilities."

Premier Printing & Letter Service

Thanks

Thanks—is a beautiful word. Most of us who are thoughtful, kindly, or who have good manners, use the word quite often. However, companies or corporations so often forget their manners. A thank-you card, folder, letter or personal note is good advertising. Some would call it public relations. But whatever you want to call it, "Thanks" works. Here's a fabulous story of how it worked for one printer. L.U. Kaiser started a small letter shop in 1925 in Houston, Texas. He had one multigraph and four old automatic typewriters. He bought a letterpress in 1928, and worked long hours, "eight days a week," as he puts it. Luke Kaiser added a 10 x 15 C.P., then a B Kelly, and a 12 x 18 Kluge to his pressroom. The depression hit Premier Printing and Letter Service as it did everyone else but it weathered the storm, which is in itself a point of distinction.

In the forties, the lithography department was born. It started with one multilith. Vic Green, a cartoonist of a nationally syndicated comic strip, now a vice president, came on the scene about that time. With lithography, the department grew, and Premier was making money. In 1951, at Christmas time, they wanted to thank their customers for their business.

So, Mr. Kaiser and Mr. Green collaborated on a generous, share-the-wealth rebate without parting with real money. They designed a corny, oversized "Texas Buck"—play money, good for nothing but a laugh. They enclosed two $100 Texas Bucks with this letter:

"Dear . . ., It is a pleasure at Christmas to include with messages of cheer and happiness . . . appreciation.

"As you know, we have no regular outside salesmen and rely entirely on our good friends and customers to solicit our 'contracts' for us.

"Since you have been kind enough to send some nice business our way, we believe that, due to adverse publicity, you might be reluctant to accept a 'mink coat' or 'deep freeze' for your 5%. Therefore, we are enclosing your commission in cash in the form of crisp new big Texas Bucks.

"Yes, we've made some 'big money' here at Premier this year, and we want to share it generously with our friends.

" . . . with the hope that you will make some REAL big money in '52 and enjoy personal happiness and health, we are

Most gratefully,
L.U. Kaiser and all the folks at
PREMIER PRINTING & LETTER SERVICE"

That "thank-you" letter really put Premier in business. It showed their appreciation for past business. It got the desired laughs but what is most astounding and what they didn't expect was the snowballing popularity of the Texas Bucks.

Cartoonist Green designed the Buck. Luke wrote the "copy." The result was a "Black Gold Certificate" signifying that "There is on deposit unlimited amounts of good will in the treasury of The Magnificent Empire of Texas." Serial numbers on "The Buck You Can't Pass" included "U 8 D Bar BQ" and "TNT 42 Series." Cavorting on the 13 x 5-inch bill were jack rabbits, long horn steers and a bronc buster superimposed on the face of George Washington. Rattlesnakes, the Alamo and a gushing oil well graced the reverse side. Signatures were: "L. Useless Kaiser, Premier Prestidigitator of Mazuma" and "Vic 'Long' Green, Custodian of the Cache."

It was all very corny, but Americans like corn. On the very day after the letters were mailed out, December 18, 1951, the deluge began. Kaiser spent hours answering phone calls from folks who wanted more Texas Bucks. Many wanted them in such quantities that they insisted upon paying for them. That is when Mr. Kaiser knew that they had someting.

A couple of days later, Kaiser jokingly told a buyer in a giant Houston department store that he was missing a bet by not selling "money" in his stationery department.

"Why not?" the buyer grinned. "Leave 500 for a trial." Before closing time, Kaiser got a frenzied phone call: "This is the darndest thing I have ever heard of, selling a printer's advertisement in a department store . . . but people are taking them away from us . . . rush 5,000 more!" Foley's sold more than 150,000 Texas Bucks.

Within a week, orders were pouring in so fast from all over the country that Premier's presses couldn't deliver fast enough. A Kansas City lumberman ordered 1.25 million. Bankers, clergymen and displaced Texans throughout the nation flooded Premier with orders. In less than a month the crazy currency found its way overseas. Each day's mail brought requests from such faraway places as Korea, Japan, Rome, London, Scotland, even South Africa and Indo-China.

After three months, Premier had been paid almost $30,000 for some three million pieces. Then the bubble burst—almost.

In March, 1952, Luke received a polite phone call from a U.S. Secret Service agent. They were afraid people might mistake Texas's illegal tender—grossly exaggerated though it was—for real $100 bills. The Treasury Department ruled that Texas Bucks were a violation of the federal statutes. Kaiser and Green watched the G-men destroy 440,000 Texas Bucks. That, with other delays and complications, cost Luke perhaps $100,000 in the year '52.

News of Premier's trouble hit the newspapers all over the nation. It was considered quite a joke. The New York Herald Tribune editorialized: "The Treasury people are becoming a little too paternalistic. After all, even the most unsophisticated dollar watcher . . . would be a little startled if he encountered a note that measured 13 inches by 5. He might not know what the Latin on the Great Seal of the United States signifies, but with a little care he could work out 'in hock furplenti' on the Texas production . . . if the Treasury is going to take the law . . . that literally, there is danger of barring all likenesses of Alexander Hamilton, all Arabic numerals and everything that's green . . ."

After attorneys and Messrs. Kaiser and Green went around and around with new designs and wording, they were able to fully cooperate with the Treasury Department. They substituted a likeness of Texas hero, Stephen F. Austin, for that of Washington, and they were back in business. The new bill had a line which read, "This bill is strictly fictional. Any resemblance to actual currency, living or dead, is purely coincidental."

A sheet was printed advising all those who had purchased the old bills that they were illegal, that they should be destroyed and to purchase the new Texas Buck. Again the presses started rolling and to this day they are still shipping Texas Bucks and many other novelties built around the crazy money, such as the first insurance policy that pays off immediately. They attach a $500 Texas Buck. Green has given up his comic strip and devotes full time to the zany end of the business now called Texantics Unlimited.

Premier now occupies more than 52,000 square feet of space and employs 135 people. There are no outside salesmen as such. They have two customer contact men who go out when a customer calls. But advertising, good friends and Texas Bucks have built their thriving business. "Thanks" was a beautiful word for Luke Kaiser. It will work for you, too.

Moxie

L.U. Kaiser and Premier Printing and Letter Service continuously advertise. They never stop. They use mottoes, first-day covers for new postage stamps, broadsides, anniversary books (they recently celebrated their 50th), enclosures with invoices, booklets, you name it and Premier has probably used it. One folder that we like was sent in a heat sealed plastic bag. The pasted-on label corner card asks, "Does Your Printer Have Moxie?" On the reverse of the address side, you see a large old-fashioned type display printed in four colors which asks the same question.

In case you are too young to remember, "Moxie" was the first carbonated soft drink invented by a doctor in 1873. Today, "Moxie" is an accepted slang expression for vigor, verve, pep, aggressiveness.

The folder is printed on a white 7" x 25¾" sheet, scored and folded twice. Pages 1, 2 and 3 are 7" x 10¼", while page 4 is just 5¼" wide. It is printed in four colors.

On page two, over a background of bottles painted in various water colors, are the words, "Premier Has Lots Of It!" In fact, we're the only printer in town who has!!!" Then page five, folded in, shows an old framed photograph of two children and an older man with cases of Moxie in front of a small striped tent. The headline is "Serving Houston for nearly half a century with old fashioned Moxie!" Below the picture was this caption, "Long before Premier Printing was founded by our president, L.U. Kaiser, he had moxie! Here at the tender age of six, he was 'moxie-minded' at his grandfather's bottling works in Freemont, Ohio. He's still a stockholder in the Moxie Corporation! No wonder we've got Moxie!" Now, someone reading this is probably saying—that's fine, but we don't have a photograph like that of our president. Our point is that you must always be awake and looking for advertising ideas. Every one of us has something in the old picture album that we could adapt to tie into a nostalgic promotion.

On pages three and four, there's bright copy giving the Random House Dictionary definition of moxie and going on to explain that at Premier they define moxie as something they have or else they don't work there. They invite the customer to come in any day that is convenient to enjoy a cool drink of "Moxie" and to see the plant. There's a large reply card enclosed in case the reader wants information on some of their 15 services.

On the last page of this folder, they have reproduced an old photo of the first drive-in restaurant in Houston where everyone in the younger set congregated after theaters and dancing—1918-1935. This place stood on the location of Premier's main office and plant now.

This is a great folder showing real imagination and creativity. It proves to customers that Premier has what they need.

Printing Center

Humor

Paul Tonsing is the president of Printing Center, Fort Worth, Texas. We would prefer to reprint Paul's letter in regard to his paperback book that he produced for his company. However, he has written after one of his statements, "for gawd's sake don't quote that!" So we won't.

The first five paragraphs of his letter told us of all the difficulties he had getting the job done. His experiences were typical of every printer who tries to do a great job of advertising for his own company. It is probably what makes so many printers give up. They do beautiful work for customers. The employees are so proud of some of the sheets that they hang them up on the wall for a while. But when they start work on their own advertising everything seems to go wrong. Nothing looks right. So many printers are perfectionists that they never are satisfied with anything they do for themselves. We suggest you keep at it and it will all come out right in the wash!

Mr. Tonsing first hired a public relations firm to write a book for his company, explaining what they did, how they did it and to tell about their employees and equipment (web offset). It was quite an expensive proposition. They published the book, it was stone sober and tried to give a description of the plant, page layouts and production helps and hints. It was sent out and Mr. Tonsing says, "It was as if we had never gone to the trouble . . . it didn't create a ripple."

So, Paul undertook the job himself and decided to write another book. He says he was under the influence of diet pills. He decided that a little light humor mixed in with the facts would help make the book readable. With the paper crunch, a big surge in business, pictures to be taken, it took some doing to get the book through their own plant. However, it was accomplished, and what a book it is. It is educational but it's fun. It has 112 pages, plus cover. The cover is printed in four process colors and shows a caricature of Paul Tonsing driving a golf cart. The subject of the book is, "The Odyssey of Printing Center." There wasn't room enough for the word "Center" so it runs down along the edge of the cover. There's a price of $1.00 scratched out and reductions to 82¢, 75¢, 26¢, 10¢ and finally, "Free." On the back cover is this copy: "This book is Free! When we first started the project of writing this book, the bookkeeper said we should get at least a dollar for it . . . when we started to show a series of proofs around the shop for candid opinions we couldn't get a unanimous vote . . . part of the boys thought we should tape a quarter to each book and give 'em away, and part thought a dime would be enough. So . . . we'll try just free. Yes, Virginia, there IS a Printing Center!"

The copy inside is both serious and humorous. When it comes to preparing layouts, inks, stock and things of that nature, it is serious and explained in detail with very little printers' jargon. When pictures of the employees are used and biographical material printed, it is humorous. It is a very readable and helpful book.

All the photographs were exaggerated. Paul's picture shows him with his feet on the desk, no shoes, a hole in his socks, a sailor's hat, a cigar in one hand and a drink in the other. We understand that he keeps his shoes on at all times during business hours; he has never had a drink of liquor in his life and never smoked a cigar or anything else. He hates hats.

Here are some of the things we learned about Printing Center from reading just one page. It is independently owned. Employs 75 people. Expected gross about $2.5 million. Prints from 75 to 100 different publications a week. Averages around two million impressions a week. Uses five trucks of newsprint weekly. Sheet offset is also done in the job shop partly to supplement the webs.

Mr. Tonsing says, "I think the humor was the key to the whole thing, and plan more of it in future advertising. It gets attention as nothing else does. Of course, the key is to have an efficient organization with a good reputation, as we have, so people know it is not a looney bin. We have always had the philosophy that you can work as well with a smile on your face; that anyone coming in the door is greeted warmly as a friend; and that anyone working here is entitled to a happy place for the 8 to 12 hours they put in here per day. We had a lot of fun with the book and I think it did us nothing but good."

If humor is handled as Paul Tonsing handled it, it will be successful. Just be careful of off-color humor and bad taste. It won't work.

Humorous Calendar

The Printing Center, Fort Worth, used humor in a calendar, also. They produce an 8¾" x 14½" plastic-bound calendar using cartoons for illustrations. The calendar is called, "Saddle Sore by Cowboy Cole." The 12 cartoons drawn by the same artist are all Western scenes and have humorous captions. There is one of two cow hands branding a steer and a city dude or tourist asking, "Why're you branding them? . . . can't you remember their names?" Another shows two cow pokes on their horses with the caption, "I'm laying off tranquilizers 'cause I was bein' nice to people I hate!"

Each page is of a similar nature and the calendar is easily read.

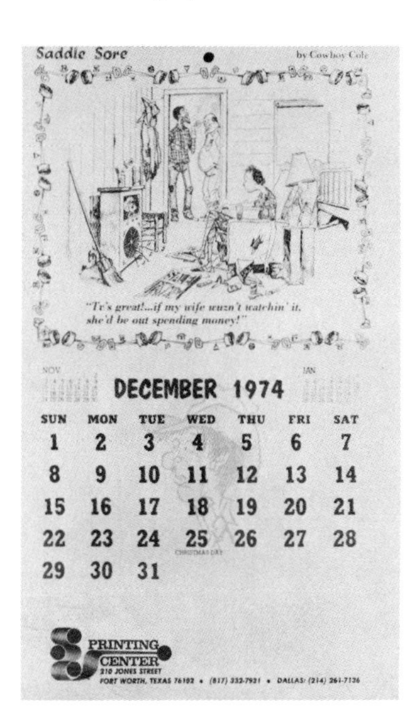

Printing Service, Inc.

House Organ

Martin J. Struhar, president of Printing Service, Inc., Madison Heights, Michigan, says, "P.S. Ink has never won a Benny but it's done a nice job for us." "P.S. Ink Magazine" is published quarterly by his company. It's 16 pages, 5¼" x 8½", printed on a heavy white bond stock. It isn't the slickest magazine in the world but it is friendly, informative and fun to read. We would recommend a similar house organ for any printer.

Printing Service plant covers 84,400 square feet on four acres. The company specializes in print business forms, custom bank checks, writing board systems and advertising printing. A conglomerate acquired PSI in December, 1969. After that, everything went wrong. Within nine months, five of the six top executives left the company because of policy changes. Employment decreased from 220 to 129. In the last two years that the conglomerate owned the plant, the operation lost more than $700,000. They decided to close the plant since they couldn't find a buyer. The employees got together with Mr. Struhar and 103 of the 129 employees pledged for stock purchases. So, they bought the company back in December, 1972. The details of the story are very interesting but that will give you a rough idea of what happened.

"P.S. Ink Magazine" hadn't been published for three years, and when Mr. Struhar came back the magazine came back because it was a communication tool between the plant and its many customers. Here are a few paragraphs from the Fall, 1973, issue. Notice the friendliness of the copy. It was written by Mr. Struhar and headed, "It's Good To Be Back Where The Action Is."

"When the leaves are falling, I autumn-atically think ahead to Thanksgiving. And I hope you'll forgive the pun.

"We at PSI certainly will count our blessings. Just a year ago, things looked grim. We were negotiating reacquisition, and everything was riding on how well we estimated the strength of our hand.

"If we failed, it was the end of a great company. Back to 'Stifling Gulch' for me. And hard times for a lot of loyal PSI guys and gals. Once you've had to worry—really worry—about the livelihood of 130 people, you know how it can tear you up. George Langlet, Don Roebert and I lost more than several months' sleep—and more than a few pounds.

"Well, somebody up there—and out there—must like us. Because the deal went through. We bought PSI back last December. And good things began to happen.

"Thanks to the way customers rallied around, PSI again is a healthy, on-the-ball printing team and growing like Topsy. Your patronage and confidence have been largely responsible. We are particularly grateful and proud that so many buyers of business forms, bank checks, multicolor advertising and accounting systems work continue to call on us. Your support has increased to such a point that 1973 will be PSI's best year yet.

"In fact, we're planning to expand again. A long range plan to step up capacity, sharpen product efficiencies and reduce costs already is under way.

"Which brings us to accountability. Something we welcome at PSI. No customer nor its supplier can afford the waste that results from weak management or poor job performance. The profit squeeze today demands greater achievement and productivity from everybody—at all levels.

"PSI people especially know that *past* successes in printing mean little. What you are doing for customers *today*, and what you will do for them *tomorrow* are the things that really count. We all have to measure up to this challenge. Marginal producers simply don't belong in the exacting printing industry.

"That's why I'd like to pay tribute to PSI's greatest asset: our people. Their record to date leaves no doubt in anyone's mind that our people are second to none. They, Langlet and Roebert, join me in saying, 'It's good to be back where the action is.' And all of us look forward to each opportunity to be of service to you."

There are jokes scattered through the pages and they are sent in by the readers. Five dollars is the grand prize, with plenty of two-dollar winners. There are short paragraphs of news briefs. Page articles about different types of forms, tax information, and messages from the P.S.I. sales manager. The pages are sometimes tinted. There are small thumbnail sketches scattered around and plenty of pictures to make it interesting and very readable. There's no doubt that it does what they want it to do—communicate. Short excerpts from those who write to the company prove that.

Puget Press/Multiple, Inc.

A Single Sheet

Puget Press/Multiple, Inc., Everett, Washington, has a wonderful idea for a series of mailings. We have five of the pieces. They are all very well printed, dignified, interesting and we imagine its customers approve of them 100%.

The pieces are printed on a 9" x 12" white enamel sheet, folded twice, for a No. 10 envelope. Both sides of the sheet are printed in solid colors. The background, in some cases, has been cut out to print a good black-and-white halftone.

The first fold has a quadrilateral panel printed in black with the words, "Know Your Neighbor" in reverse, and a reverse arrow pointing to a die-cut quadrilateral window from which the printing on the next fold shows through. The next fold has copy headed, "Introducing . . ." and then the name of the person or thing that is being introduced in a halftone on the right of the sheet. This is the halftone that shows through the die-cut window. On this fold is also some copy describing or explaining the picture.

When the inside of the sheet is unfolded, there are one or two halftones and extensive copy about the thing they are introducing. The back fold is used for one word such as, Quality, Craftsmanship, Service, and then the company name and trademark are shown. There is just one problem on the five copies we have. There is no address or phone number.

They have introduced their new logo, a large grinding wheel manufacturer, a man who directs a rehabilitation center called Work Opportunities, Inc., an office equipment manufacturer and a frontier village

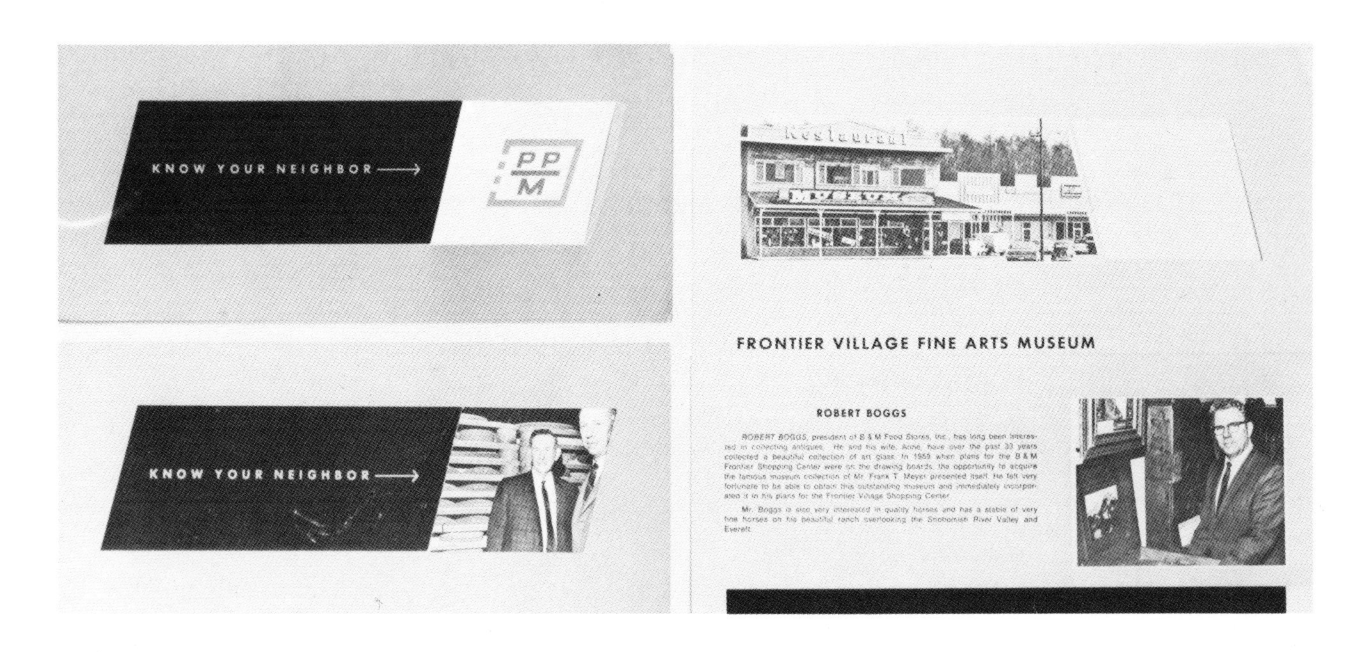

fine arts museum. All of these companies are no doubt customers or prospects of Puget Press/Multiple. This seems like a great idea. Bob Overstreet, the general manager, says these folders have kept their name in front of people and given them some ideas. They have also helped the company's image. He thinks he probably should have sold the idea to a bank. We surely agree.

Puget Press was founded in 1906. It has 22 employees and specializes in form printing. Its sales are approximately $500,000. It, like all printers, has trouble getting its advertising printed because its advertising work comes second.

Renown Printing Company, Ltd.

Merchandising An Award

"For a number of years we have been practitioners of self-advertising. The feedback we get from customers shows that we are known for quality printing," says Peter Hayes, sales manager of Renown Printing Company, Ltd., Niagara Falls, Canada.

The quality of its printing surely shows through in a four-page, long, narrow folder that was produced about the awards won in a P.I.A. competition. The four-pager is 8½" x 14", folded on the 14" side. The headline is, "Above and beyond the call of duty." The first page is a large halftone bleeding three sides, printed in blue ink of a young man in foreign officer's uniform. It is a head and full shoulder picture with a little over one-half of his left side showing. The brass and braid are quite apparent. In the background flies a banner with Renown Printing's trademark.

On page three is this same halftone but printed in four process colors, and on the man's chest are three actual gold seals with actual blue ribbons pasted on. The copy is good so we will print it here: "A soldier can risk his life, save his country or conquer an enemy and receive a ribbon and a shiny medal as a visible sign that he put forth an effort above and beyond the call of duty. In business life, we rarely receive any tangible evidence of excellence in our field. But the craftsmen of Renown Printing have earned three awards from the Printing Industries of America in competition with the best printers in North America. Why not let this award winning quality work for you? Ask for the Sales Department of Renown Printing at . . . " Then followed telephone numbers and address. The copy was set in 18-point type, ragged right and printed in perfect register in four process colors.

On page four there was a large blue trademark with a listing of the awards and, again, the company name, address and phone numbers.

Here, again, is a small company doing a beautiful job of advertising and printing. There seems to be no doubt that the small printers try harder. The large companies that advertise produce more costly jobs and impress the reader with grandeur. The smaller companies come up with creativity and inventive presentations. Renown Printing has 16 employees, including one-and-a-half salesmen. They aren't sure of the mailer's effectiveness, yet they say it did attract one large customer and kept their name in front of prospects and clients. We believe it was very effective.

Above and beyond the call of duty

A soldier can
risk his life,
save his country
or conquer an enemy
and receive a
ribbon and a
shiny medal
as a visible sign
that he put forth
an effort above and
beyond the call of
duty.

In business life, we
rarely receive any tangible
evidence of excellence
in our field.

But the craftsmen
of Renown Printing
have earned
three awards
from the
Printing Industries of
America in competition
with the best printers
in North America.

Why not let this award
winning quality
work for you.
Ask for the Sales Department
of Renown Printing at
416-356-7721
or write Renown Printing Co. Ltd. at
4112 Bridge Street,
Niagara Falls, Ontario

Rolph-Clark-Stone, Ltd.

Involving The Prospect

Rolph-Clark-Stone, Limited, Montreal, Canada, won a P.I.A. award for its campaign to promote folding cartons and machine forming systems. The campaign featured a small folding box viewer and film strips to use with the viewer. Since most humans are curious, we are certain that this was a campaign that was used. One surely couldn't throw it away without first seeing what were on the film strips.

Rolph-Clark-Stone was founded in 1845, as lithographers, specializing in 1955 as folding carton producers and printers. It employs 250 and has 10 salesmen. This campaign was produced in its own plant.

There were six mailings in No. 10 envelopes. One was sent every two weeks. The folders were printed on heavy stock in blue and black ink. The sheet size was 8½" x 11", scored and folded twice. On one side the message was in French and on the reverse side in English. The film strip or long slide was held in place by three die-cut flaps on a 3¾" x 9" heavy stock panel or card.

The first mailing, plainly marked "1" (each mailing was numbered), contained the folder, the slide holding card and a folded flat viewer with

flaps to be folded to form a box. On one end of this viewer was a printed eye which had a die-cut hole and a lens pasted in. On the opposite side of the box was an oblong die cut and a translucent screen pasted over it. The box was 2" x 2" x 2½" when folded to make the viewer. It was also printed in blue and black. The slide card noted that the viewer should be kept as there were more to come.

The copy on each folder referred to the slides marked A, B, C, etc. Each slide had eight full-color transparencies showing boxes or men at work planning and designing packages, or machines erecting cartons, or machines printing. The copy was well written and informative. Each folder had a line on which a salesman could write his name. There were also the company trademark, addresses and phone numbers.

This campaign took hours of planning, writing, photography and printing. It was felt that the salesmen found it easier to talk about folding cartons and machines after the clients received these mailings. There is no doubt that the customers and prospects had to become involved in this campaign. There was no way they really could get the complete story without seeing the slides.

Rothchild Printing Company, Inc.

A Numbers Campaign

Tags and labels are the printing products of Rothchild Printing Co., Inc., Elmhurst, N.Y. It employs 65, including six salesmen. Its numbers campaign was just a part of its continuous advertising program. The campaign found the company about 30 new prospects and eight customers.

Each mailing was in the shape of a giant number (1 through 2) and as such had continuity. However, each mailing was a complete message by itself. Each number had a string attached to somewhat resemble a tag. The mailings were sent once a month. The first number was 5" high and 6" wide and die cut to make four "pages." All of the numbers were printed on a cast coated paper.

Page one of the figure one was printed in a glossy black with type in reverse and in gold. The copy was, "Subject: Tags. Object: To point out the benefits of dealing with Rothchild." Page two contained this copy printed in two colors, black and red. Every other line was red. "This is the beginning of a campaign to obtain a share of your tag business. It will be brief, to the point and persistent. We know that we must earn the right to become your tag source. In subsequent mailings, we will provide sound reasons why our background, skills and experience of over 60 years warrant your consideration. You will be hearing from us next month." The third page contained the company name, address and telephone number.

The second number was printed in a bright red. It was 5½" high and 8½" wide. It was die cut and the copy was printed on the reverse side. Samples were sent with the number.

The third was a four-pager with the fold at a small flat space at the top of the figure which was 5¾" high and 8¾" wide. This copy, printed on pages two and three, was about "Color: Its contribution to commerce." Every other line was either green or black. There were also samples enclosed with this mailing, including some printed in 4-color process.

The inventory program and drop shipments were the subjects of the fourth mailing. The first page was printed in magenta. The fold was at the top of the figure four, which was 5¼" high and 8⅝" wide. The copy was printed with every other line black or magenta.

The five was 5½" high and 8⅝" wide. Reversed on a mustard colored background were the words, "Quote and Unquote." On the reverse side were mentioned some flattering stories that had appeared in some trade journals and also some special studies the company had made. There were reprints enclosed.

And so the campaign went for 12 months. A very attractive and unusual approach.

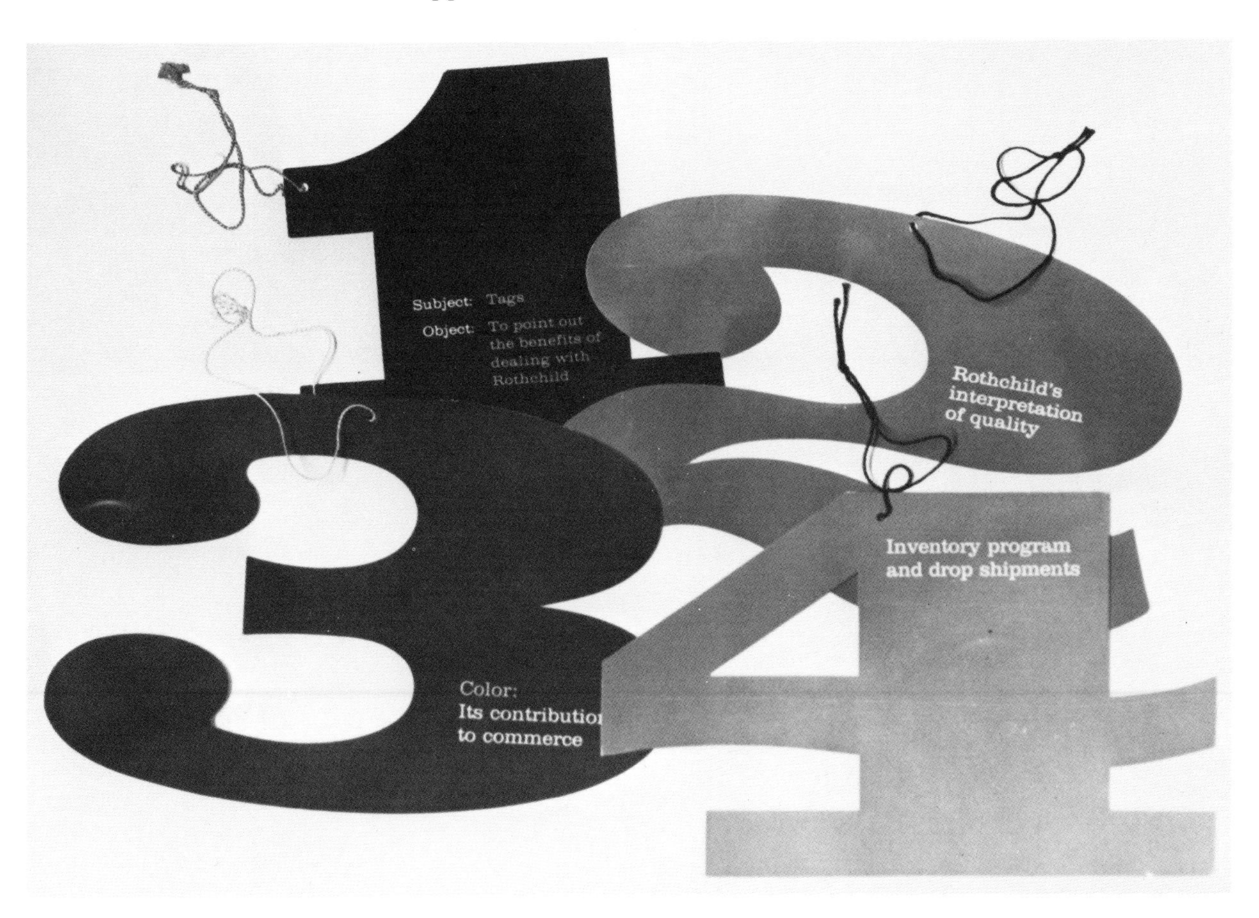

Sayers Printing Company

Annual Report Planning

Herbert M. Sayers, president of Sayers Printing Co., St. Louis, has always believed in good advertising. He believes if it is good for his customers it is good for his company. Please note, we said good advertising. We have seen Sayer's advertising for years and we have never seen a poor piece. It is of the highest quality. We doubt if they receive many compliments about their advertising because they are just expected to come up with super pieces.

"Fastract" is one of those super pieces. It was planned and produced for a targeted specific need: to help the financial printing buyer. The layout and design was done in-house; the copy was written outside. The copy writer had to have the assistance of the people who had been working with and printing annual reports. The copy was too pointed to have been written by an outsider without great assistance.

The "Fastract" material was contained in a jacket or, rather, file folder die cut, gold-leaf embossed, blind embossed, perforated, printed in four colors, scored and folded from a cast coated 15¾" x 24" heavy stock. The inside was printed in blue with a perforated reply card. When the card was folded up it helped to hold the material in. There was a cutout tab for using if the folder was placed in a file.

The business reply card could be used to ask for more information, have a Sayers financial printing expert call, receive three other annual report books or award-winning annual report portfolios.

Attached to the inside of the jacket cover was a hand written note from Mr. Sayers. It read, "We at Sayers hope you will enjoy and put to good use the enclosed material for 'Fastracking' your Annual Report. The charts should help you produce and schedule your Report in record time, skirting costly overtime and expensive do-overs at the last minute."

There was a six-page fold-out bound into a cover which was entitled, "Fastrack, Inc., Annual Report." The illustration on this cover was the same as was used on the file folder. It was a beautiful brown-toned photograph of a speeding racing car with a blind embossed puff of smoke coming from its exhaust.

The copy was written with tongue in cheek and for those who had ever worked on an annual report it had to be delightful reading. The president's letter was signed by Rip Van Dretti. Rip Van Winkle's picture was used. All of the six inside pages were printed with an overall design not too dissimilar from safety paper. We will copy a few of the paragraphs from the president's letter so you can get a feel of the copy. "Your Company profited handsomely by virtue of a very successful and restful year.

"As you know, the sole corporate activity of Fastrack, Inc., consists of putting out The Annual Report . . . summarizing our experiences to those of you who share our penultimate interests in such things.

"The ultimate objective, of course, is in doing the job well, in record time so that all employees concerned can enjoy an extended sabbatical leave. This year, using our new approach to the task, we were able to extend the previous year's vacation from six months to ten months . . . a resounding improvement in return-on-effort of 66.6%.

"This improvement was of such magnitude that the Board boldly changed the company name from the dreary: Make Work Company to the more dynamic: Fastrack, Inc.

"Altruists that we are (including all the fine folk at Sayers) this booklet is offered as a helpful guide as you start this year's Grand Adventure of The Annual Report. If you should want further assistance . . . we can always call someone back from vacation."

There was more copy than the above but that will give you an idea of how the copy was written. The other five pages continued with copy on how to organize to start the report, how to schedule the many requirements, how to get people thinking about the report and what the report would cost.

Then enclosed in the packet was a flow chart for the work covering every page. This was a 21" x 32½" sheet. There was also another Fastrack Flow Chart with columns representing one or two week increments covering Concept; Research; Writing; Financial; Design Photography; Illustrations: Artwork and Charts; Typography and Pasteup, Printing and Mailing.

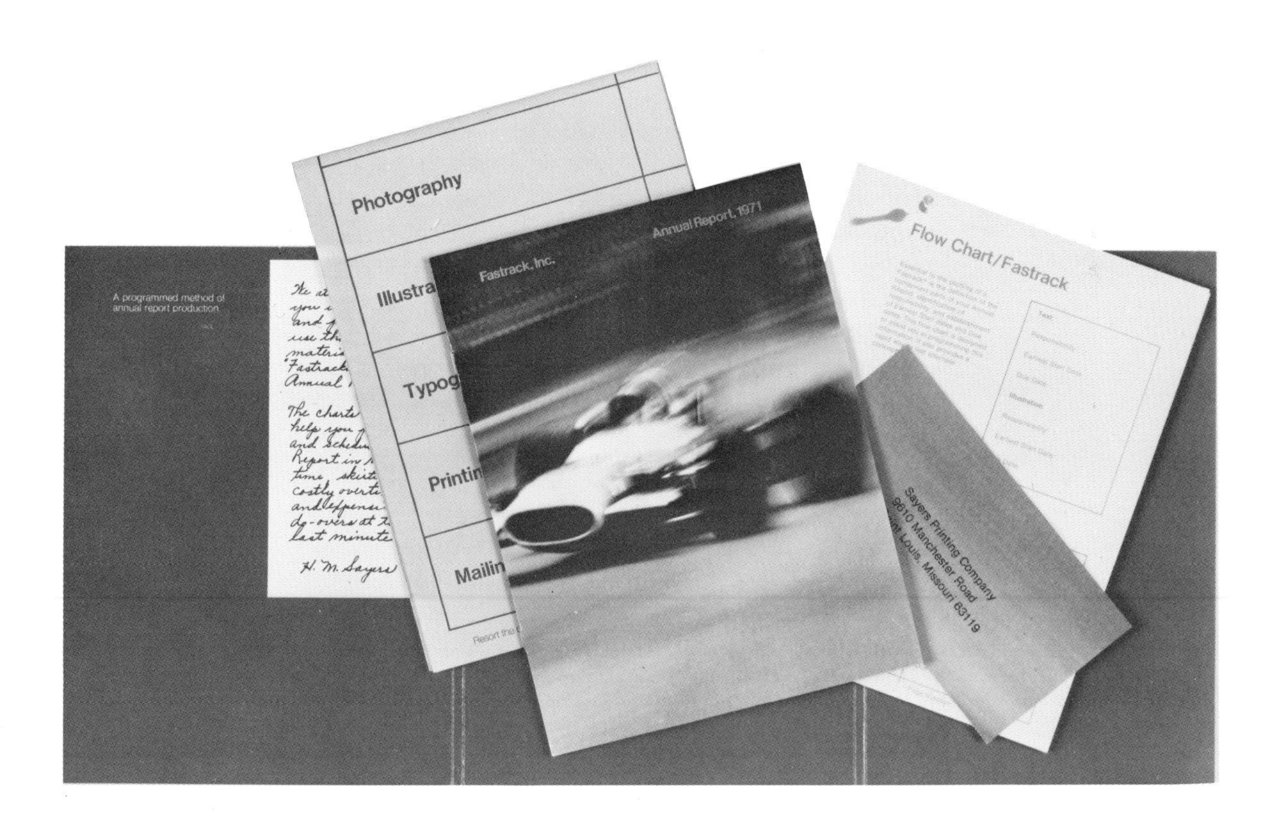

Mother Goose Book

There is no wonder that Sayers Printing Co., St. Louis, has no difficulty in publicizing its award-winning advertising pieces. They get notices in local magazines, newspapers and even radio. Their advertising is fabulous! Herb Sayers, president, tells us they received over 350 letters about their Mother Goose book. They mailed 1,000 copies. Seven new customers were found and business increased by $100,000. At least 20 good prospects were developed. If you could see the 12-page book you would wonder why more customers weren't acquired.

The book was contained in a very heavy box covered with a white text paper. The box alone was beautiful. There was a three-inch diameter circle cut out of the box cover so you could see Mother Goose's head showing through from the cover of the book. The box cover was hot gold-leaf stamped with the words, "The House that Craft Built."

Inside the box on a gold foil covered piece of corrugated board was the book, which was wrapped in a gossamer handmade Japanese paper and a gold velvet ribbon so it could be easily removed from the box.

The book is 11" square. The cover is printed in four colors and elaborately embossed on a heavy Beau Brilliant cover stock. Both front and back covers are embossed. The art is a contemporary rendering in watercolor of a typical Mother Goose scene. The copy on the cover is, "A Reconstructed Rhyme from Sayers Printing Company."

The inside cover is blank but the embossing is decorative. Page one is covered with medals, ribbons and award medallions printed in black line with four-color stylized flowers from the cover drawing, over-printed at the bottom of the page. The copy line reads, "These are Awards."

Pages two and three are an overall full-color halftone, in perfect register at the binding edge, of a wall covered with many framed awards and plaques. The flowers from the cover again appear on these pages at the bottom. Every page has been lacquered or laminated with a film. The coating is so heavy we aren't sure which it is. The copy is "These are the Awards that Sayers won."

Pages four and five are two pages of a halftone showing another wall with beautiful printing samples posted thereon. In the foreground are some flowers and a palm plant but overprinting these are the flowers from the front cover. The one line of copy reads, "These are the Pieces that won the Awards that Sayers won."

On pages six and seven, the center spread shows a group picture of the employees. We counted 41 present, although they have 53, including five salesmen. Their annual sales in round figures are $3 million. The flowers from the cover continue to appear on the bottom of the page. This continues throughout the book. The copy which now goes over onto two pages reads, "These are the people who printed the pieces that won the awards that Sayers won."

Pages eight and nine are headed, "These are the presses run by the people who printed the pieces that won the awards that Sayers won." On a solid jet-black background is a cutout photograph of a five-color press. There are eight other small photographs in full color of other presses and equipment on these pages. It is a beautiful layout, wonderful printing and binding.

On pages ten and eleven there is a full-color photograph of the Sayers Printing Company sign with trees in the background. Since the sign is in red, white and blue, with the type in gold, it is very attractive. The copy: "This is the place where the presses are run by the people who printed the pieces which won the awards that Sayers won."

On page twelve, on a magenta background, is Mother Goose. The copy reads, "A Further Note: Award winning printing just looks like it costs more."

Of course, small printers can not economically produce a piece like this that must have cost at least six or seven dollars each. However, they can work towards this end by making their small pieces just as attractive and creative. Sayers Printing was not always able to afford such pieces but we are sure that Herb Sayers will tell anyone that their advertising was one of the things that helped them grow. Please notice, we said one of the things. You must be able to produce quality printing if you are going to grow.

Schneiderith & Sons

"Brains At Work"

For at least 20 years, Schneiderith & Sons, Baltimore, Md., has been publishing monthly a six-page, 4" x 9" folder, printed in two colors, entitled, "Brains At Work." There are 30 or 32 short paragraphs in this publication, reporting new and stimulating ideas in science and industry. If the readers wish to know the source of any item, they can write to Schneiderith, whose address and phone number are on page one. Page five carries the advertising message or comment. If the message grows too long, they just enclose another sheet or four-pager. This happened recently when they tried to explain the origin and development of the alphabet.

This mailing is copyrighted and controlled by Schneiderith, and they sell the service to companies in other industries. The paragraphs cover everything from a flotation vest for a dog to how the noise level in a city could be minimized. Every paragraph is interesting. One never knows what he will find and we understand the number of requests for further information are quite gratifying. It is an excellent piece of advertising to keep the company name in front of buyers of printing every month.

Starline Creative Printing

Magazine Ad

Starline Creative Printing, Albuquerque, New Mexico, hasn't used its advertising dollars to produce super deluxe brochures. Probably its most expensive pieces are its twice-a-year reproductions of paintings it purchases for hanging in its Southwestern Art Gallery. These are four-color reproductions in a 9" x 12" folder of a heavy linen-textured stock. They are quality pieces, in good taste, not flamboyant.

The other pieces that we have seen are nicely done, well executed, with excellent copy that sells, and are comparatively inexpensive. Starline made its dollars work.

One ad that was no doubt used as a magazine page and then folded for a mailing piece made use of a big photo of Bob Dye, its printing consultant. Notice that he isn't a salesman, he is a consultant. The headline, "I guarantee 100 percent interest" is surely a provocative one for this day and age. We will take the space to show you the copy because it is good.

"I'm Bob Dye, printing consultant. I've been with Starline for almost a year, and I'm continually amazed at the extra effort everyone expends to serve our clients. Every one of my Starline associates cares about deadlines, about quality, about ideas, about good results.

"That's why I can unhesitatingly promise you 100 percent interest in your business and in the problems that can be solved, the goals attained with creative printing.

"You ask, 'But isn't that 100 percent interest expensive?' No. Starline is expensive only when you don't use us.

"We're expensive when you're publishing a catalog that's amateurish in appearance and thus futile in the marketplace. Expensive when you're using shabby, ill-designed stationery to represent your company. Expensive when your printed advertising makes your product or service appear to be an inferior substitute for the real thing.

"That's when that 100 percent interest is expensive: When you don't allow us to work for you.

"Starline has the creative people-artists and skilled craftsmen to produce the kind of printing you need. I guarantee it. Starline guarantees it. One hundred percent!"

Custom Christmas Greetings

Here is a field that has hardly been tapped by printers. Some wonder where the new markets are. What about holiday greeting cards designed especially for a particular customer or industry? Starline Creative Printing sells them.

We have seen two pieces of Starline's that sell the design and production of custom Christmas greetings. The copy mentions "In business, of course, thanking one's friends and clients at Christmastime is nearly indispensable to good customer relations." How true—and how few companies bother to have a card designed that is truly their own. There is a large amount of business yet to be developed by the printing industry through custom-made greeting cards.

Deliveries

Starline Creative Printing also sells its ability to deliver. Here is some more honest copy that follows a large picture of its delivery man, and a headline that reads, "A Winner—98.85 percent of the time.

"Our philosophy is right out of Robert W. Service: 'A promise made is a debt unpaid,' When we accept your order, we accept an obligation to you to deliver on time.

"And we do it. Last year we did it 2,532 times out of a possible 2,561.

"Those 29 misses still bug us. We've analyzed each of them carefully and installed corrective procedures. So far they're working fine. As a sage once remarked, 'The harder I work, the luckier I get.' We're getting luckier every day.

"Deadlines don't bother us at all. We live with them constantly. Squish them around and savor them. And deliver—the finest printing in the Southwest—to you, on time."

The advertising ideas, all produced within the plant, are excellent, the copy is top notch, and proof of their effectiveness is the steady increase in the company's business. The walls near the reception room are covered with awards. We counted 65 plaques. As some of their copy states, "The national awards that Starline is winning are not the result of four-leaf clovers. They are the result of bringing together the best commercial artists and printing craftsmen in a nationally recognized creative combination."

We asked how Starline managed the consistency. It has never mailed less than once each month since 1958. Bob Walker, President, came right back with the correct answer. "Starline advertising will always be mailed on time. If overtime is required, overtime we work. Our advertising has the same priority as the critical materials we produce for our largest accounts."

Steck-Warlick Company

Micro-Scent

Steck-Warlick Company, Austin, Texas, produced a good 8½" x 11", four-page mailer selling Micro-Scent, "A New Dimension For Direct Mail Advertising." It employs 600, has 30 salesmen and has $15 million sales. It produces color work, magazines and large sheet-fed and web printing.

The folder was printed in four colors on a white cast coated sheet. On page one was a drawing of an egg-shaped world globe. In large type, the copy read, "In our 75 years in the printing business . . . we've laid our share!" On page three, in the same type, " . . . but this is our first real lemon." Below the type was a picture of a lemon with a note below it to "Scratch and Smell."

On page two were seven paragraphs about the Micro-Scent process and how "This folder illustrates dramatically how design, art and good printing can be reinforced with a new graphics tool—Micro Scent." The last paragraph suggested that "For more information on printing that 'smells good'—get in touch with Steck-Warlick Company, by mailing the enclosed card."

On page four were printed the trademark, address and phone numbers.

This was a nice image-building piece and they say it stirred up some interest about the process.

Tulsa Litho Company

Celebrations

Anytime you can latch on to a local or national celebration in planning your advertising it is good to do so. The promotion other sources give to the occasion will help your advertising. Tulsa Litho Company, Tulsa, Oklahoma, tied in with the nation's bicentennial year and mailed an American heritage portfolio entitled, "The American Revolution." The program started in the summer of 1973, and promises to continue through the spring of 1976. A piece is mailed every quarter and is built into a file, 11" x 11½", with a tab cut for each season. We will describe two or three pieces of this excellent campaign.

The first mailing was contained in a box with a wrap of 80-lb. Warren Lustro Gloss Enamel cover. The wrap was printed in two colors. One red was hit twice in the same area to get an interesting effect. One line was red foil hot stamped and a gloss varnish was applied overall.

The box contained a master divider sheet. It was a black mezzotint of a log entitled, "200 Years Of Freedom," printed over seven flat colors on a Champion Huskey Cover. The logo was a carved linoleum block, photographed and then shot as a mezzotint. A letter from President R.D. Lengacher, describing the series, and a reply card were also enclosed. Also, a tab divider sheet on a Gold Carrara Text cover. On one side appeared the logo again. On the other side were production notes that are very interesting to buyers and creators of advertising. In the box was also a six-panel folder entitled "Richard Henry Lee."

The panel folder was printed on 65-lb. Simpson Lee Wild Blue Coronado Text Cover. Two tones of blue seemed to be used to reproduce the charcoal pencil, three-page high drawing of Mr. Lee. Some cursive hand lettering was used on the cover and an initial letter on page five. A large amount of type was set in 10-point with a measure of 42 picas on page five, and it described the "Cicero Of The Continental Congress." On page six, we found a map showing the 13 original colonies and some important dates during the summer of 1773.

Inside the folder was a beautiful 22" x 27¼" fold-out poster, printed on 80-lb. Warren Lustro Gloss Enamel book stock entitled, "The Birth Of A New Nation." The acrylic printing on gesso was an outspread eagle. At the base of the poster was a broken egg painted to represent the British flag. There was also some copy explaining the headline and Richard Henry Lee's part in forming the Committees of Correspondence.

This entire presentation showed imagination, creativity, excellent color work and fine printing.

The autumn mailing was about the "Penman of the Revolution," John Dickinson. He was the Pennsylvania farmer who refused to sign the Declaration of Independence. This folder cover was printed 4-color process on pages one and four. The two inside pages were printed using six colors. There was a sketch of Dickinson holding a pen and a drawing of a case of tea in the ocean water. The story or copy was printed on four pages of parchment wire stitched into the cover. There was also a tab-cut divider sheet and reply card. Another excellent job of design and printing.

The winter mailing with the tab-art divider sheet and reply card was about Josiah Quincy, Jr. It was an 11" x 37", 80-lb. offset dull enamel cover sheet folded and scored three times into a 9¼" x 11" folder. There were six colors used on the inside pages and four process colors printed on the reverse side. On each presentation, the logo was used and, of course, the Tulsa Litho signature. The copy must have taken quite a bit of research because they portrayed the lesser known patriots. Naturally, this made for more interesting reading.

THE BIRTH OF
A NEW NATION

Bob Lengacher tells us the company was founded in 1935, and they produced their first small advertising booklet in 1936. The early pieces of advertising were fairly simple and generally in one color. In 1965, Tulsa Litho decided that the Tulsa market was ready to move toward 4-color process. So, they hired a color-separation craftsman from Switzerland. When they were sure of their ability they mailed their first promotion piece and it resulted in two specific large sales from totally new customers which more than paid the cost of the mailer.

Tulsa Litho has had steady campaigns going with the emphasis on creativity. They have a three-person art staff. Since they have started promoting four-color process work, sales volume has tripled and the color jobs have accounted for 75 percent of the growth. Profits are up and Mr. Lengacher definitely thinks advertising has played a very important part of this growth.

Three-Dimensional Calendar

Tulsa Litho Company, Tulsa, Oklahoma, had another quarterly mailing that was well designed and printed. They mailed three-month calendars that were die cut, scored and printed. The recipient had to fold them according to instructions on the reverse side. When folded, they made very interesting boxes and tubes which could be placed on the desk for easy reference. They were printed in three to five colors on various kinds and weights of stock, including one piece of heavy film. The art theme was the various signs of the zodiac. There were small blocks of copy describing the person born under each sign. The campaign was very well handled. Instead of sending one year's calendar, they spread it out and were able to "talk" to their customers and prospects every three months. A good idea.

E.S. Upton Printing Company

Photographic Prints

E.S. Upton Printing Company, New Orleans, are creative printers who produce brochures, menus, annual reports and advertising pieces. It has annual sales of $1.3 million, employs 50 people, which include five salesmen. It was founded in 1889.

One piece of a continuing self-advertising effort is a large folder entitled, "The Southern Vista." Within the 14¾" x 19¾" heavy, white coverstock folder is a fine print of a photograph of the interior of the "Church Of Silence." It is quite suitable for framing.

On page two of the folder is printed a signed message from William Bell, President. It reads, "Seven years, silent years, have passed since a hurricane closed St. Mary's Assumption Church. The old Redemptorist church of the Irish Channel still stands in its baroque German splendor, tended by devoted priests.

"But in the meantime a sensitive photographer has given it momentary life, vitality in glowing, rich color, a tonal interpretation unachieved by the human eye.

"And in turn, Upton craftsmen have given this accomplishment exquisite fidelity. They can do this because they are capable of the best. Not only do they draw from that ancient resource, pride, but they are constantly abreast of the latest contemporary technology.

"Printing from Upton lives . . . because quality is not anonymous."

Mr. Bell tells us that $100,000 in increased sales can be traced to this mailer and approximately 25 new customers were found. They have always been practitioners of self-advertising.

George Waters Color Productions, Inc.

Award Merchandising

George Waters Color Productions, Inc., won a first award for one of its advertising campaigns and then produced, in very good taste, a 4" x 8½" four-page folder printed on a heavy embossed enameled stock. They reproduced a full-color photograph of the Benjamin Franklin statuette and the reproduction was beautiful. We have never seen a better one and there have been many reproductions made. The short copy on page two explained the award they won in the category for a company employing 19 persons or fewer.

On page two was this copy: "Gilbert & Sullivan had Robin Oakapple sing almost 100 years ago in his ditty from Ruddigor (politesse for Bloody Gore),

'My Boy Take It Frome Me!
If you wish in the world to advance,
Your merits you're bound to enhance,
You must stir it and stump it,
And blow your own trumpet,
Or, trust me, you haven't a chance!'

"And this stanza is just as applicable to our business life today. Here at George Waters Color we share in receiving this award for putting our best foot forward in a tasteful manner. Perhaps these talents can help you and your organization in preparing and producing a graphic statement." The last page showed the company name and address.

This was an excellent way to merchandise the award. All printers who win awards should do likewise!

Wolf Envelope Company

Magazine of Letters

The Wolf Magazine of Letters has been published every other month for 41 years. That is consistent advertising. It is published by the Wolf Envelope Company, Cleveland and Detroit, and is written by H. Jack Lang, who is employed by a Cleveland advertising agency. It is 12 pages and cover, and measures 4⅜" x 6⅝". The cover is printed in two or three colors on a heavy enamel stock. The inside pages are printed on an ivory text paper.

All of the material consists of letters with short explanations of why or when they were written. Most are very amusing. Interesting letters are requested from readers. If published, they send a Webster's New World Dictionary with a phonoguide record telling the correct pronunciation of words.

Let us give you one idea of a letter in a recent edition: "Stuart Levin, when president of New York's Four Seasons gourmet restaurant, received this letter from camp from his 11-year-old daughter. (As reported by Cleveland Amory).

"Dear Dad—

The food is awful. I can't even get snails.

A."

The inside covers and back cover always contain selling messages for the many printed products manufactured by Wolf Envelope. This is an excellent example of consistent advertising.

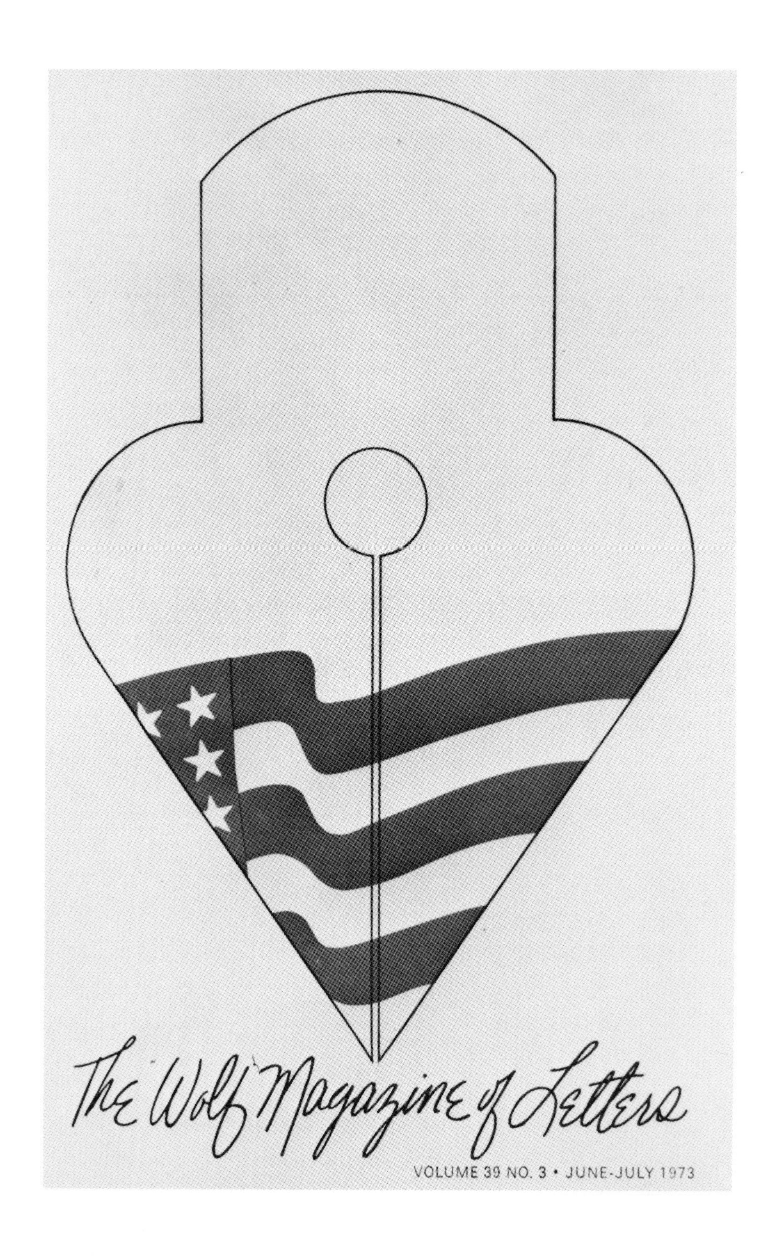

Bibliography

Many books in regard to advertising are available. The partial listing that follows will assist you in becoming more knowledgeable. Consult your public library for a more detailed list.

Ayer Glossary of Advertising and Related Terms. Chicago: Ayer Press, 1972.

Ayer Public Relations and Publicity Style Book, 5th ed. Chicago: Ayer Press, 1972.

Book, Albert C. and Norman D. Cary. *The Television Commercial.* Chicago: Crain Books, 1973.

Cutlip, Scott M. and Allen H. Center. *Effective Public Relations.* Englewood Cliffs, N.J.: Prentice-Hall, Inc., 1971.

Hodgson, Richard S. *Direct Mail and Mail Order Handbook,* 2nd ed. Chicago: The Dartnell Corp.

Kleppner, Otto and Stephen Greyson. *Advertising Precedure,* 6th ed. Englewood Cliffs, N.J.: Prentice-Hall, Inc., 1973.

Littlefield, James E. and E.A. Kirkpatrick. *Advertising,* 3rd ed. Boston: Houghton Mifflin Co., 1970.

Mandell, Maurice. *Advertising,* 2nd ed. Englewood Cliffs, N.J.: Prentice-Hall, Inc., 1974.

Sales Promotion Handbook, 6th ed., ed. Ovid Riso. Chicago: The Dartnell Corp.

Stansfield, Richard H. *Advertising Manager's Handbook.* Chicago: The Dartnell Corp., 1969.

Stone, Bob. *Successful Direct Marketing Methods.* Chicago: Crain Books, 1975.

Young, James Webb. *Technique for Producing Ideas.* Chicago: Crain Books, 1940.

Media Directories

Ayer Directory of Publications (Newspapers-Magazines)
N.W. Ayer & Son
W. Washington Square
Philadelphia, Pa. 19106

Business Publication Rates and Data (Monthly)
Standard Rate & Data Service, Inc.
5201 Old Orchard Road
Skokie, Ill. 60076

Canadian Advertising Rates and Data (Monthly)
Standard Rate & Data Service, Inc.
5201 Orchard Road
Skokie, Ill. 60076

Consumer Magazine and Farm Publication Rates and Data (Monthly)
Standard Rate & Data Service, Inc.
5201 Old Orchard Road
Skokie, Ill. 60076

Direct Mail List Rates and Data (2 Issues)
Standard Rate & Data Service, Inc.
5201 Old Orchard Road
Skokie, Ill. 60076

National Mailing List Houses
Superintendent of Documents
Government Printing Office
Washington, D.C. 20402

Network Rates and Data (6 Issues)
Standard Rate & Data Service, Inc.
5201 Old Orchard Road
Skokie, Ill. 60076

Newspaper Rates and Data (Monthly)
Standard Rate & Data Service, Inc.
5201 Old Orchard Road
Skokie, Ill. 60076

Newspaper Circulation Analysis (Annually)
Standard Rate & Data Service, Inc.
5201 Old Orchard Road
Skokie, Ill. 60076

Print Media Production Data (Monthly)
Standard Rate & Data Service, Inc.
5201 Old Orchard Road
Skokie, Ill. 60076

SBA Small Business Bibliography No. 29
Superintendent of Documents
Government Printing Office
Washington, D.C. 20402

Spot Radio Rates and Data (Monthly)
Standard Rate & Data Service, Inc.
5201 Old Orchard Road
Skokie, Ill. 60076

Spot Television Rates and Data (Monthly)
Standard Rate & Data Service, Inc.
5201 Old Orchard Road
Skokie, Ill. 60076

Transit Advertising Rates and Data (4 Issues)
Standard Rate & Data Service, Inc.
5201 Old Orchard Road
Skokie, Ill. 60076

Weekly Newspaper Rates and Data (2 Issues)
Standard Rate & Data Service, Inc.
5201 Old Orchard Road
Skokie, Ill. 60076

Associations

Association of Direct Mail Agencies
1509 22nd St., N.W.
Washington, D.C. 20037

Assoc. of Industrial Advertisers
41 E. 42nd St.
New York, New York 10036

Canadian Direct Mail Assn.
130 Merton St.
Toronto, Canada M4S 1A4

Direct Mail Marketing Assn.
6 E. 43rd St.
New York, New York 10017

Envelope Manufacturers Association
1 Rockefeller Plaza
New York, New York 10020

Magazine Publishers Association, Inc.
575 Lexington Avenue
New York, New York 10022

MASA International
7315 Wisconsin Ave.
Bethesda, Md. 20014

Mail Adv. Ind. League (MAIL)
100 Indiana Ave., N.W.
Washington, D.C. 20001

Mailing List Brokers Professional Assoc.
541 Lexington Ave.
New York, New York 10022

Marketing Communications Executives
2130 Delancey Pl.
Philadelphia, Pa. 19103

National List Compilers & Managers Assn.
541 Lexington Ave.
New York, New York 10022

National Public Relations Council
419 Park Ave., So.
New York, New York 10016

Outdoor Advertising Association of America
625 Madison Avenue
New York, New York 10022

Radio Advertising Bureau, Inc.
555 Madison Avenue
New York, New York 10022

Specialty Advertising Association International
740 North Rush Street
Chicago, Ill. 60611

Transit Advertising Association
1725 K Street, N.W.
Washington, D.C. 20006

Index